M000114010

Praise for
The A.B.C.'s of Behavioral Forensics: Applying Psychology to Financial Fraud Prevention and Detection

"Fraud is an important part of enterprise risk. Although it falls in the finance and accounting function it is also a people issue. The authors have taken an important step forward in helping organizations by examining issues of relationships, emotions, narcissism, and larger group and organizational dynamics that will help leaders understand and deter fraud."

—Harry M. Jansen Kraemer
Former CEO, Baxter International and
Professor of Leadership, Kellogg School of
Management, Northwestern University

"I have known Sri for 25 years and have found him to be one of the most eclectic thinkers I have ever known. He draws his insights not only from his formal accounting and psychology education but also from a wide range of philosophic sources not often read by business students and practitioners. He has given considerable thought to a wide range of topics, including ethics, governance, and auditing. In *A.B.C.'s of Behavioral Forensics*, you will find that he and his coauthors have been adept at bringing a broad view of their diverse interests to bear on the emerging discipline of behavioral and financial forensics. You will, upon reflection, note that they have not only addressed the narrower issues of forensics but also the broader issues of philosophy, ethics, and governance. This book can be read usefully at the surface level or, given more time and thought, a reader will be led to think more deeply about how society is impacted when otherwise good people, particularly our leaders, violate their trust. Reading this book will be a good and profitable use of your time."

—Andrew D. Bailey, Jr., PhD, CPA, CMA
Professor of Accounting Emeritus,
University of Illinois at Urbana-Champaign,
and former Deputy Chief Accountant,
U.S. Securities & Exchange Commission

"Daven, Sri, Joe, and Kelly have done a great job of helping us understand the importance of recognizing the very personal and individual human factors that can drive someone to fraudulent behavior. They also provide insights and guidelines that can help us recognize the potential fraudster."

—Peter Pesce
Partner Emeritus, A.T. Kearney

"This excellent work forces us beyond any easy and dangerously narrow examination of fraud to the understanding of complex motivations that set in motion results that can be startling in their financial consequence. With recognizable and pertinent case studies, these exceptionally qualified authors demonstrate how certain human behavioral factors precede and enable a fraud—be it carried out by one person, a colluding group, or by suggestions from leadership. What the authors then do is thoroughly describe these defining emotions, the essential relationship between the fraud perpetrator and the victim, and what can lead an individual to reverse his or her 'honesty course.' With certain knowledge that fraud is theft, even though it is not carried out by force, and struggling with the question of why do people cross the line, the reader is moved to an understandable and professionally sophisticated discussion of the factors attributable to the human mind followed by the delivery of methods for identifying early-stage fraud and for mitigating its consequences. This critically important and highly readable book is essential for anyone responsible for or caring about businesses and organizations today, or for anyone desiring deeper insight into certain explanations for the considerable fraud that surrounds our daily lives."

—Jameson A. Baxter
Chair, Putnam Funds

"Leaders with integrity attempt to define and determine the personality characteristics of truth and honesty in themselves and others. However, it's a search often fraught with uncertainty. *The A.B.C.'s of Behavioral Forensics* will help you to be aware of the signals of devious behavior. Most important, it will increase your sensitivity to the importance of the issue. Corrupt activities are often allowed to continue due to our own indifference."

—Duane R. Kullberg
Former CEO, Arthur Andersen & Co.

"As a fraudster, I succeeded for almost two decades because I understood how to exploit the psychological and emotional weaknesses of my victims. This book teaches auditors and anti-fraud professionals about fraud psychology, the "soft underbelly of fraud"—the emotional manipulation, big and small lies, and other behavioral cues that fraudsters employ to success-fully execute their crimes. I call it the art of spinning, and the authors have described it as the predator-prey dance. Without such an understanding of the behavioral dynamics of fraud, victims will always be doomed to lose (lots of money) and fraudsters will always have the upper hand."

—Sam E. Antar
Former Crazy Eddie CFO, former CPA,
and a convicted felon

"This is a brilliant idea for a book on the topic of fraud, which isn't always obvious to those being victimized. Understanding the psychological elements of how we rationalize behaviors associated with fraud enables our understanding of why even those whom we trust the most are capable of committing fraud. The authors have done a magnificent job of simply explaining the psychological and sociological characteristics of a fraudster. If you work with money, this book is a must read."

—Russ Cancilla
Vice President & Chief Security Officer (retired), Baker Hughes

"Our profession has a rich body of literature on the subject of fraud. Unfortunately, the litera-ture has had a significant gap in understanding all elements of fraud and its motivation and execution. This book identifies and closes this gap by focusing on what is perhaps the most important key: psychology."

—W. Ken Harmon, DBA
Provost and Vice President for Academic Affairs,
Professor of Accounting, Kennesaw State University

"I'm often asked, 'What is the difference between an accountant and a forensic accountant?' and 'What distinguishes a forensic accountant from a good forensic accountant?' I've pon-dered these questions for years, but the answer to both questions invariably circles back to profiling the white-collar criminal. While all accountants focus on numbers (the quantita-tive), the forensic accountant must be in tune with the qualitative. In other words, to be a successful forensic accountant or fraud investigator, it is absolutely essential to understand the psychological mindset of the fraudster and the intangible attributes that cannot be captured on a balance sheet or income statement.

"In *A.B.C.'s of Behavioral Forensics*, Dr. Ramamoorti and Dr. Morrison, along with Joe Koletar and Kelly Pope, introduce us to several intriguing characters—all of the characters are real-life fraudsters—and take us on a journey through the concepts of psychology and psychiatry. Building and expanding on Cressey's fraud triangle, the authors do a wonderful job of weaving the clinical aspects of 'mind science' into a practical application of criminology, on a personal and attention-keeping level. With easy to understand language along the way—and literally providing the A.B.C.'s and building blocks for profiling corruption and white-collar crime—this book is a must read, whether fraud examination is just an interest for you, you're new to the profession, or you're a seasoned expert."

—David Sawyer, CPA, CFF, CITP
Partner and Practice Leader,
Forensic Services, Frazier & Deeter LLC,
and four-time president of the
Georgia chapter of the Association
of Certified Fraud Examiners

"This book is an important addition to the literature on behavioral forensics. At a time when corporate governance and risk mitigation are at the top of the agenda for governments and private enterprises in all sectors, the authors have skillfully dissected several ideas at the intersection of accounting and psychology. Of particular value are the several topical examples and anecdotes that elucidate the concepts discussed."

—Ramesh Venkat
Chief Executive Officer, Reliance Private Equity, India

"Brilliant! With the depth, integrity, and passion we have come to expect from Sri, this important work by an eminently qualified team of authors teaches us about ourselves—why we, as humans, do what we do. Anyone interested in understanding the contributing factors that affect the potential for fraud will benefit from the compelling insights contained herein and enjoy Sri's instructive storytelling. G. R. Moorti was certainly prescient!"

—Michael J. Powell
Intellectual Property Attorney and Registered
Mediator, Baker Donelson

"Excellent book that is immensely thorough and a must read for accountants, auditors, investigators, senior management, and audit committee members. This book is very well organized and does a superb job of blending the key theoretical/behavioral aspects of forensics with very good practical examples. It is eminently readable and right on the mark."

—Alan N. Siegfried, MBA, CPA, CIA
Former Auditor General, Inter-American Development Bank

"I really enjoyed reading the book. It presents an interesting insight into the deep recesses of mind. A difficult subject has been presented in simple terms."

—V. Varadarajan
Director, Compliance and Money
Laundering Reporting Officer (MLRO),
Kotak Mahindra (UK) Limited

"This study examines the psychological fabric of fraud, which has reached epidemic proportions in contemporary society. It is particularly illuminating when it examines the relationship between the destructive charismatic corporate executive and his or her ever-gullible followers."

—Jerrold Post, MD
Professor of Psychiatry, Political Psychology, and
International Affairs, Director of the Political
Psychology program, Elliott School
of International Affairs, George Washington University

"'This doesn't make any sense to me.' Or 'Something's not right here.' These have frequently been the words of a junior auditor, compliance officer, or junior staff employee to me that are the beginning of a long, in-depth investigation of fraud. Often, they have not been expressed by the 'smartest guy in the room,' nor have they been spoken by an experienced management executive. Yet they have a 'gut feeling,' a 'women's intuition,' or a keen awareness that something is simply *wrong*. At long last, there is a book about the psychology of fraud that will guide us in the understanding of why it is that some people whom we 'like' and, even more important, trust, commit frauds. The text also guides us toward the next steps forward. *A.B.C.'s of Behavioral Forensics* is an essential read for anyone working in the field of accounting, auditing, compliance, and operations management."

Marjorie A. Maguire-Krupp, CPA, CFA, CIA
Former Vice President, Enterprise Risk Management,
Compliance & Audit, International Consumer
Finance Division, AIG

"I wish I could have read this book when I was in the early stage of my accounting career. People at the average age of a fraudster, between 45 and 55 years, had many years of professional experience compared to me. I looked up to them, knowing little about their vulnerability to committing or condoning fraud during mid-life transition and even less about the psychology and interpersonal dynamics at play."

Brigitte W. Muehlmann, PhD, CPA
Associate Professor, Sawyer Business School, Suffolk University

"Understanding why fraud happens is as important as understanding what happened. *A.B.C.'s of Behavioral Forensics* offers important insight into the mind of the white-collar criminal. It's good reading for accounting professionals, journalists, lawyers, psychiatrists, and laypeople alike."

Bethany McLean
Coauthor, *All the Devils Are Here* and *The Smartest Guys in the Room: The Amazing Rise and Scandalous Fall of Enron*

A.B.C.'s of Behavioral Forensics

A.B.C.'s of Behavioral Forensics

APPLYING PSYCHOLOGY TO FINANCIAL FRAUD PREVENTION AND DETECTION

Sridhar Ramamoorti
David E. Morrison III
Joseph W. Koletar
Kelly R. Pope

Cover image: © iStockphoto.com/4X-image
Cover design: Wiley

Copyright © 2013 by John Wiley & Sons, Inc. All rights reserved.

Published by John Wiley & Sons, Inc., Hoboken, New Jersey.
Published simultaneously in Canada.

No part of this publication may be reproduced, stored in a retrieval system, or transmitted in any form or by any means, electronic, mechanical, photocopying, recording, scanning, or otherwise, except as permitted under Section 107 or 108 of the 1976 United States Copyright Act, without either the prior written permission of the Publisher, or authorization through payment of the appropriate per-copy fee to the Copyright Clearance Center, Inc., 222 Rosewood Drive, Danvers, MA 01923, (978) 750-8400, fax (978) 646-8600, or on the Web at www.copyright.com. Requests to the Publisher for permission should be addressed to the Permissions Department, John Wiley & Sons, Inc., 111 River Street, Hoboken, NJ 07030, (201) 748-6011, fax (201) 748-6008, or online at http://www.wiley.com/go/permissions.

Limit of Liability/Disclaimer of Warranty: While the publisher and author have used their best efforts in preparing this book, they make no representations or warranties with respect to the accuracy or completeness of the contents of this book and specifically disclaim any implied warranties of merchantability or fitness for a particular purpose. No warranty may be created or extended by sales representatives or written sales materials. The advice and strategies contained herein may not be suitable for your situation. You should consult with a professional where appropriate. Neither the publisher nor author shall be liable for any loss of profit or any other commercial damages, including but not limited to special, incidental, consequential, or other damages.

For general information on our other products and services or for technical support, please contact our Customer Care Department within the United States at (800) 762-2974, outside the United States at (317) 572-3993 or fax (317) 572-4002.

Wiley publishes in a variety of print and electronic formats and by print-on-demand. Some material included with standard print versions of this book may not be included in e-books or in print-on-demand. If this book refers to media such as a CD or DVD that is not included in the version you purchased, you may download this material at http://booksupport.wiley .com. For more information about Wiley products, visit www.wiley.com.

Library of Congress Cataloging-in-Publication Data:

Ramamoorti, Sridhar.
  A.B.C.'s of behavioral forensics : applying psychology to financial fraud prevention and detection / Sridhar Ramamoorti and David E. Morrison III with Joseph W. Koletar and Kelly R. Pope.
     pages cm
  Includes bibliographical references and index.
  ISBN 978-1-118-37055-1 (cloth) — ISBN 978-1-118-42058-4 (ePDF) —
ISBN 978-1-118-41724-9 (ePub) — ISBN 978-1-118-74042-2 (O-Book) 1. Fraud. 2. Criminal psychology. 3. Fraud—Prevention. I. Title.
  HV6691.R36 2013
  363.25'963—dc23

                         2013013997

Printed in the United States of America
10 9 8 7

For my father, G. R. Moorti (1927–2011), who was persuaded that I would be the psychologist among the accountants and the accountant among the psychologists

For Dr. Gil Geis (1925–2012), reputed University of California–Irvine criminologist and president of the Association of Certified Fraud Examiners (1992–2002) for his mentoring and encouragement

With apologies to the Reverend Charles Lutwidge Dodgson, aka Lewis Carroll of *Alice in Wonderland* fame,

"The time has come," the Walrus said,
"To talk of many a thing:
Of shoes and ships and sealing-wax
Of psychology and accounting!"

Imagine how hard physics would be if particles could think!
—Murray Gell-Man, Physics Nobel Laureate

Contents

Foreword

In more than a quarter century as a forensic accountant, I have encountered many corporate executives, managers, and staff who allegedly committed fraud. Every one of these "characters" has been fascinating and somewhat mysterious, like the protagonist in a whodunit. Each person apparently decided to falsify records or give untruthful or misleading answers to questions. Nevertheless, in every case, an objective analysis suggested to me it was inevitable that they would, in time, get caught. Their actions conflicted with basic common sense, but these apparently smart businesspeople went ahead anyway. Why? That is the riddle that hooked me on a career fighting fraud.

Data analytics now offers powerful tools and techniques to help deter or more quickly detect potential wrongdoing, reaching into huge populations of data and identifying anomalies that merit further investigation. Behavioral forensics has similar potential to help businesspeople identify anomalous behaviors that may indicate a heightened risk of fraud or other wrongdoing. In terms of widespread practical implementation, behavioral forensics may be some years behind data analytics, but its potential is just as exciting.

The authors of *The A.B.C.'s of Behavioral Forensics* have both academic credentials and extensive business experience. This helps to make their material more accessible and more practical than a textbook or academic paper. This book will likely introduce you to new terms and to ways of thinking that may seem quite alien at first, but, trust me, you will warm up to it. Confirming much of what you intuitively know about people and human nature, your patience will be rewarded with valuable insights and "Aha!" moments as you recognize and understand better the behavior of a former customer or supplier, boss or colleague. Medical diagnosis should be left to the professionals, but understanding behavioral forensics could help you to more effectively prevent, deter, and detect fraud.

Fraud is a human act and both influences and is influenced by the prevailing culture and society—the twin conceptual towers on which the field of anthropology is founded. I am enthusiastic about the prospects for behavioral forensics in the coming years as the societal and cultural aspects of fraud become a greater focus of research in economic anthropology. This book is a great introduction to a topic that accountants, auditors, compliance officers, lawyers, fraud examiners, financial managers, and other business professionals could benefit from understanding more as we all work to help combat the costly global scourge of fraud.

Toby J. F. Bishop
Director, Deloitte Forensic Center
Deloitte Financial Advisory Services LLP
and former president and CEO
Association of Certified Fraud Examiners

Preface: A Serendipitous Journey to This Book

The man who knows how will always have a job. The man who also knows why will always be his boss.

—Ralph Waldo Emerson

Advances are made by answering questions. Discoveries are made by questioning answers.

—Bernard Haisch
Director, Calphysics Institute

Fraud, especially financial fraud, has become a global concern for governments and societies all over the world, and it shows no sign of abating. Instead, we remain largely helpless, watching what seems to be a growth industry. The United States has no monopoly on it, either. To try to explain this complex phenomenon is to set a grand goal, yet part of what our team set out to do was to follow Bernard Haisch's insight quoted in the epigraph to the preface and question answers. At the core is the answer that all fraud is greed and that the fraud of one mind is the same as the fraud of many minds.

This preface will have an autobiographical flavor to better describe how it is that such a team of authors came together to write this book—there's a story that runs through it. Genesis stories are important, as American philosopher George Santayana emphasized, for you can't know where you're going until you know where you've been.

Autobiographical narratives can be interesting, but mine (Sri speaking) is unusual because the luck element seems so compelling—including the serendipity in meeting Dr. David "Daven" E. Morrison III, a psychiatrist by training, who knows so many of my ex–Arthur Andersen colleagues and has greatly influenced my thinking over the years. As coauthor, he has made significant contributions to this book.

After training to be a chartered accountant from India and working for Ernst & Young in the Middle East, I came to the United States as a student in the Ph.D. program in accounting and management information systems at The Ohio State University in Columbus. After four years in the Ph.D. program, as luck would have it, and because my second Ph.D. advisor was hospitalized and couldn't supervise my dissertation, I made the momentous decision—really by accident—to switch my disciplinary focus to quantitative psychology.

In transferring to psychology, I was fully supported by my first advisor, Professor Andrew D. Bailey Jr., who had since moved on to the University of Arizona. When I earned my Ph.D. in psychology in 1995, I simultaneously became the first—to the best of my knowledge—certified *psychological* accountant in the United States. I wasn't planning to be the "shrink" among the CPAs, nor am I "certifiable," but I do know something about how the human mind works.

My foray into the behavioral sciences opened my eyes. It did for me what Marcel Proust described in this profound observation: "The voyage of discovery is not in seeking new landscapes but in having new eyes." My "eyes" as a professional accountant were focused on the *how* questions: how the books are "cooked," how the evidence is concealed, and how trust is violated, all from investigations after the fact. It was not until the first few years of this century, watching the prestigious firm of Arthur Andersen collapse while I was employed there, that I came to realize the significance of understanding the *why* question.

My understandings were cemented through interactions with professional colleagues at Ernst & Young's forensic and investigative practice with former FBI Special Agent Dr. Joseph Koletar (a coauthor of this book); David Stulb, now global leader for Ernst & Young's Fraud Investigation and Dispute Services (FIDS) practice; and Michael Emmert, then the E&Y FIDS managing partner. With David Stulb offering commentary, I was a member of the in-house Ernst & Young faculty that conducted training seminars on "Fraud Risk: Assessment and Response" to more than 1,000 U.S. audit partners and principals across the country. By this time, I was also persuaded that future generations of accountants should take relevant psychology courses—not by accident like me, but by design.

Again as luck would have it, through Madhavan Nayar, the cofounder of the Information Integrity Coalition (IIC), I met Daven Morrison at an IIC meeting. I later served with him on the board of the organization and subsequently became president. Daven and I immediately connected, especially when I found out that his father, Dr. David Morrison, a distinguished psychiatrist, had had a consulting relationship with Arthur Andersen in the 1970s and 1980s. In my quest, I simply couldn't have met a better person than Daven to help me continue thinking seriously about the *why* question. Of course, I appreciate the reciprocal causation—the fact that the *why* and *how* questions may frequently be connected.

Bringing Joseph Koletar into our conversations allowed us to submit a proposal to the newly founded Institute for Fraud Prevention (IFP), a joint initiative of the American Institute of Certified Public Accountants and the Association of Certified Fraud Examiners (ACFE). Our topic was "Bringing Freud to Fraud: Understanding the Mind of the White Collar Criminal." It is in this IFP-funded 2009 research paper that we laid out the core A.B.C. ideas: the bad apple, the bad bushel, and the bad crop. Numerous "psychology of fraud" presentations internationally confirmed that the A.B.C. characterization resonated with many in the antifraud professional community.

At his alma mater, West Virginia University, Ernst & Young's Chuck Owens, also a former FBI agent, introduced me to Professors Richard Riley and Timothy Pearson, both active with IFP. They got me to write the article on the psychology and sociology of fraud that appears as an appendix in this book.

For some time, Toby Bishop from Deloitte and I served as fellow IFP board members. Toby and I worked together at Arthur Andersen. Brad Preber of Grant Thornton is an ex-Andersen colleague as well. As luck would have it (the third time now), these valued, talented, and seasoned professional colleagues from whom I have learned so much graciously agreed to write the foreword and the afterword, respectively, to this book.

It is a motley crew that constitutes the book's authoring team: an accountant, psychologist, former accounting-firm partner, and now professor; an organizational psychiatrist who has consulted with many C-suite executives; a veteran FBI special agent; and an accounting professor who has done a series of interviews with convicted white-collar felons. Indeed, I am convinced that only when people with different backgrounds apply their minds to answering hard questions will we have an opportunity for breakthrough ideas to surface. But this is also a point of view firmly held by my coauthor Daven Morrison. He will take the baton from me at this point and conclude this preface.

• • •

Research emphasis on fraud prevention and detection entered my (Daven speaking) world by way of Sri, who invited me to the renaissance of the IFP. This was a delightful meeting of inquiring minds: ACFE founder and chairman Joe Wells; Tim Pearson; Dick Riley; John Warren; and Mary-Jo Kranacher, editor of *CPA Journal*; and others. They found my psychiatry background surprisingly relevant to their efforts in gaining a better understanding of the criminal mind.

As Sri noted earlier, we hit upon the A.B.C. configuration in work done for the IFP by colliding our ideas the way the Fermi lab smashes atoms, fully cognizant there were so many answers to be questioned. Personally intrigued by questions about tone at the top, the history of Andersen's origins and its downfall, and the parallel and tragic story of Continental Bank in Chicago, I was hooked.

The ideas were new, but they brought back memories of my training in psychiatry. I was deeply familiar with the many ways people deceive one another. At times, early in my training, my colleagues and I felt like mercenary soldiers standing guard against malingerers. We knew—or least thought we did—who was really ill and who was just looking for food and shelter (or what was called "three hots and a cot"). As an intern, during my very first Veterans Administration rotation, I had the good fortune of having Phillip Resnick, M.D., as my supervisor. He taught me a fundamental truth about the dance between people caught up in deception and deception detection: The only way to truly know if someone is malingering is if you catch the person in the act or if he or she confesses and tells you.

Despite all the technological advances, this fundamental tenet remains true today, more than 20 years later.

Before and after my medical education, I worked with David Morrison, my father. He has always had a medical mind-set underpinning his consulting practice. Recruited to Chicago to work with Continental Bank, he consulted with Arthur Andersen as well as

Amoco and other organizations. The following principles from medicine remain at the core of our shared approach:

- Make the right diagnosis through listening and quality assessment.
- Pursue primary prevention (one can do more good avoiding problems than dealing with them after they manifest).
- Treat the person; don't force-fit the theory backward.

My interests in completing training and joining my father's consulting practice full-time allowed me to find a niche on the team. This niche was related to the "derailing" executive: the executive who had to either change his or her performance or leave. Deception, including large doses of self-deception, and half-truths are common in this arena. Challenges of performance feedback processes and methods were also exposed like a receding tide. Working with derailing executives helped me understand the power of emotion and the importance of having a language and theory that would help others see what I saw with great clarity. These dynamics must apply to fraud, I surmised. And this experience is what I brought to IFP.

Although Joe and Sri generally agreed with my intuitions, it helped me greatly to see and hear the emotions and motivations we had suspected in the interviews of felons conducted and filmed by coauthor Kelly Pope. Being able to see shame, hear about how and why real people chose to commit fraud, and discuss it all with a professional colleague like Dr. Pope was a wonderful opportunity.

Perhaps the most personal tie Sri and I have is to Arthur Andersen. However, we also have a behavioral science connection—after all, the disciplines of psychiatry and psychology are close cousins. If not for Enron, the dynamics around that organization, and its relationship to Andersen, many of us would have had distinctly different career paths. In my efforts to understand what happened, I talked with journalist Bethany McLean, who broke the Enron story. On the question of why C-suite executives aren't more curious about what the implications of Enron are for their organizations, she noted, "There is virtually no concern for fraud. They don't worry about it because they don't think it could ever happen in their company." Yet the odds are undoubtedly that it will, and continued self-deception only guarantees that it won't be stopped until it is too late. Humility and the ability to understand fraud risk and consider the potential for fraud will be necessary for future leaders.

There but for the grace . . .

For all of us on the team, we really want to understand the human being who commits fraud, the ultimate domain proper for the nascent field of behavioral forensics.

Acknowledgments

Any book is hardly the work of a single author. This book, involving a multidisciplinary team of authors, has considerably benefited from the detailed reviews and comments of several distinguished practitioners and academics. Indeed, it is their encouragement about topics that are quite distant from the everyday concerns of (forensic) accountants, auditors, and business leaders that kept us focused and going.

The following individuals (in alphabetical order) provided helpful review comments on earlier drafts of the manuscript that improved it in both substance and style: Lauren Abramson, Ph.D.; Michael Apter, Ph.D.; Raj Bagga; Dr. Andrew Bailey; Usha Balakrishnan; Jennifer Baskin; Jameson Baxter; Toby Bishop; Clyde Bowles, J.D.; Katherine Brummel; Russ Cancilla; Dr. Bruce Clements; Dr. Rich Clune; Chetan Dalal; Dr. Kathryn Epps; Dr. Barry Epstein; R. Luke Evans; Jeanette Franzel; Peter Freeman, J.D.; Karen Garner; L. S. Giridhar; Dr. Audrey Gramling; Dr. W. Ken Harmon; Victor Hartman; Dr. Dana Hermanson; Vernon "Vick" Kelly, M.D.; William P. Kovacs; Harry Kraemer; Margie Maguire Krupp; Duane Kullberg; Neeraj Kumar; Jake Lambert; David Landsittel; Robert Martin; Fred Masci; Tracy McBride; Tom McGahey; David Morrison (Daven's father); Dr. Brigitte Muehlmann; Bill Olsen; Charles Owens; Pete Pesce; Jim Peterson; Jerrold Post, M.D.; Michael J. Powell, J.D.; Brad Preber; Debra Richie; David Sawyer; Ron Schouten, M.D.; Kurt Schulzke; Mohammed Siddiqui; Alan Siegfried; Steve Smalt; Paul Sobel; Dr. Eugene Soltes; Daniel Street; Karthik Swarnam; Robert Thornton; Connie Valencia; V. Varadarajan; Dr. Ramesh Venkat; Neel Venkatachalam; Raj Vijh; John Warren; Monica Weaver; Sheila Weinberg; and Alan "Phil" White.

In addition, we have benefited from conversations on this topic with numerous friends, relatives, and professional colleagues, including Dr. Rashad Abdel-Khalik; Dr. Mohammed Abdolmohammadi; Chris Adonis; Adi Agrawal; Dr. Anurag Agarwal; Imran Akbar; Dr. Conan Albrecht; Dr. Steve Albrecht; Art Alderson; Dr. Nayef Al-Hajraf; Abdulqader Ali; Dr. Gopesh Anand; Dr. Sowmya Anand; Richard Anderson; Dr. Urton Anderson; Naren Aneja; Natarajan Arjun; Savithri Arjun; Dr. Bala Balachandran; Dr. Ramji Balakrishnan; Sandeep Baldava; Amy Barrett; Dorsey Baskin; Joseph Bell; Dr. Daniel Beneish; Debbie Benson; Denny Beran; Denny Beresford; Dr. Sanjai Bhagat; Anil Bhandari; S. Bhaskar; Shyam Bhatter; Dr. Gary Biddle; Martin Biegelman; Jennifer Birtz; Jeannot Blanchet; Peggy Boisonneau; the Hon. Charles Bowsher; Adil Buhariwala; Larry Brown; Tom Bussa; Michael Cangemi; Rhoda Canter; Dr. Joseph Carcello; Krishna Chaitanya; Anthony Chalker; Dr. Dennis Chambers; Richard Chambers; Vishesh Chandiok; Sunil Chandiramani; Dr. Akhilesh Chandra; S. Chandrasekhar; Angelina Chin; Jeff Chin; Stephen Chipman; Dr. Robert Colson; Dr. Joseph Comprix; John Covell; Dr. Karen Cravens; Dr. Larry Crumbley; Dr. Srikant Datar; Vikram Das; Nilesh Dattani; Elizabeth Davis; Dr. Jeff Davis; Dr. Roger Debreceny; Jim DeLoach; Mark DeLong; Dr. Don Delves; Dr. Susela Devi; Rhea Dignam; Dr. Mortimer Dittenhofer; Dr. Rajib Doogar; Darrell Dorrell; Dennis Duquette; Angsuman Dutta; Dr. Martha Eining; Michael Emmert; Julie Erhardt; George Farragher; Jon Feig; Curtis Fields; Annie Flatz; Randy Fletchall; Bill Foale; John Fogarty; John J. Fontana; Dr. Dana Forgione; Jonny Frank; Tony Fuller; Dr. James Gaa; Dr. Jagdish Gangolly; David Garfield, M.D.; Hal Garyn; J. Russell Gates; R. Trent Gazzaway; John Geron; John Gill; Dr. Jon Glover; Steve Goepfert; Gary Goolsby; Jim Green; Craig Greene; James Greene; Chris Grippa; Dr. Parveen Gupta; Sandeep Gupta; Sanjay Gupta; Dr. Karl Hackenbrack; Oliver Halle; Michael Hamilton; Fred Harburg; Dr. Govind Hariharan; Taylor Hawes; Mike Head; Greg Heffington; Dr. John Hepp; Paul Herring; Linda Hertog; Jan Hertzberg; Eric Hespenheide; Scott Hilen; Bob Hirth; Robert Hodgkinson; Nick Hodson; Dr. Chris Hogan; Marie Hollein; Chuck Horstmann; Richard Howell; Muhannad Ismail; Dr. Varghese Jacob; Dr. Richard Jagacinski; Dennis Jancsy; Dr. Daniel Jensen; Greg Jonas; Graham Joscelyne; Mike Joyce; Scot Justice; Manoj Kabra; Nitin Kabra; Paul Kanneman; Kathi Kedrowski; Dr. Jay Kesan; Dr. J. Edward Ketz; Dr. Saleha Khumawala; Robert Kiely;

Dr. Don Kleinmuntz; Lisa Koblinski; Rick Kokoszka; Bobby Koritala; Frank Koster; Dr. S. P. Kothari; Mary-Jo Kranacher; Richard Kravitz; Dr. Jagan Krishnan; Dr. Jayanthi Krishnan; Dr. Jack Krogstad; Dr. George W. Krull; Mike Krzus; Chris Ksoll; Mohan Kumar; Suresh Kumar; Bob Kutsenda; Steve Kuzma; Dr. Alex Lajoux; Paul Lapides; Dr. Rob Larson; Hee Lee; Dr. Linda Leinicke; Dr. Morley Lemon; Dr. Tom Linsmeier; Brian Loughman; Dr. Timothy Louwers; Tom Lydon; David MacCabe; Jagdeep Makkar; Pavi Mani; Steve Mar; Norman Marks; Kevin McCabe; Mike McGuire; Francine McKenna; Mike McLaughlin; Betty McPhilimy; Rajiv Memani; Steve Minder; Dr. Theodore Mock; Anna Mok; Sam Mok; James A. Morel; Iyad Mourtada; Richard Mueller; Dr. Jane Mutchler; Dr. Jay Myung; Madhavan Nayar; Dr. Belverd Needles; Dr. Mark Nelson; Roger Nelson; Dr. Frederick Neumann; Robert Newsome; Dr. Mark Nigrini; Dr. Sumit Nijhawan; James O'Donnell, Pharm.D; Thomas Olivieri; Edith Orenstein; Dr. Joyce Ostrosky; Scott Paczosa; Sriram Padmanabhan, Dr. Venkatesh Padmanabhan; Michael Pakter; Prabha Parameswaran; Dr. Jagdish Pathak; Dave Peacos; Dr. Tim Pearson; Jeff Perkins; Dr. Karen Pincus; Nagesh Pinge; Dr. Hasan Pirkul; David Pleasance; John Polarinakis; Mike Popovits; Dr. Les Porter; N. S. Prasad; Dr. Doug Prawitt; SanDee Priser; Liza Prossnitz; John Radford; Anita Raghavan; Sundaresan Rajeswar; Dr. Ram Ramakrishnan; T. N. Ramakrishnan; Sridhar Ramamurthy; Dr. Kasi Ramanathan; Pratima Rao; Shrikanth C. R. Rao; James Ratley; Dr. Kurt Reding; Dennis Reigle; Phil Resnick, M.D.; Dr. Zabi Rezaee; David Richards; Dr. Richard Riley; Amy Ripepi; Ram Rishi; Dr. Larry Rittenberg; Dr. Jack Robertson; Jeff Robertson; James Rose; Robert Rudloff; Mark Ruppert; Dr. Fleming Ruud; Rajendra Saboo; Mark Salamasick; Dr. Michael Salvador; Anant Sampat; Michael Santay; Michael Savage; Dr. Katherine Schipper; Andre Schnabl; Stephen Seliskar; David Sems; Jerry Serlin; G. V. Seshagiri; N. G. Shankar; Ruby Sharma; Mahesh Shetty; Scott Showalter; V. Shrinivasan; Bob Shultz; Dr. Tommie Singleton; Bill Sinnett; Dr. Ira Solomon; Dr. Theodore Sougiannis; L. Srinivasan; Dr. Shiva Srinivasan; Dr. Rajendra Srivastava; Mike Starr; James St. Clair; J. Larry Stevens; John Stewart; Warren Stippich; Dr. Dan Stone; Brenda Stopher; Dr. Donna Street; David Stulb; Dr. Shyam Sunder; Dan Swanson; Dr. Natan Szuster; Tom Tam; Scott Taub; Bill Taylor; Dr. Donald Tidrick; Tom Tischauser; Sheri Toivonen; Daniel Torpey; Dr. Richard Traver; Andreas Trogsch; Lynn Turner; Dr. Relmond Van Daniker; Anton van Wyk; Dr. Miklos Vasarhelyi; Dominique

Vincenti; Dr. Manu Vora; the Hon. David Walker; Clarke Warren; Phil Wedemeyer; Dr. Marcia Weidenmier-Watson; Dr. Thomas Weirich; Dr. Joseph Wells; David Wetmore; Dr. Ray Whittington; Mike Willis; Mary Wilson; Rod Winters; Rick Wood; Dr. Arnie Wright; Dr. Arthur Wyatt; Owen Youngman; Dr. Tarik Yousef; Kevin Yu; Mark Zabel; Parul Zaveri; Gary Zeune; Dr. Douglas Ziegenfuss; Dr. Richard Ziegler; and Paul Zikmund.

We would also like to acknowledge the support of Betty Ricksecker and Sally Imboden, who have helped coordinate the conference calls and calendars of the authors.

The perspectives provided by convicted felons Diann Cattani, Sam Antar, and Walt Pavlo were particularly useful; Antar and Pavlo have been quoted in Appendix B.

At John Wiley & Sons, our esteemed publishers, Tim Burgard was an early and avid supporter of the concept behind this book and has championed the book throughout its development. Jennifer MacDonald, Judith Antonelli, and Kimberly Monroe-Hill have been terrific editors and helped convey our message with clarity and polish. We genuinely appreciate Kimberly Monroe-Hill's gentle nudges from time to time to get us to the finish line. Helen Cho cheerfully assisted with manuscript reviews and in securing endorsements. Overall, we were impressed with the professionalism and excellent demeanor of the Wiley team.

In particular, Daven and Sri would like to acknowledge the Committee of Work and Organizations of the Group for the Advancement of Psychiatry (GAP). In 2008, the GAP committee invited Sri and Bethany McLean as special guests for an afternoon discussion of aspects of psychiatry, leadership, fraud, and organizations. The committee at that time consisted of Joshua Gibson, M.D. (chairman); Barrie Grieff, M.D.; Steven Heidel, M.D.; Robert Larsen, M.D.; Barbara Long, M.D.; and David and Daven Morrison. Sri would like to thank David Sawyer, Vic Hartman, and Dave Peacos for inviting him to speak on the topic of behavioral forensics at the 2012 Georgia ACFE Chapter Conference.

Daven would like to acknowledge David Morrison, the "elder" who presented to large and small groups of financial services professionals and found a way to connect. Many of the ideas in our book had their start with his sharp and incisive insights. Sri fondly recalls several insightful conversations with his father, G. R. Moorti, and Dr. Gil Geis, both of whom are now deceased and to whom this book is dedicated.

As always, the support of our loved ones merits mention. Sri's mother and sisters have been a constant source of encouragement his entire life. His wife, Binu Ramamoorti, has been the wind beneath his wings (despite her occasional caustic inquiry, when he was a hapless, struggling Ph.D. student in psychology, "Honey, how was la-la land today?"). As for the little one, Sarita, she has by now surely concluded that her father is some kind of typist! Similarly, Jeanette, Daniel, and Henry Morrison have graciously tolerated the work demands of the "fraud" book.

Both families have endured many missed meals, long phone calls, and intrusions on vacation and holiday breaks over the last several years—we hope you think it was worth it. It was your efforts and sacrifice that allowed us the space to work and to bring this book to life.

Introduction

This is a book about fraud. To be more precise, it is a book about the psychology of fraud. It focuses on human behavior, because the central fact behind all fraud is the existence of one or more individuals and their questionable, egregious, unethical, or even illegal, behavior.

This book is largely unlike any other you may have ever read on this topic. It covers an important aspect of fraud, for even though we think we know fraud, in reality we know only part of it. It is like the old analogy about the iceberg: What is known is usually visible, seen above the surface, but most of it remains hidden beneath the surface. Unfortunately, it is what is beneath and unseen that causes the most harm.

More than a century ago, Sigmund Freud brought our attention to the fact that the conscious part of ourselves is like the tip of an iceberg.[1] The unconscious part is what lies underneath. Although unconscious motivation was first introduced by Freud as part of his psychoanalytic theory, more recently, neuroscientists have done extensive research on how consciousness and emotions drive decision making. It is not a case of "What you see is what you get" (WYSIWYG), but rather it's "What you *don't* see is what you get." Think of fraud, then, as a two-sided coin. On one side is the economics of fraud. Fraud has enormous consequences, economically speaking, so this is what we usually focus on: the numbers, the losses, the techniques, the forged documents, the wire transfers, the shady deals, the adjustments to the general ledger, and so on. The latest (2012) *Report to the Nations* from the Association of Certified Fraud Examiners estimates that the typical organization loses 5 percent of its revenues to fraud each year. Applied to the 2011 gross world product, this figure translates to more than $3.5 trillion annually.

With much effort devoted to examining the economic results of fraud, accounting as a profession has developed some skill at examining these hard facts.[2] They are numbers on a piece of paper or on a computer screen. We can slice and dice them, detect patterns, and gather evidence to ascertain whether fraud has taken place. In the process, we might even uncover how the fraudsters went about their fraudulent acts and their associated concealment activities. In other words, we know quite a bit about how fraud is perpetrated.

Looking at the economics is important work, but we rarely turn the coin over to look at the other side: the hidden human factor. How do we understand the behaviors and actions that lie behind and motivate fraud?

The Human Factor

An article on the human factor in fraud asserts the following:

> Fraud is a human endeavor, involving deception, purposeful intent, intensity of desire, risk of apprehension, violation of trust, rationalization, [and so on]. So, it is important to understand the psychological factors that might influence the behavior of fraud perpetrators. The rationale for drawing on behavioral science insights is evident from the intuition that one needs to "think like a crook to catch a crook."[3]

Many business professionals—particularly those in the accounting, auditing, and finance arena, who are analytically minded—tend to discount behavioral explanations.[4] They think they already know what fraud is; after all, as Judge Edwin R. Holmes observed in 1941, "The law does not define fraud; it needs no definition; it is as old as falsehood and as versatile as human ingenuity."[5] As the incidence of fraud continues to grow, however, placing the spotlight on behavioral factors may be an important approach not only to fraud detection but to fraud deterrence as well.[6]

Consider a reality check: In the history of human existence, no general ledger or computer has ever committed a fraud. People certainly use these tools and other mechanisms to commit fraud, but

Like a gun in wrong persons hand

the instruments themselves are inert. They are insentient; they have no motive, no desire. They are just things. It is also not about the process, it is about the people!

Such is fraud. We have tended to look at the instruments but not the motivations. It is all quite simple: Fraud is a result of human behavior, actions unique to human beings—nothing more, nothing less. Thus, in this book, we seek to turn the coin over and to look at the hidden part of the iceberg. We begin to examine the simple but crucial question of *why*.

In doing so, we enter precarious and largely uncharted territory. The human mind is perhaps the most complex and powerful "mechanism" on the face of the earth. In the human mind, the power exists to do good or harm. This book explores the human mind's propensity to engage in the harm of fraud. We often think we know someone when in reality we do not. People often wear masks when facing the world and may exhibit themselves in ways that belie their true natures.[7] Aspects of their personalities or characters may drive their actions in maladaptive ways.

Not only are there complexities of the human mind, there are also nuances in all of us as we move through adulthood and face developmental challenges, just like children who must learn to manage the different challenges of kindergarten and high school. As with the iceberg, we believe that the part of someone we can see is his or her true being when it is not. And when it comes to motivations and strivings, psychologists and psychiatrists will tell you that even fraud perpetrators themselves may be unaware of why they engaged in certain behaviors.[8] Even when they talk about it later.[9]

Adding to the complexity is the interplay of minds. Besides the interplay of fraud perpetrator and victim, there is gang behavior, in which individuals, as a result of a dominant gang leader or perhaps groupthink, get caught up in a unique set of warped ethics (frequently outside what is legal). This leads to a group activity that is to the group members' long-term personal detriment. Upon reflection, many convicted white-collar felons are able to track exactly when they transgressed their own internally set psychological thresholds relating to their values and beliefs. At other times, organizations and shareholders run after charismatic leaders only to find themselves operating in a delusional system with its own closed-system logic that cannot be challenged. This provides a toxic culture that is a fertile soil for fraud and other human action that puts an organization at risk.

A toxic culture can drive fraud, and complexity can help to mask fraud. Just as pioneers exploring a new continent seek new understanding, in order to understand the human aspects of fraud, we must have some foundational points of reference. We need a guide to the "lay of the land"—the topography.

Trust Violation and Its Consequences

Criminologist Donald Cressey deserves much credit for his writings about the root causes of fraud and the so-called fraud triangle. Just as the fire triangle is shown with the components of heat, oxygen, and fuel, the fraud triangle has three vertices: opportunity, pressure or incentive, and rationalization. What often goes unrecognized is that all three elements of the fraud triangle are fundamentally behavioral constructs. Personal incentive and perceived pressure drive human behavior, and the need to rationalize wrongdoing as somehow defensible is very much psychologically rooted. To some extent, even the assessment of the opportunity to commit fraud—including the likelihood of being caught—is a subjective, behavioral assessment.

Therefore, to understand the root causes of fraud, psychological explanations should be sought. The decision to deviate from the norm and commit fraud is not taken lightly; it involves the ability to justify one's questionable actions to oneself and to others. When the consequences of our actions lead to exposure, the effect on individuals can be devastating.

Fraud is not always a "soft" crime. A tragic example is Enron Corporation's Cliff Baxter, who couldn't come to terms with what had happened and took the extraordinary step of committing suicide.[10] It is not clear whether he was aware of the crimes at Enron or ashamed at being associated with them. No court of law would see fraud as a capital offense, but for Baxter it was worthy of a death sentence. In his case, judge, jury, and punishment existed in his own mind, which wrought its own justice and brought great tragedy to those who cared for him and survived him.

This Book's Approach: The A.B.C.'s of Behavioral Forensics

Corporate governance reform legislation, such as the Sarbanes-Oxley Act of 2002 and the Dodd-Frank Act of 2010, can certainly help to limit the opportunity for fraud. However, the possibility of individuals succumbing to perceived pressure and their ability to rationalize fraudulent acts remain outside the scope of law. Better governance imperatives in the form of improved rules and regulations have an inner flaw: They are created by people and thus can be outmaneuvered by people.

Fraud deterrence and detection should therefore focus on how to deal with the underlying behavioral dynamics: the psychology of fraud perpetrators; the psychology of those responsible for governance, including auditors; and the psychology of fraud victims, especially what makes them vulnerable to the charm-offensive of con artists. Thus, we intend to explore the psychology of the predator and the prey as well as the overseers of governance and risk management processes. We must also pay attention to the manner in which fraud is perpetrated: by individuals, such as rogue traders or executives operating alone; by groups of executives, or colluding "bad boys"; and by a culture that seems to be forgiving of bad behavior and at times even encourages egregious behavior. These considerations constitute the basics of the previously defined A.B.C. theory: bad apple, bad bushel, bad crop.[11]

An understanding of what motivates the fraudster, whether acting alone or in collusion with others inside or outside the organization, can go a long way in identifying the behavioral risk factors that may indicate fraud. A simple analysis of motive, opportunity, and means (MOM) shows that motives are the crux of the matter, because fraud requires the establishment of intent to deceive another. So it is crucial to know what the potential motives are—what it is that a fraud perpetrator desires:

- **Greed.** Money or other financial incentives, such as a bonus or stock-based compensation.
- **Status.** "Keeping up with the Joneses," fame, or fear of losing status.
- **Revenge.** "The organization owes me" and crimes of passion (the victims of such fraud may not be entirely innocent).
- **Excitement.** The thrill of a catch-me-if-you-can game or a gambling frame of mind.
- **Parity with others.** "Everybody else is doing it, so why can't I?"
- **Loss of moral compass.** "Noble cause corruption"[12] is behavior arising out of a mind-set or subculture that fosters a belief that the ends justify the means and so forth.[13]

If opportunities do not exist, the motivated fraud perpetrator can create them by a careful analysis of weaknesses in controls or by exploiting a generally lax environment. Once fraud perpetrators take the initial steps, they quickly reach the proverbial point of no return and frequently find themselves unable to turn back and escape the ruinous consequences. Even convicted fraudsters, in candid interviews and reflecting in retrospect, admit to having crossed the line or overstepping a self-determined ethical or behavioral norm.[14] We will say more about this later.

An Interdisciplinary Approach

As a team, the four authors of this book bring diverse yet specialized perspectives to understanding the phenomenon of fraud in all its complexity. They share a combined experience of more than 100 years in diverse areas related to financial fraud, having served many of the Fortune 100 companies and smaller clients across industries. These include accounting, auditing, internal controls, ethics, information integrity and corporate governance, psychology, psychiatry, criminology, executive risk management, and forensic accounting and fraud prevention, deterrence, detection, investigation, and remediation. The authors have worked for three of the big four accounting firms and Grant Thornton at different points in their careers and are members of many professional organizations appearing in the following list.

- American Institute of Certified Public Accountants
- Association of Certified Fraud Examiners
- Institute of Internal Auditors
- Association of Government Accountants
- American Society for Industrial Security
- Financial Executives International
- Information Systems Audit and Control Association
- Institute for Fraud Prevention
- Group for the Advancement of Psychiatry
- National Association of Certified Valuators and Analysts
- Society of Former Special Agents of the FBI
- International Association of Chiefs of Police
- Association of Former Intelligence Officers
- Tomkins Institute

- Academy of Organizational and Occupational Psychiatry
- National Association of Corporate Directors

Our combined expertise thus provides a comprehensive interdisciplinary lens through which to view the fraud phenomenon and generate helpful insights.

This book has the modest goal of introducing new thinking about the behavioral forensics of fraud while using the A.B.C.'s of behavioral forensics as a backbone to explain the breadth of effects to the reader. We are persuaded that the combination of behavioral forensics, financial forensics, and computer forensics will result in a synergy that can be a powerful antidote to combat fraud and white-collar crime internationally.

Notes

1. S. Ramamoorti, J. W. Koletar, and D. Morrison, *Bringing Freud to Fraud: Understanding the State of Mind of the C-Level Suite/White-Collar Offender through "A-B-C" Analysis.* Institute for Fraud Prevention (IFP), 2009, http://www.theifp.org.
2. See, for instance, H. M. Schilit and J. Perler, *Financial Shenanigans: How to Detect Accounting Gimmicks & Fraud in Financial Reports* (New York: McGraw Hill, 2010); Mark Nigrini, *Forensic Analytics: Methods and Techniques for Forensic Accounting Investigations* (Hoboken, NJ: John Wiley & Sons, 2011); Mark Nigrini, *Benford's Law: Applications for Forensic Accounting, Auditing, and Fraud Detection* (Hoboken, NJ: John Wiley & Sons, 2012); and D. D. Dorrell and G. A. Gadawski, *Financial Forensics Body of Knowledge* (Hoboken, NJ: John Wiley & Sons, 2012) for methods and techniques of forensic accounting, auditing, and fraud detection.
3. S. Ramamoorti and W. Olsen, "Fraud: The Human Factor," *Financial Executive* (July–August 2007): 53–55.
4. We might come up with several reasons for such discounting: Most accounting and finance professionals have not taken courses in the behavioral sciences as part of their undergraduate or graduate education; touchy-feely topics do not readily lend themselves to quantitative and analytical approaches; in conventional economics, human emotions have been kept out of decision analysis; and behavioral economics is only now emerging as an influential discipline. See, for instance, M. Altman, *Behavioral Economics for Dummies* (Hoboken, NJ: John Wiley & Sons, 2012); R. H. Thaler and C.R. Sunstein, *Nudge: Improving Decisions About Health, Wealth, and Happiness* (New York: Penguin Books, 2009); and D. Kahneman, *Thinking Fast and Slow* (New York: Farrar, Straus and Giroux, 2011).
5. In *re Weiss v. United States*, 122 F.2d 675, 681 (Ct. App. 5th Cir. 1941). For a fuller appreciation of this line of reasoning, see Appendix A, "The Psychology and Sociology of Fraud."
6. Ramamoorti and Olsen, "Fraud: The Human Factor."

7. Erving Goffman, *The Presentation of Self in Everyday Life* (New York: Anchor Books, 1959).
8. It is important to note that *subconscious* and *unconscious* are not synonyms. The subconscious seems to lie somewhere between the conscious mind and the unconscious; it contains information that is at the margins of attention, that one is only vaguely aware of. See A. S. Reber, R. Allen, and E. S. Reber, *Penguin Dictionary of Psychology* (London: Penguin, 2009).
9. It is instructive to view the ACFE's 2011 video *Inside the Fraudster's Mind* and read the accompanying self-guide to get an appreciation for the common "thinking errors" that fraudsters make. Refer to the summary of the video in Appendix B.
10. "Former Enron Exec Dies in Apparent Suicide, CNN, January 26, 2002, http://articles.cnn.com/2002-01-25/us/enron.suicide_1_cliff-baxter-philip-hilder-enron-north-america?_s=PM:US.
11. The A.B.C. concept was originally developed by Ramamoorti, Koletar, and Morrison as part of an IFP-funded project as stated in note 1. The working paper, as of December 2009, is posted at http://www.theifp.org.
12. Steve Rothlein, "Noble Cause Corruption," *Public Agency Training Council,* 2008, http://www.patc.com/weeklyarticles/print/noble-cause-corruption.pdf. An interesting aspect of "noble cause corruption"—done for love of country, office, or position—is that the individuals engaging in such activity may not be "bad apples" but may in fact be "golden apples," or the best officers of a government agency, for instance.
13. Social comparison theory asserts that people evaluate their own abilities and opinions by comparing themselves to others; other people help us to define ourselves. See L. Festinger, "A Theory of Social Comparison Processes," *Human Relations* 7 (1954): 117–40; and C. H. Cooley, *Human Nature and the Social Order* (New York: Schocken Books, 1902). For the catch-me-if-you-can-game, see F. W. Abagnale, *Catch Me If You Can: The Amazing True Story of the Youngest and Most Daring Con Man in the History of Fun and Profit* (New York: Broadway Books, 2000).
14. The original Danish adjective, *grænseoverskridende,* meaning "border-crossing," is used exclusively to describe a violation of social norms (contrary to what the English phrase "crossing the line" might suggest).

PART I

WHEN FRAUD IS COMMITTED

Reading the headlines about another fraudulent scam is upsetting on many levels. When the story is one in which the money stolen is in the billions—and thus beyond conceptualization for the average person, who never crosses paths with such large sums—the media accounts stoke rage and provoke calls for justice.

In the allied professions of management and accounting, similar feelings are aroused. Such outrage is more complex in reality and includes feelings of betrayal by peers, colleagues, or even management or capitalist heroes. Legislatures are called upon, grand speeches are delivered, and references are made to times when people were honest, a man earned a living with his hands, and communities (and markets) were based on trust.

In the end, the widespread loss of trust, personal and corporate reputations, and market confidence is the greatest casualty of a catastrophic fraud.

As more and more resources are put into addressing the problem of fraud, sometimes it just looks as though too little is being done too late, and at other times the efforts don't seem to make a dent at all. The fraud problem simply seems to be increasing in scope and frequency, and newspaper headlines continue to highlight how the last major financial loss has just been surpassed by the most recent.

Consider this curious case of theft. A man named Arthur "the Brain" Rachel gained notoriety for stealing the 45-carat Marlborough diamond from a London jewelry store three decades ago. He was sentenced in 2012 to eight and a half years in prison for racketeering. He had already served many years in jail for other crimes, and he was 73 years old when he received this sentence. When the judge announced the sentence, he asked Rachel why he continued to commit crimes after so many years in prison. Rachel reportedly replied that he and his comrades were bored and had nothing better to do.[1]

Fraud is theft, and it is often explained in the media as being motivated by greed. For instance, Pedro Espada Jr., a former New York State senator recently convicted of tax evasion and stealing from a health care network he founded, truly had a "rags-to-ill-gotten-riches" story. He survived homelessness in his youth to rise to the highest echelons of state government and brazenly abused his position, perhaps motivated by greed. Before he was indicted, Espada remarked, "There's no way there's a chapter in this story that includes me going to jail. . . . It's surreal. Not a part of my plan or my script." Commenting on his grandiose sense of entitlement, Eastern District of New York U.S. attorney Loretta E. Lynch called him a "thief in a suit." She concluded, "Pedro Espada Jr. could have chosen the high road. Every time he had a choice, Pedro Espada chose himself."[2]

In contrast, as noted earlier, Arthur Rachel stole items of immense value, but he was not motivated by greed. In both of these cases, might criminal investigations and psychology shine a new and more brilliant light on fraud motivations to broaden and deepen our understanding?[3]

Beyond the solutions currently applied, new ones are needed. With personal computers becoming popular in the 1980s, computer crime (including hacking) also flourished. This naturally led to the new field of computer forensics viz., forensic methods of examining digital media for identifying, preserving, recovering, analyzing, and presenting facts and opinions, which collectively constitute electronic evidence. Financial forensics has made impressive gains and is also rapidly evolving as a specialized discipline. Financial forensics refers to the plethora of tools, techniques, methods, and methodologies— with a primary focus on analysis and surgically precise dissection of numbers and scenarios—applicable to virtually any large or small economic or financial matter, whether civil, criminal, or involving dispute.[4] With the rising incidence of fraud and the realization that fraud is committed by sentient human beings, there is an urgent need for the field of behavioral forensics to exploit the insights of the behavioral disciplines to understand, address, and respond to fraud and perhaps even preempt it.

To understand how fraud happens, new thinking is required to answer this simple question: Why do people commit fraud?

Notes

1. "Jail for Chicago's 'Brain' in Racketeering Case," *Wall Street Journal*, June 8, 2012.
2. Mosi Secret, "Ex-Legislator Guilty of Theft Gets 5-Year Prison Sentence," *New York Times*, June 15, 2013.
3. For instance, psychologist Michael Apter argues that it is to keep boredom at bay that youths in wolf packs engage in the practice of "wilding"—an expression that seems to mean "being wild for its own sake," or being violent. He proceeds to ask, "But how is it that hurting others can produce thrills?" See Michael J. Apter, *Danger: Our Quest for Excitement* (Oxford, UK: One World Publications, 2007), 6. We will discuss some of Apter's theories later in this book.
4. D. D. Dorrell and G. A. Gadawski, *Financial Forensics Body of Knowledge* (Hoboken, NJ: John Wiley & Sons, 2012).

CHAPTER

1

Fraud Is Everywhere

F raud is an interesting concept, because it is both so common and so serious. Fraud is generally everywhere around us; most people do something fraudulent, unwittingly or not, in their lifetimes.

Even such an innocuous thing as two employees chatting for a few minutes in the workplace about last night's baseball game can be a minor form of fraud. After all, they are on company property and are being paid to do other things. Assuming that they are being paid for their time, and that biological needs as well as needs for breaks are provided—many professional service firms bill by the hour—they are defrauding their employer if they are aware that they should be working rather than talking.[1]

This example may be considered a small infraction, and few people would think of it as fraud, but it could become so, depending on the degree. Association of Certified Fraud Examiners (ACFE) founder and chairman Joseph Wells wrote in the prologue to his autobiography, "Everyone [has lied]. Everyone. We do so for two basic reasons: either to receive rewards or to avoid punishment (or a combination of both). Although lying is not endemic to the human species, we learn it very early in life. Fraud, though, is a lie with a special twist—it is committed to deprive an innocent victim of money or property."[2]

Of course, in cases of revenge fraud, the victim may not be so innocent after all.

The Pervasiveness of Fraud

If you ask a room full of midcareer professionals whether they have committed a crime in the past week, almost no one will respond (and perhaps understandably so). Some will be offended by the very nature of the question. But if you then ask them whether they drove just one mile over the speed limit in the past week, they will become sheepish.

"Of course," they will reply, "but it was only a couple of miles an hour. The cops don't care." That may be true, but legally speaking, it is a violation of well-understood traffic laws—and therefore a crime. In most cases it may be unintentional (speedometers tend to be subject to margins of error), but in cases of reckless driving, intentional violation of traffic laws unambiguously makes it a crime.

Tom Tyler, Macklin Fleming Professor of law and a professor of psychology at Yale Law School, provides two useful perspectives on legal compliance. The first is the *instrumental perspective*, wherein he argues that people who take this view obey the law because they fear punishment. The second is the *normative perspective*, wherein people who believe in social norms and perceptions around equity and fairness feel morally obliged to comply with the law, regardless of the fear of punishment.[3] Authorities prefer that citizens hold the normative perspective because it removes the need for law enforcement. Nevertheless, it must be pointed out that people espousing the normative perspective may still decide not to pay their taxes if they believe the tax authorities are unjust. As for those holding the instrumental perspective, their decision primarily relies on weighing the pros and cons of compliance with the law. Stricter enforcement is the only way to dissuade such people from breaking the law.

Fraud, in various small ways, is so common we cease to recognize it. It is just the way people are. It is the normal course of human behavior. Distinguished behavioral economist Dan Ariely makes compelling arguments to provide answers to the following unsettled questions:

- Does the chance of getting caught affect how likely we are to cheat?
- How do companies pave the way for dishonesty?
- Does collaboration make us more honest or less so?[4]

More than three decades ago, sociologists Edwin H. Sutherland and Donald Ray Cressey offered the "differential association principle" as an explanation for why people act this way. They argued that "people violate the law because the world, the nation, and even the family have multiple moralities." Consequently, subjectivity and contextual interpretation make "learning to behave in terms of a morality which could land you in jail . . . as easy as learning how to drive your car faster than 55 miles an hour."[5] They concluded that we can only persuade people to follow the right course of action especially true for those people who adopt the instrumental perspective when deciding whether to obey the law.

David Saunders of the Behavioral Sciences Department of Mathtech, a strategy and consulting services firm, asserted that management fraud can be thought of as a "perversion of effective management behavior"—of executives turning to the dark side. He persuasively described the resulting scenario as follows:

> Nobody would deny that our system of economic incentives rewards imagination applied in the pursuit of profit, and that it rewards managers who exploit profit opportunities. Nobody would deny that this should be so. Yet this often has the effect of encouraging managers to operate as closely as possible to the borderline between legality and illegality—the borderline between what is ethical and what is unethical. And it follows, in turn, that for any of a variety of reasons, an individual manager or management group may *cross over the line* [emphasis added].[6]

Former Securities and Exchange Commission (SEC) chairman Arthur Levitt echoed these ideas in a 1998 speech titled "Numbers Game" delivered at New York University:

> [Too] many corporate managers, auditors, and analysts are participants in a game of nods and winks. . . . Managing may be giving way to manipulation; integrity may be losing out to illusion . . . how difficult it is to hold the line on good practices when their competitors operate in the gray area between legitimacy and outright fraud. A gray area where the accounting is being perverted; where managers are cutting corners; and where earnings reports reflect the desires of management rather than the underlying financial performance of the company.[7]

On Making (Up) the Numbers

Many human beings use cosmetics to enhance their appearance—the color of their lips, skin, or hair—or to improve the way they smell. Cosmetics are also called *makeup*. To make up is to pretend, to create a false impression—to create a new reality, much as a child may create an invisible friend in the course of play. Misleading others by creating a false impression is called *apple polishing* for a fruit seller, *puffery* in advertising, and *window dressing* when used in financial statements that portray a rosier picture of the financial position than is warranted. Actor George Burns famously observed, "If you can fake sincerity, you've got it made." Erving Goffman, probably the most influential twentieth-century sociologist, labeled this "self-presentation" by human beings as part of an elaborate game of "impression management."[8]

One may think that considering such things is silly and a waste of time, but we are citing them to make a point. We all deceive to some degree and in some aspects of our lives. The question then becomes one of magnitude. There is certainly a huge difference between talking about last night's baseball game on company time and crafting a scheme to defraud your employer of millions of dollars. Similarly, there is a big difference between fraudulent financial reporting ("cooking the books") and theft and embezzlement. Explicitly considering these differences helps us to better understand the associated characteristics and statistics.

What are the possible psychological factors that cause some people to commit a big fraud? These fraudsters often seem normal in every way. They are married, loving parents, pillars of the community, active in civic and religious affairs, supporters of good causes, and pleasant to be around. Yet they can do terrible things.

Ken Friedman is a corporate attorney in Manhattan. When asked about who owns fraud risk in corporations, he replied, "When things are going well, nobody does. When the train runs off the tracks, *everybody does*."[9] This is in line with the quip that is humorously titled Zimmerman's Law of Complaints: Nobody notices when things go right.

Consider the following historical facts:

- Enron used to be a wealthy and powerful company—the seventh largest in the United States, with more than $100 billion in revenue.

- Arthur Andersen used to be a premier accounting firm, widely regarded as the "gold standard" in the auditing profession.
- WorldCom was a mammoth telephone services provider, among other sprawling interests.

There were many other companies like these, besides the Silicon Valley technology companies preceding the dot-com crash of 2000–2001, in what is sometimes called the Enron era.

Thousands of people worked in these organizations. When they collapsed, pensions were wiped out, investments were lost, reputations were damaged, and various civil and criminal legal actions were set in motion. Pretty much everyone shared the pain because of the actions of a relative few—who probably seemed normal in every way until the train ran off the tracks.

After the passage of the Sarbanes-Oxley Act in 2002 as a result of the Enron, WorldCom, and Arthur Andersen accounting scandals, we all thought that we had a comprehensive regulatory fix. Soon after the 2002 wake-up call, Leonard Sayles and Cynthia Smith presented their well-researched views on how corporate America was on a dangerous course:

- **How the tail started wagging the dog.** The unanticipated consequences of large-scale executive stock ownership.
- **The technology of deceit.** How information technology makes abuse easier to execute and easier to hide.
- **The silence of the lambs.** How the media and academia contribute to the problem.
- **The mythic executive.** Overwhelming greed, excessive compensation, and feet of clay.[10]

Indeed, the inner workings of corporate America had been shockingly revealed in the Enron and WorldCom scandals. Leading business journalist Roger Lowenstein, who previously reported for the *Wall Street Journal,* made the analogy that it is "as if an attic trapdoor had been flung open exposing the family's supposedly demented aunt, and all of her cousins, nieces, and nephews had seen a ghostly reflection of themselves."[11]

And then came the Wall Street financial meltdown of 2008. The Lehman Brothers collapse, in the amount of $759 billion, alone dwarfed what happened at Enron and WorldCom by ten times.

Moreover, we still do not have any major developments around culpability. The argument seems to be that because so many "bad actors" were involved, it is unfair to single out any particular group, be they bankers, lawyers, accountants, or even politicians.

For instance, a 2012 Rand Corporation study found that hedge funds did not appear to have been a primary cause of the Wall Street financial crisis. In 2011, however, the Financial Crisis Inquiry Commission, concluding that the meltdown could have been avoided, did point to "reckless" Wall Street firms and "weak" regulators as the primary drivers of the financial crisis.[12]

The hugely controversial Dodd-Frank Act of 2010 has been passed, but do we really believe that legislation can prevent fraud? If the collapse was about a corrosive Wall Street culture, then won't it happen again?

This book seeks to address the fact that the devastating outcomes of accounting scandals and massive frauds affect pretty much everyone: boards of directors, audit committees, C-suite executives, internal and external auditors, regulators, investors, employees and their families, and local communities. The damage can be both immense and long-lasting. So we are inevitably led back to these questions:

- Why does fraud happen?
- Could it have been prevented?

The latter question, while difficult, is perhaps the easier to answer. Internal and external controls, monitoring systems, due diligence, professional skepticism, and other mechanisms of corporate governance either failed or were overridden. Management override of internal controls as a critical risk factor has been recognized by the auditing profession and enshrined in professional guidance from the American Institute of Certified Public Accountants (AICPA). The guidance is particularly relevant for audit committees and refers to management override of internal controls as the "Achilles' heel" of fraud prevention strategies.[13]

These corporate governance failures do not happen overnight. There are always warning signs. An analogy can be made to a person's health. We are supposed to get annual physicals because unlike the proverbial canary in the coal mine, very few people drop dead for no apparent reason. Doctors are trained to detect the early warning signs and recommend actions to prevent them from leading to more serious consequences. So it is with corporate "health."

In the financial train wrecks discussed here, the warning signs were certainly there, but they were ignored, overridden, or deliberately suppressed. Thus, it only *seemed* that when what appeared to be "once-great" organizations disappeared overnight, we can see that the warning signs were all there on closer inspection. For instance, the Hon. David M. Walker, former U.S. comptroller general and a former Arthur Andersen partner, made the following remarks:

> The Andersen story illustrates how a few people can do the wrong thing with catastrophic consequences for many innocent parties. It was not long ago that Arthur Andersen was viewed by many as the premier professional services firm in the world. For years, Andersen had the reputation of "thinking straight and talking straight" and doing what it felt was right in connection with challenging accounting and reporting issues—even if the client didn't like the answer. *From global gold standard to GONE in less than two years!* What happened? [emphasis added][14]

The first question, why fraud happens, is the more difficult to answer, because it is there that we enter the realm of the human mind. Most of the people involved in these financial collapses were highly educated, experienced, and well paid. Yet in retrospect, they did things that seem foolish, if not criminal.[15]

We must begin to think of ways to monitor human behavior, to pick up warning signs before the disease becomes fatal, and to be able to take necessary action before a problem becomes too large. But this can be a tricky task.

A Slippery Slope

In the study of ethics, the idea of the slippery slope is fairly simple. It holds that a small infraction or indiscretion, if not detected and dealt with, will probably lead to even more serious infractions and indiscretions over time. There is an old saying among experienced antifraud professionals: "Did you ever hear of somebody stealing a million dollars and working their way down?"

All frauds tend to start small and get bigger with time. There is much speculation on why this occurs. You get used to the "free" money. You take pride in having beaten the system. You believe a number of others are doing it and have yet to be caught. According to the *Report to the Nations* survey published by the ACFE, the average workplace fraud lasts about 18 months and gets bigger with time. These frauds are often detected because they simply become so large that they are too difficult to hide. From the *Report to the Nations* data, we also know that fraud perpetrated by senior management is 16 times as expensive as fraud perpetrated by an average employee. Generalizing, we can assert that the cost of fraud is a function of time as well as the position held by the fraud perpetrator(s).

We know that learning by imitation occurs in the area of ethics. That is, people learn to behave ethically by watching others. However, it turns out that people are more likely to accept others' unethical behavior when ethical degradation occurs slowly over time rather than in one abrupt shift. In terms of the psychological process underlying the slippery slope phenomenon, much of the effect occurs because people simply fail to notice minor violations and infractions, especially when they occur gradually.[16]

Imitating others serves an important social function: it improves interpersonal interactions by signaling that you are in sync with the others in your pace, posture, mannerisms, facial expressions, tone of voice, speech patterns, and other behaviors. Such social mimicry can be conscious or unconscious; it also is not limited to humans but extends to other mammals.[17]

There is another question just beneath the surface that the behavioral sciences have already uncovered: Why does fraud bother us so much?

For example, why is it that we are so disturbed by a theft by senior officers? From research on trauma victims, it is well-known that it is harder to understand, forgive, and adapt when we believe we have been wronged by another human being. When a natural disaster wipes out lives and causes the loss of hundreds of millions of dollars, we are not as troubled as when the loss results from dishonest human beings cheating others. It becomes a question of fairness, and the hardwired, human-primate tendency of inequity aversion is forcefully exhibited.[18]

Being a victim of a crime is one of the most unsettling of all traumas, and when the leaders of an institution are accomplices, it rocks us to the core. Similarly, there is a lot of discussion today about the growing vast disparity between C-suite and rank-and-file compensation.

Noting that compensation was most inflated at the higher levels of the investment banking organization, Roger Lowenstein remarked that CEO incentives were biased toward maximizing short-term profits. Concerning bankers, he observed, "Bankers who took home these enormous paychecks were crafty financiers, but their cleverness served their personal interests first, their clients and shareholders second, and the economy barely at all. The bankers learned to fool the system: to game the rating agencies, [fool] their compensation committees and society, [but] ultimately, the bankers fooled themselves."[19] Here are some actual compensation figures from company proxy reports: "In 2006, Ken Thompson earned $18 million for his handiwork in acquiring Golden West; Daniel Mudd netted $15 million from Fannie Mae; Angelo Mozilo, $43 million at Countrywide; John Mack, $41 million at Morgan Stanley; Lloyd Blankfein, $55 million at Goldman; Richard Fuld, $28 million at Lehman; and James Cayne, $40 million at Bear Stearns."[20]

It is instructive to note that after 2006, each of the organizations named here was acquired because of financial distress, had to be bailed out, or is in conservatorship (Fannie Mae), or went bankrupt. So in retrospect, such excessive compensation packages seem to have only encouraged reckless, risk-taking behaviors. Certainly, the inflated compensation packages created a "false sense of entitlement and invincibility: If their personal fortunes were guaranteed, how could the fate of their institutions be otherwise?"[21]

From Slippery Slope to Broken Windows

Now let us return to the two employees discussing last night's baseball game. Do we censure them immediately? Do we monitor employees' phone calls to make sure they are not chatting about who is going to pick up Melissa after school? There are unresolved practical aspects of the slippery slope concept, but the theory has found strong advocates in law enforcement.

First promulgated in a magazine article about thirty years ago as the "broken windows theory," the slippery slope concept has been modified and adapted over the years.[22] It is widely credited with reducing crime rates, especially in major cities. The theory holds that if a window is broken in a building and not repaired, other windows in that neighborhood or community are likely to be broken. If they too are not repaired, more damage to the neighborhood is likely to occur. As the neighborhood goes downhill, crime is likely to increase. The theory has been modified and adapted by various police departments over time, and it is often called community policing or quality-of-life policing.

Here is a case in point from the New York Police Department. For many years, New York City's vast subway system was a major scene of crime. Robberies, assaults, rapes, and even murders were not uncommon. The police responded in the normal manner. They put more uniformed officers in the stations and on the trains. They deployed undercover officers in civilian clothes on the trains. Nothing much changed, however. Then they came up with the "broken windows" approach. Most of the subway crimes were committed by young males, fare beaters, who would vault over the subway turnstile without using a subway token. The police put cops at the turnstiles and arrested the fare beaters. It was a fairly minor crime, but once the police started doing this, the crime rate as a whole dropped by well over 50 percent.

The police reduced the problem significantly not by studying the crimes but by studying the behavioral patterns of those committing the crimes. Thus, they affected the crime rate and kept the citizens safer.

Let us move from New York City and criminal issues to the organizations in which most of us work. Does someone seem to have a behavioral pattern of calling the same number each morning on a company phone and talking for an hour? Why? Is the person being called a customer? It would seem odd for this to happen every day. Is it Aunt Sally in Omaha? Does one salesperson always have expenses for "business lunches" that are 30 percent higher than their peers' expenses? If so, why?

The study of human behavior can be frustrating, because we all differ a bit. But it can also be quite helpful if insights from the behavioral sciences are used properly. As Michael Apter observed, "In some very real sense we are all different kinds of people at different times, with different needs, feelings, emotions, and ways of seeing things."[23] Hence, the theme of individual differences—of the different ways in which, and the degrees to which, individuals need, experience, and respond to situations is a critically important, underlying building block of behavioral forensics.

Social psychologist Kurt Lewin remarked, "Close cooperation between theoretical and applied psychology can be accomplished . . . if the theorist does not look toward applied problems with highbrow aversion or with a fear of social problems, and if the applied psychologist realizes that there's nothing so practical as a good theory."[24]

Fraud Is a Human Act

For our collective efforts on the problem of fraud to make progress, we need to understand human beings better. Specifically, despite our technophilia (i.e., love of computers), we should not rely solely on computers to provide solutions, for they too are built by humans.[25] Nor should we assume that once we take a technical solution to its highest refinement, we are done. A fuller comprehension requires that we appreciate the contributions of both the human being and the technology; this challenge requires an understanding of human beings, computers, and human-computer interactions.

Finance and accounting professionals seem to discount the value of the behavioral sciences; this explains why the field of behavioral finance is still in its infancy. For some reason, there is a perception that behavioral science is less than real science and has nothing to offer. This view is extremely unfortunate, because most fraudsters, as we will discuss in this book, are quite the applied psychologists. And, as is well-known, fraud is a crime in which the victim participates—voluntarily. We will present convincing arguments for why utilizing behavioral science insights is critically important to addressing the fraud problem, including developing defenses against being deceived.

Another misconception seems to be that greed is the root cause of fraud. In fact, we assert that greed as the sole explanation for fraud does little to advance our understanding of why a fraud occurred and what preemptive steps we can take to avoid fraud in the future. The right questions to ask about greed are the following:

- If there is something more than greed, what is it? What lies beyond greed outside our perception?
- If greed is the cause, what are the categories and variants?
- If fraud is practically infinite in its variety, how does greed interact with the personality and behavior of the fraudster?
- Most important, are there different gradations of greed? What is within bounds, and when is greed excessive? How can we tell the difference?
- How does the greed factor interact with group dynamics? How is it accentuated or constrained by social and cultural norms?

Conclusion

We possess some general knowledge about perpetrators and cost mostly from ACFE data from the biannual *Report to the Nations* (1996–2012). We know that the fraud committed by senior executives exceeds employee fraud by a factor of 16. We also know that given the exponential growth of technology, access, and computing powers, the opportunity for fraud will increase greatly (internationally). It is only when the river runs dry that the rocks begin to show. Hence, during a worldwide period of financial stagnation or decline, fraud incidence will only grow more rampant, with its economic effects becoming more visible.

In terms of the emotional costs (at a societal level), being defrauded is more upsetting than being a victim of natural disasters. This is because an act of fraud is humiliating for the victims: they conclude that "we were taken for fools" (consider the investors in Bernard Madoff's Ponzi scheme).[26] Although a fraud can be a group or industry phenomenon, there are generally thought leaders or head honchos—specific individuals who make it happen, people of significant power or influence who either reside in or have inordinate influence over the C-suite; hence, it is ultimately a "tone from the top" issue.

Despite possessing this knowledge, we have not progressed far in ascribing motivation because of our blind eye to the relevance of the behavioral disciplines. In fact, we have made many assumptions that get in the way, such as rational markets, cognitive dissonance, the purity of the study of economics or finance, and, worst of all, that the behavioral disciplines do not matter, when in fact every fraud is perpetrated by people. Ultimately, fraud is a human act.

Notes

1. In this context, consider Yahoo CEO Marissa Mayer's recent company policy, beginning in June 2013, that company employees hitherto telecommuting, or working from home, will be required to come into the office. Specifically, the memo sent out to Yahoo employees stated that speed and quality "are often sacrificed when we work from home. . . . Being a Yahoo isn't just about your day-to-day job, it is about the interactions and experiences that are only possible in our offices."
2. Joseph T. Wells, *Fraud Fighter: My Fables and Foibles* (Hoboken, NJ: John Wiley & Sons, 2011), xiii.

3. See Tom R. Tyler, *Why People Obey the Law* (New Haven, CT: Yale University Press, 1990).
4. D. Ariely, *The (Honest) Truth about Dishonesty: How We Lie to Everyone—Especially Ourselves* (New York: HarperCollins, 2012).
5. Donald Ray Cressey, "Management Fraud, Accounting Controls, and Criminological Theory," in *Management Fraud: Detection and Deterrence*, ed. R. K. Elliott and J. J. Willingham (New York: Petrocelli Books, 1980), 118.
6. David R. Saunders, "Psychological Perspectives on Management Fraud," in *Management Fraud: Detection and Deterrence*, ed. R. K. Elliott and J. J. Willingham (New York: Petrocelli Books, 1980), 108.
7. Arthur Levitt, "Numbers Game," speech delivered at New York University, September 28, 1998, http://www.sec.gov/news/speech/speecharchive/1998/spch220.txt.
8. Erving Goffman, *The Presentation of Self in Everyday Life* (New York: Anchor Books, 1959).
9. Based on a personal conversation that coauthor Joseph Koletar had with Ken Friedman.
10. Leonard R. Sayles and Cynthia J. Smith, *The Rise of the Rogue Executive: How Good Companies Go Bad and How to Stop the Destruction* (Upper Saddle River, NJ: Prentice Hall, 2006).
11. Roger Lowenstein, *Origins of the Crash* (New York: Penguin Press, 2004).
12. "Don't Blame Hedge Funds for Financial Crisis, Study Says," *Wall Street Journal*, September 19, 2012, http://blogs.wsj.com/marketbeat/2012/09/19/dont-blame-hedge-funds-for-financial-crisis-study-says; and "Crisis Panel Report Pins Blame on Wall Street, Washington," Bloomberg, January 26, 2011, http://www.bloomberg.com/news/2011-01-26/crisis-panel-report-pins-blame-on-wall-street-washington.html.
13. American Institute of Certified Public Accountants (AICPA), *Management Override of Internal Controls: The Achilles' Heel of Fraud Prevention* (New York: AICPA, 2005). Similarly, in the late 1990s, AICPA's Fraud Task Force did an excellent job of incorporating the fraud triangle components into its Statement on Auditing Standards (SAS) 99, "Consideration of Fraud in a Financial Statement Audit," which emphasized the need to exercise a higher degree of professional skepticism and suggested brainstorming as a useful planning strategy before commencing auditing fieldwork.
14. The Hon. David M. Walker, "Integrity: Restoring Trust in American Business and the Accounting Profession," speech given to the American Institute of Certified Public Accountants' leadership conference, November 2002, http://www.gao.gov/cghome/2002/acpro122.pdf.
15. All this certainly seems true of former New Jersey governor and MF Global CEO Jon Corzine who was charged in June 2013 by the Commodities and Futures Trading Commission with the alleged misuse of over $1 billion in customers' funds.
16. F. Gino and M. H. Bazerman, *Slippery Slopes and Misconduct: The Effect of Gradual Degradation on the Failure to Notice Others' Unethical Behavior* (Cambridge, MA: Harvard Business School, 2007), http://www.people.hbs.edu/mbazerman/Papers/Gino-Baz-06-007-Slippery%20Slopes.pdf.

17. Humpback whales off the coast of Maine use lobtail feeding, a complex behavior that traps fish. First observed in 1981, this behavior had been adopted by 50 percent of the whale population in the area by 1989. See L. Rendell and H. Whitehead, "Culture in Whales and Dolphins," *Behavioral and Brain Sciences*, no. 24 (2001): 309–82.

18. Sarah F. Brosnan and Frans F. de Waal, *Monkeys Reject Unequal Pay* (Atlanta, GA: Emory University Yerkes Primate Research Center, 2003). A brown capuchin monkey (*Cebus apella*) will toss a cucumber to the ground if she is offered the inferior item at the same time that her partner is unfairly favored with a more delectable grape. The experimenters concluded that aversion to inequities—a hardwired sense of fairness—is probably innate not only in humans but also in other species.

19. Roger Lowenstein, *The End of Wall Street* (New York: Penguin Press, 2010), 75.

20. Ibid.

21. Ibid.

22. James Q. Wilson and George L. Kelling, *Broken Windows: The Police and Neighborhood Safety* (New York: Manhattan Institute, 1982), http://www.manhattan-institute.org/pdf/_atlantic_monthly-broken_windows.pdf.

23. Michael J. Apter, *Danger: Our Quest for Excitement* (Oxford, UK: One World Publications, 2007), 10.

24. Quoted in S. Kassin, S. Fein, and H. R. Markus, *Social Psychology*, 8th ed. (Belmont, CA: Wadsworth, Cengage Learning, 2011), 29.

25. Richard Dooling, "Rise of the Machines," *New York Times*, October 12, 2008, http://www.nytimes.com/2008/10/12/opinion/12dooling.html?pagewanted=all&_r=0.

26. A particularly interesting perspective is provided by a Madoff victim, Stephen Greenspan, clinical professor of psychiatry at the University of Colorado. See his opinion piece from Tuesday, December 23, 2008, in eSKEPTIC, the e-mail newsletter of the Skeptics Society, www.skeptic.com/eskeptic/08-12-23/#feature.

2

The Sins of Quantification and Other Mind-Set Impediments

As people in organizations assemble to discuss their work, they often ask, "How will this affect the bottom line?" and apply this question to virtually any decision or plan of action. Behind this question, though, is a question about the numbers.

How often, in the course of a business day or in the offices of senior leaders, does the conversation stop when someone asks about the numbers? How many times does a business leader interrupt a presentation and ask, "So what do the numbers say?" As many chief executive officers (CEOs) and chief financial officers (CFOs) will tell you, the real power behind the organization is determined not by them but by the numbers. Our preoccupation with the bottom line seems excessive and unhealthy.[1]

Numbers are thought of as cold, hard facts. In accounting, the numbers are what they are, and we have to deal with them—or rather, we have to deal with the reality they create. What lies behind this statement may be difficult for financial professionals to get their minds around, because numbers are not real—they are an abstraction. An auditor who reviews a balance sheet is dealing not with reality but with symbols and abstractions of reality.

Now you are reading this book (let's assume you're reading the hardcover version). The book you are holding is tangible and concrete. You can feel it, smell it, see it, and hear the pages turning. Let's also assume you are reading this book with other tangible things nearby such as a phone, a pencil or pen for writing, and a case to carry what you need for work or school. You can experience them with your senses, and others can experience them, too.

This changes with numbers. The book you hold in your hand is real, but once we talk about all the books in your collection, dozens or hundreds, that now becomes a representation. The pencil you write with is real. If you have one more, then you have two pencils. These two pencils are real, but only the pencils, not the number, exist. "*Two* pencils" is an abstraction. The number is merely a symbol representing reality. Accountants understand the ideas presented here quite well when couched in terms of tangible and intangible assets appearing on the balance sheet. They also know how difficult it is to measure and report on intangible assets, such as company brand or reputation.

In other words, numbers are a mirror of reality, but they are not the reality itself.[2] What *is* very real, though, is the human costs of the actions of fraud perpetrators—to others as well as to themselves: the loss of employment and future employability, a criminal record that accompanies perpetrators (perhaps for the rest of their lives), and the significant loss of money and opportunity that creates real pain for the victims.

Although the numbers are important in many ways, even as abstractions, we must be cognizant of another basic fact: No number ever created itself. All numbers are created by humans, and humans operate from a variety of psychological foundations. For instance, a stock price is the result of how people feel about a given stock at a given time. Some degree of analysis was probably involved, but so was psychological disposition. So too with credit card use. Were we in a rush to buy a present? Were we seduced by a clever advertisement? Were we confident that since we did not have to put cash on the counter, we would eventually find the money to pay the charge? There is a whole literature on the psychology of money.[3]

Once we begin to allow for the noneconomic, psychological aspects of hard numbers, a lot of interesting things begin to happen. We start looking beyond the numbers and into the source and root cause. For instance, stock price may fall because of reports that the CEO is ill (witness the Apple stock price movements associated with Steve Jobs's health condition in the year preceding his death). Banks and credit card companies may agree to renegotiate a debt or pay stupendous amounts to settle pending litigation. They can do this because their profit margins are so high to begin with, and they want to keep their good reputations and their customers. Corporate reputation and brand image are intangible but nevertheless significant drivers of value.[4]

However, this does not negate the usefulness of numbers when we cite statistics to understand the nature and scope of the fraud problem—they do have great utility in the right contexts. Where "hard numbers" are available to support accounting assertions, there is no better evidence to provide a basis for valuation.[5]

The Danger of Numbers

In March 2013, the SEC accused the state of Illinois of securities fraud. The state had seen its pension fund steadily eroding, and the severity of underfunding grew as the recession deepened. Specifically, the SEC alleged that Illinois had misled investors about the condition of its public pension system from 2005 to 2009. As a result, the debt kept growing, and Illinois had become the second state—after New Jersey—in five years to be accused of fraud. This had never happened before.[6]

In the lives of the people of Illinois (and perhaps in the United States as a whole), this was seen by many as "Oh well, another day, another scandal." Illinois, already notorious for organized crime, had recently been the center of an investigation of murders inside the Chicago crime syndicate. In addition, the state has had as many as four governors in recent memory convicted and sent to prison: Rod Blagojevich (2003–2009), George H. Ryan (1999–2003), Dan Walker (1973–1977), and Otto Kerner Jr. (1961–1968). In April 2012, U.S. Attorney Patrick Fitzgerald reported that Dixon, Illinois, CFO Rita Crundwell, 58, allegedly defrauded the city's 15,000 residents of more than $30 million to fund her lavish lifestyle, which included a stable of 150 horses and a $2.5 million American Express bill.

What happened to bring about this pension fund fraud charge, and why was the SEC involved? The details of the case were intriguing. The state had been accused of underfunding the state pensions for several years while also raising state bonds. The SEC's report noted the following:

> The (pension funding) schedule proved insufficient to cover both the cost of benefits accrued in a current year and a payment to amortize the plans' unfunded actuarial liability. The statutory

plan structurally underfunded the state's pension obligations and backloaded the majority of pension contributions far into the future. This structure imposed significant stress on the pension systems and the state's ability to meet its competing obligations—a condition that worsened over time.[7]

The current Illinois governor, Patrick Quinn, who became governor after Blagojevich's conviction and imprisonment, was not ignorant of the problems. "Without pension reform," he said, "within two years, Illinois will be spending more on public pensions than on education. As I said to you a year ago, our state cannot continue on this path."[8]

What happened here? How did an entire state merit an investigation of securities fraud and prosecution by the SEC? The SEC had harsh words for the state of Illinois and why the decision was made to get involved.

"Municipal investors are no less entitled to truthful risk disclosures than other investors," said George S. Canellos, acting director of the SEC's Division of Enforcement. "Time after time, Illinois failed to inform its bond investors about the risk to its financial condition posed by the structural underfunding of its pension system."[9]

According to the SEC, the state had not done a reasonable amount of work keeping track of the money. As a result of various institutional failures, Illinois lacked the proper mechanisms to identify relevant information about its pension systems in its disclosures. Somehow, millions of dollars were not properly accounted for, and an entire state had placed its public employees' retirement and investment money at risk. How did this come to pass?

Benjamin Disraeli, the former British prime minister, once supposedly said, "There are three kinds of lies: lies, damn lies, and statistics." Numbers can be inflated or deflated as necessary to try to influence human behavior (as seen in the recent Wall Street scandals, which point to the danger of using statistics to support invalid or weak arguments). One may argue that machines often produce numbers, and these are precise in a scientific sense. A machine does not make mistakes and has no interest in the outcome produced by the numbers it delivers.

It is a seductive argument, at least until one takes a step back. No machine ever built itself. Machines are built by humans and programmed to act the way they do. They are not sentient, or conscious, so no machine ever decided what to do. Humans did that. No machine ever decided what was important and what was not. Humans did that. No machine ever decided what size, color, and texture of clothing was adequate as it moved down the conveyor belt. Humans did that.

No matter how swift or accurate machines are, they can only do what humans tell them to do.[10] Once we get into the human arena, things can change. Emotions such as pride, greed, and excitement along with misperceptions and falsehoods are fully capable of being influential. Many machines are excellent at what they do, and many humans are honest and upstanding citizens, but not all are. Human beings, however, can change over time, including in their desires and motivations.

Roughly 1 percent of the population of the United States is in prison or on probation or parole. Not everyone plays by the rules, and this percentage is just those who got caught. How many more rule breakers are out there?

The danger of numbers is that they have the inherent potential to influence human behavior. They are unreal things that, when acted upon, can produce real consequences. Consider the pernicious influence of numbers in the context of suicide committed by a financial advisor who could not get the results he had promised or expected. A bad number on your credit card statement does not mean that the credit card company did anything illegal. Most likely, you simply spent more than you intended! Everyone agrees that owing to time and cost constraints, a "perfect" audit probably never gets done. We nevertheless assume that the longer a company's audited financials remain uncontested, the more they are likely to have presented fairly the company's financial condition. A good stock price may indicate the financial performance of the company, or it may reveal (usually far down the road) that the numbers reported had been "dressed up." Indeed, managers with strong incentives to "make the numbers" may decide to simply make *up* the numbers. (Think Enron.)

Data Analysis Is Not Enough

There is a simple test that can be used to highlight the limits of raw numeric analysis. It is a pair of questions that has been given to groups of financially sophisticated professionals in the last 20 years: certified public accountants (CPAs), accounting professors, CFOs, lawyers, CEOs, and other people immersed in the world of numbers, who make their living with them and are good at them. To these people, a number is either x or y. When the analysis is complete and the final numbers are in, the chapter is closed and the discussion halts. There is no room for further discussion or debate. Therefore, the test they are given is basic: They are asked to go home and create a quantitative analysis on the two most important decisions they ever made in their lives:

1. Whom did you choose to marry?
2. How many children did you choose to have?[11]

There has yet to be a valid and defensible response from anyone who has been asked these questions. The point of the exercise is simple: Even though people live in a world of numbers and often treat them with near-religious devotion, they often make decisions based on other, psychological factors. Many of those who study the human mind believe that people operate at two or three levels of consciousness. Thus, it is unclear what compels us at any given time to take or not take a given action. The mind is a complex and tricky thing.

Many fraud schemes cannot be effectively found using data-driven approaches and sampling, such as corruption, bribery, and kickbacks. Searching relevant transaction data for patterns and unexplained relationships often fails to yield results because the information may not be recorded per se by the system. Behavioral concepts and qualitative factors frequently allow the auditor to look beyond the data, both data that are there and data that aren't. It is important to look for data that should be there but aren't as well as to question why certain data that aren't supposed to exist do exist.[12]

The noted *New York Times* columnist David Brooks did an excellent job in discussing the expanse of human experience in his 2011 book, *The Social Animal: The Hidden Sources of Love, Character, and Achievement.* Building relationships, even those that turn out to be romantic and long-lasting, is rarely a totally logical process.

There is no accounting for why tastes differ. Think of ice cream. Why does one person like peach ice cream and another like strawberry?[13] Just try to explain the logic and rationale for each person's choice. In social science research, this is called a *criterion problem.* There is simply no yardstick with which to measure the issue. Favorite color is another example. We don't know why some people like red and others like blue; this might well be the reason why we have vanilla *and* chocolate. Human behavior just works that way. We cannot provide a logical and coherent explanation for many of our choices.

This brings us back to fraud, and it will allow us to better appreciate some of the radical ideas of Sigmund Freud.

Hard Numbers versus Reality

As noted in Chapter 1, most of us commit innocuous traffic violations, like speeding, every day. We do so because experience has taught us that we can get away with it. We *follow* a law if we believe there is a good reason for it based on principles of equity and fairness (normative perspective), but we merely *obey* the law if our sole motive is to avoid punishment (instrumental perspective). In order to commit a crime, we begin to learn the minds of others in order to avoid punishment. In the speeding example, we know that a police officer is unlikely to stop us and give us a ticket if we are only a mile or two over the speed limit. We accept this implied "permission" and take advantage of it. We are still guilty of a traffic violation, but we are not likely to be punished for it. Of course, there are people who base their decisions on the normative perspective and rarely exceed the speed limit unless there is an emergency or defensible need to do so.

Now apply this behavior to the financial aspects of organizations. Auditors do not have the time to look for every dollar or cent, and such an effort would be too expansive in scope and too expensive to carry out. Certainly they will look closely at big issues, but they will generally ignore the smaller ones. Accountants use the term *materiality* to cover this gap. It means that an issue has to be of a certain potential or actual size before it gets attention. But we are still dealing with supposedly hard numbers.[14] Clever fraudsters know when and how to fly below the radar and escape detection.

A useful example of the difference between hard numbers and reality is illustrated by the following dialogue on a syndicated consumer affairs show hosted by Clark Howard.

Caller: Clark, this is Bob from Omaha.

Howard: Yes, Bob, how can I help you?

Caller: Clark, my wife and I moved into our new house
           18 months ago. Our builder told us the appliances he
           put in had the lowest repair rate in the industry. They

are all made by the same company. In 18 months, our dishwasher, refrigerator, washer, and dryer have all broken down.

Howard: Well, Bob, your builder didn't lie to you, but he didn't give you the full picture, either. That company's appliances do have the lowest repair rate in the industry. That's because they are so poorly made it's cheaper to replace them than repair them.[15]

So much for the supposedly hard and scientific numbers in providing an accurate understanding. To truly understand numbers, you need to take the time and make the effort to look at how and why they were produced. They may look fine on the surface, but what do they *really* mean? What incentives did the people who produced them have? Were there numbers that would benefit some people to produce? Was it easy or difficult to produce the necessary numbers? What proof lies behind them? Do they fit the reality in a reasonable way? And perhaps most relevant to fraud, what people have access to the numbers?

The following two case studies may be instructive.

The Bank: An Ingenue Shall Lead Them—into Fraud

In this case study, the assignment was to look into the erratic behavior of the CFO of a major credit card company that had purchased a small local bank to process payments from its card holders. The behavior noted was the CFO's constant irritability and short temper, which seemed to be getting worse in the context of some unusual financial results.

Paul, the CFO, was in charge of 94 accounts, with a total of $938 million in credit card debt. He had performance metrics, one of which was write-offs, or identifying irrecoverable amounts (i.e., how many bad debts had to be discarded).

At the bank where Shirley, the president, processed the write-offs on behalf of the CFO, the story began to go from bad to worse. In one year the CFO's target for bad-debt write-offs was $750,000—on almost $1 billion in credit card debt. That's less than 1 percent target reserve for the write-offs. Such a small percentage appears to be quite ridiculous. But the results recorded were even more shocking. Shirley brought the final total to $5,000. This is well-nigh impossible.

The next year her given target from the CFO on the same volume of debt was $500,000—ridiculous again, but she brought down the write-offs to an outrageous $250. The on-site investigation was a treasure for understanding the underlying dynamic for how so much damage could be done so easily. If one were to enter her organization, one would not have seen the walls of her office. They were covered with company awards and pictures from presentation ceremonies for her stellar performance in managing to keep the write-offs within such low tolerances.

Curiosity on the part of the investigator led to the human resources department, since an award from an organization is usually justified by a memo of some sort. This is normally found in the personnel file for the individual in question. The investigator found the memos in the file. That made sense. What didn't make sense was what the awards were recognizing.

When Shirley was later interviewed, she ducked and dodged for about eight minutes, then finally admitted that it would be possible to change the age of a receivable by moving it from one account to another. Since she had 94 accounts to play with, it was a simple game of moving bad debt around every 90 days. This involved very few write-offs. It was not a particularly ingenious solution, but it fooled the system.

A first-year accountant should be able to spot this in about 10 minutes, yet it was not caught. Why? The company was so enamored with this continued stream of good news that it just could not honor Shirley enough.

We all like good news and good numbers, but they can blind us to reality.

Shirley had no college degree and no history of experience with financial matters. She had been the secretary of a senior executive of the credit card company. Whoever placed her in that position had most likely had an agenda. This brings us to the importance of understanding the role of background information and psychology in a heightened fraud risk environment.

The Plants: "Let's Manufacture More Than Widgets. Let's Make the Numbers!"

In this case study, the client was a manufacturing company with 11 plants around the United States. The CEO was aggressive and wanted to reach his financial targets. He told the CFO what the numbers should be; how the CFO achieved them was of little interest to the CEO.

To keep his job, the CFO had to pressure the corporate controller to pressure the plant controllers to move numbers around. The plant controllers were not uninformed and naive; they knew what was going on, but they wanted to keep their jobs even though they knew that what they were being forced to do was wrong.

Accordingly, they formed a plan. For three years, the 11 plants came within $100 of budget each quarter, a result that is simply too good to be true. Everybody was happy until one day it all fell apart. It was bound to fail eventually, because the numbers were made up and not based on real business items, products, and sales.

Case Discussion: Challenging Questions

What was the driving motivation in these cases? The usual answer given for the motivation for fraud is greed. Yet there is some vagueness in both of these cases.

In the first case, the uneducated and essentially unsupervised bank president was like a kitten in a spider web, wreaking havoc on a delicate system with no sense of the damage done. Perhaps at some level she knew that it was not the right thing to do. But with more awards and honors than she had wall space, and with a minimal education, she must have also had the impression that she was doing more good than harm. Was this a case of an intentional plant of someone incompetent in order to make gains elsewhere? Perhaps. What is clear, however, is that in this large complex system, the financial reality (the life blood of the parent organization) was put at risk by an organizational environment that was fertile soil for fraud. How long had this been going on, and why?

To accomplish any goal requires aggression. In the second case, the aggressiveness may not correlate with monetary greed. But it was a very aggressive promotion of a certain narrative about the company designed to positively impress shareholders. Was the CEO aware of the potential consequences of what he was asking? Probably. Did he do so because he needed the money and was greedy? Maybe, but maybe not. Perhaps he needed something more than just more money. Perhaps he was greedy for something unique to those in the C-suite: a level of success, a drive to outperform a sibling, a desire to be the savior to his people—any of these could be possible and doesn't require his greed for more money. And there are more aspects to greed in this second case. Clearly, the subordinates were not necessarily greedy, and they probably did not benefit (at least not very much) financially from manufacturing the numbers. Why did they cooperate? What was the role of their values and their emotions as they came to work each day? Recall also the phenomenal performance numbers: 11 manufacturing plants came within $100 of their operating budgets. This is beyond incredible; anyone who has managed a budget would know that it is usually impossible even once. These plants did it for three years—36 months straight! Where were the auditors? How does this dynamic relate to the why of fraud? Were they intimidated or otherwise beholden to their clients?

Accountants are familiar with earnings management, which is typically done to meet Wall Street analysts' expectations. In an SEC filing, USA Networks chairman Barry Diller "balked at the sophisticated art form known as managing expectations, saying publicly what many have said privately for a long time: 'The process has little to do with running a business and the numbers can become distractingly and dangerously detached from fundamentals.'"[16] Auditors must be sensitive to such brazen efforts to manage earnings expectations and exercise the appropriate degree of professional skepticism in such situations.

Conclusion

The financial numbers matter. They are seen as, and in many ways are, critical to the performance of any organization. They are at the root of the training of many professionals who manage organizations, especially ones with budgets. And most organizations have budgets. Financial forensics turns the analysis of numbers into an art form—it can help uncover and unearth financial fraud. However, we need to go beyond the numbers and reflect on the motivations of the architects of the financial statements, too. This latter consideration falls squarely into the domain of behavioral forensics.

The point of this chapter and of the two cases is simple as it relates to our trusted tools of analysis of the numbers. Just because you see a number on a piece of paper or a computer screen does not mean it is real. Numbers are, at their core, an abstraction representing reality. They are not the actual reality.

Because numbers are so familiar and because the analysis of most accounting and financial processes is done by reviewing the numbers, they may sometimes provide a sense of (misplaced) confidence. Yet as has been illustrated, they may inspire a sense of confidence because we normally assume that a number is an accurate representation of reality, but that is not always the case.

The questions evoked by the cases are a portal into new ways of thinking about fraud. They are a way to break down categories by thinking about how people are involved in fraud perpetration. As we answer them, we can gain insight into the surrounding circumstances that played a role. What factors make it easier or harder for fraud to take root in the ecology that humans work within?

The next chapter connects us to the taxonomy of the A.B.C. theory of fraud: the bad apple, the bad bushel, and the bad crop. As we go through this taxonomy, we will outline and describe the local microenvironments of individuals as well as the macroenvironments that serve to allow fraud to flourish and harm human financial systems.

Notes

1. See Tad Tuleja, *Beyond the Bottom Line* (New York: Penguin Books, 1987).
2. Philadelphia-based noted stained-glass artist Judith Schaechter has pondered over Belgian surrealist painter Rene Magritte's classic depiction of a pipe with the famous notation "*Ceci n'est pas une pipe*" (This is not a pipe). That painting powerfully conveys that representation is not reality, that the map is not the terrain. Schaechter writes in her blog, "Has everyone forgotten 'art' is the first syllable of 'artifice'? Or that Picasso once said: 'We all know that art is not truth. Art is a lie that makes us realize the truth'?" See her blogpost at http://judithschaechterglass.blogspot.com/2009/03/this-is-not-pipe.html. We should probably treat numbers in financial statements the same way as we reflect upon art, as furnishing the means to understanding what lies behind the numbers. In a similar vein, consider that an advertisement for British chartered accountants once showed the revenue and cost lines on a graph and stated, "We seek accountants who can read between the lines."
3. A. Furnham and M. Argyle, *The Psychology of Money* (London: Routledge, 1998).
4. K. Cravens, E. O. Oliver, and S. Ramamoorti, "The Reputation Audit: Measuring and Managing Corporate Reputation," *European Management Journal* 21, no. 2 (April 2003): 201–12.
5. "Although the businessman may be forced to estimate value, accounting must remain anchored to price, since it is beyond the power of accounting to express all of these 'psychological estimates.'" A. C. Littleton, "Value and Price in Accounting," *Accounting Review* 4 (September 1929): 147–54.

6. It is to draw public attention to the critically important issues of transparency and accountability in government financial management that Sheila Weinberg established the Chicago-based nonpartisan, nonprofit organization Institute for Truth in Accounting (IFTA). A coauthor of this book, Dr. Sridhar Ramamoorti, is an IFTA board member. See http://www.truthinaccounting.org.

7. Securities and Exchange Commission (SEC), press release, "SEC Charges Illinois for Misleading Pension Disclosures," March 11, 2013, http://www.sec.gov/news/press/2013/2013-37.htm.

8. Mary Williams Walsh, "Illinois Is Accused of Fraud by S.E.C.," *New York Times*, March 11, 2013.

9. SEC press release 2013-37 dated March 11, 2013, Washington D.C. See http://www.sec.gov/News/PressRelease/Detail/PressRelease/1365171513202#.Ueis2Y21Esw.

10. "To err is human, but to really foul things up you need a computer." The source of this quote is not known for sure, but American biologist Paul Ehrlich is sometimes credited.

11. These are questions used by coauthor Joe Koletar in his teaching of the limits of accounting in forensic accounting and criminal investigations.

12. See S. Ramamoorti and S. Curtis, "Procurement Fraud and Data Analytics," *Journal of Government Financial Management* 52, no. 4 (Winter 2003): 16–24.

13. The Latin expression *De gustibus non est disputandum* cautions, "Thou shalt not quarrel over tastes." The song "Let's Call the Whole Thing Off," written by George Gershwin and Ira Gershwin in 1937 for the film *Shall We Dance,* is most famous for its "You say *to-may-toes* and I say *to-mah-toes*" and other verses comparing different regional dialects.

14. Accounting and auditing standards typically apply only to material items or items involving significantly large dollar magnitudes. The attitude is: "If it doesn't really matter much, then don't bother with it." Where a departure in accounting from the recognized standard is not material, then it is presumed that it can't affect the fair presentation of the financials. For an auditor in practice, however, it is important to consider the overall effect of immaterial adjustments. "Creeping materiality" becomes relevant in scenarios in which a series of immaterial items have a combined effect that is material; cumulative materiality is relevant when items accumulate over a period of time and become material.

15. Brian Clark Howard, Episode 1214, "Planned Obsolescence," May 16, 2013, Constitutional Radio Network, Maine. This deliberately set short life span of products is what futurist Alvin Toffler referred to as "planned obsolescence."

16. J. Fuller and M. C. Jensen, *Just Say No to Wall Street.* Monitor Company, n.d., http://www.latrobefinancialmanagement.com/Research/Governance/Just%20Say%20No%20To%20Wall%20Street.pdf.

CHAPTER 3

Beyond the Fraud Triangle

TOWARD AN OUTLINE OF A.B.C. THEORY

Is it the apple, the bushel, or the crop? This is what we often ask ourselves when we learn about alleged fraud involving a staggering amount of money.

As we have discussed, fraud is a human act that often relies heavily on both an individual's emotions and his or her state of mind. For years, scholars and practitioners have attempted to study and understand these behaviors. Much of the extant literature has focused on the idea that greed is the underlying motive for most fraudulent behavior.[1] We are going to take this literature one step further by gaining a better understanding of how the behavioral sciences can be utilized to explain fraud.

The Relevance of Behavioral Approaches

One of the forensic accounting "classics" introduced the "iceberg theory" as a way of looking at fraud and enabling its detection. According to this theory, the top one-third of the iceberg (sticking out of the water) involves structural considerations, such as hierarchy, financial resources, organizational goals, personal skills and abilities, technological state, and performance measurement. However, the authors argued that like an observant Internal Revenue Service agent, a forensic accountant should be aware of the lifestyles of the employees, because this may provide clues about the possibility of fraud. According to this theory, fraud auditors should look at the two-thirds of the iceberg below the water. It is below the water line that a person's "attitudes, feelings (fear, anger, etc.), values, norms, interactions, supportiveness, and satisfaction" may be observed.[2]

Another antifraud professional gives seven examples of an employee mind-set that may be used to spot the behavioral red flags of fraud:

1. **Weak code of ethics.** If a person is willing to engage in dishonest behavior in other parts of his or her life, it often follows that the same inclination exists in the workplace.
2. **Propensity to work "outside" the system.** This means not following the rules that everyone else abides by—not following established job procedures and workplace policies and repeatedly trying to beat the system.
3. **Poor work performance.** When coupled with the rationalization or justification of a substandard performance, this can be an indicator of disrespect for the organization, which in turn can be a driver of internal fraud.
4. **Excessive drive to achieve.** Employees who desperately try to improve performance or meet certain targets may find it tough to resist the temptation to circumvent fraud controls.
5. **Overprotectiveness of data and key documents.** Dishonest employees are often reluctant to share information with coworkers or managers. To conceal their illegal activity, they may go to great lengths to ensure that sensitive documents are never out of their sight.
6. **Persistent demoralization.** When you spot an employee who shows constant dissatisfaction with his or her status in the organization, job duties, coworkers, or supervisors, it is time to keep a close eye on the person.
7. **Being the first one in or the last one out.** An employee who looks for ways to be alone in the workplace could pose a problem. Watch for those who take few or no vacations.[3]

These factors can be signs that a fraud has been perpetrated, yet they can also be fertile soil for an enriched environment for fraud. Our focus will be on what is happening inside the minds of the employees that increases the risk of fraud for an organization.

Clinical psychologist Stanton E. Samenow painted a chilling profile of the (violent) criminal in his book *Inside the Criminal Mind*. He asserted that "the criminal's way of thinking is vastly different from that of a responsible citizen" and recommended that we begin with the clear understanding that the "criminal chooses crime." Samenow explained that the criminal "chooses his associates, his way of life, the kinds of crime he commits. He rejects society long before society rejects him; he is victimizer, not victim. The criminal values people to the extent that they can be manipulated; he believes he is *entitled* to whatever he desires; he does not justify his actions to himself" (emphasis in original).[4]

In the ACFE's educational video, *Inside the Fraudster's Mind*, which presents numerous clips of interviews with convicted white-collar felons, none of those interviewed stand out as the tattooed, threatening brutes one might find at a high-security penitentiary. Instead, they are regular people—like any person one might meet in the grocery store or in the park.[5]

Nevertheless, although violent crime differs significantly from white-collar crime, it is nevertheless important that we heed a quote from the corrupt businessman Noah Cross in the movie *Chinatown*: "You see, Mr. Gittes, most people never have to face the fact that at the right time and the right place, they're capable of anything."[6]

Understanding White-Collar Crime

Fraud is a legal term and frequently involves a legal determination to be made, so the broad definition from *Black's Law Dictionary* may be the most appropriate to consider in this context:

> A generic term, embracing all multifarious means which human ingenuity can devise, and which are resorted to by one individual to get advantage over another by false suggestions or by suppression of truth, and includes all surprise, trick, cunning, dissembling, and any unfair way by which another is cheated. . . . Elements of a cause of action for "fraud" include false representation of a present or past fact made by defendant, action in reliance thereupon by plaintiff, and damage resulting to plaintiff from such misrepresentation.[7]

The Federal Bureau of Investigation (FBI) has defined white-collar crime as "those illegal acts which are characterized by deceit, concealment, or violation of trust and which are not dependent upon the application or threat of physical force or violence. Individuals and organizations commit these acts to obtain money, property, or services; to avoid the payment or loss of money or services; or to secure personal or business advantage."[8] Ever since the Committee of Sponsoring Organizations (COSO) of the Treadway Commission issued its landmark internal controls–integrated framework in 1992, corporations around the world have been concerned about implementing strong and robust internal controls to ensure compliance with organizational policies and procedures and to protect against error and fraud.[9] Section 404 of the Sarbanes-Oxley Act of 2002 brought a renewed focus to "internal controls over financial reporting."[10] It is natural to think of a system of internal controls as being somewhat people-neutral. That is, assuming an organization has competent individuals in key control positions, an adequately designed system of internal controls should operate effectively, even when people make mistakes.

However, considering that fraud involves intent to act in a manner different from what would normally be expected, another element must be considered: how unethical people might act and whether the system of internal controls is robust enough. Auditors, both internal and external, as well as risk and compliance managers, must have a heightened sense of professional skepticism and not always assume that people will do the right thing. Put another way, auditors and risk managers must instead pay heed to the maxim "Think like a crook to catch a crook." They must try to understand why an otherwise honest individual would commit a dishonest act. Gaining this understanding will increase the likelihood that they can more effectively detect, and in some cases even deter, one or more individuals from committing fraud.

Behavioral science has thus far been unable to identify a single psychological characteristic or set of characteristics that can serve as a reliable marker of the propensity of an individual to commit fraud.[11] For example, to say that "greed and dishonesty"—a commonly heard refrain—can account for all that went on during the "irrational exuberance" of the 1990s or the first decade of the current century would be overly simplistic. After all, there are many professionals in the business world who are extremely ambitious, competitive, and wealthy but who nevertheless fully abide by the law. They do not necessarily resort to fraud to achieve their goals and performance targets. But they are motivated by something, and understanding the different motives that drive fraudsters is an important starting point.

It also may help to view fraud from criminologists' perspectives. They believe that fraud, like any other crime, can best be explained by three factors: a supply of motivated offenders, the availability of suitable targets, and the absence of capable guardians—controls systems or someone to "mind the store," so to speak.[12] Familiarity with these factors may help auditors and risk managers be alert to fraud risk vulnerabilities. Under the A.B.C. typology, an individual acting alone would be characterized as a bad apple. When there are accomplices and thus collusion is involved, it is a case of a bad bushel. When the organization's leaders engage in corrupt behavior, however, and the whole culture is toxic, we have a case of a bad crop. The bad crop syndrome can even afflict an entire industry, as we have recently seen in the case of the LIBOR (London Interbank Offered Rate) rigging scandal that has tarred the reputations of many large banks such as Barclays, Union Bank of Switzerland, and the Royal Bank of Scotland, which have engaged in extremely questionable behaviors. At this point we will set the stage for the A.B.C. taxonomy while placing it in the historical context of the fraud triangle and other classic and modern theories of fraud causation.

The Fraud Triangle and Other Theories of Causation

Ever since criminologist Donald Cressey made his seminal contributions to the literature on fraud, the root causes of fraud have been traced to what he called the fraud triangle.[13] Cressey defined the core phenomenon of fraud as "a violation of position of financial trust."[14] Three elements—hence a triangle—must be present:

1. **Opportunity.** A problem that cannot be shared (e.g., gambling losses).
2. **Pressure or incentive.** The knowledge of how to solve the problem in secret through an opportunity for trust violation (e.g., a lax environment in which no one is minding the store).
3. **Rationalization.** The ability to find a way to justify the appropriateness of the behavior so that it does not conflict with the image of oneself as a trusted person (e.g., "For all the services I have rendered, the company owes me!").

To some extent, even the assessment of the opportunity to commit fraud—including the likelihood of being caught—is a subjective, behavioral assessment. The decision to deviate from the norm and commit fraud is not taken lightly. These ideas are captured well in the AICPA's standards and professional guidance, which provide auditors with the right mind-set for grappling with fraudulent financial reporting.[15]

Some antifraud researchers and professionals believe that the fraud triangle is incomplete, so in the last decade, additional factors have been suggested. In 2004, a fourth factor, *capability*, was added to turn the fraud triangle into a fraud "diamond"; this viewpoint asserts that fraud can be committed only by someone who has the expertise and ability to exploit an opportunity. The idea of capability in committing fraud is explained as follows: "Opportunity opens the doorway to fraud, and incentive and rationalization can draw the person toward it. But the person must have the capability to recognize the open doorway as an opportunity and to take advantage of it by walking through, not just once, but time and time again. Accordingly, the critical question is, "Who could turn an opportunity for fraud into reality?"[16] In 2010, antifraud professionals in the accounting firm of Crowe Horwath put forward a fraud pentagon adding *individual arrogance* and *competence* to the original fraud triangle. At the time of this writing, it remains unclear whether adding more factors is really helpful in assessing fraud risk.[17]

Compared to the fraud triangle and its more recent modifications, which typically conceive of the individual fraud perpetrator as the unit of analysis, the A.B.C. theory also considers the groups acting in concert and the influence of the environment and/or culture as perpetrators. Furthermore, we believe that it is helpful to gain insights into the psychology of the fraud perpetrators, the victims, and the governance overseers—antifraud professionals such as risk managers, compliance personnel, auditors, regulators, and forensic accounting professionals. After all, it is the psychological interaction among these segments of the population—sort of a "cops and robbers" dynamic—that gives rise to the study of white-collar crime. This perspective is extremely important in understanding the fraud perpetrator's assessment of whether the coast is clear, the available alibi (i.e., the plausible deniability defense routinely used by white-collar criminals, with the assistance of highly paid attorneys), and the risk of being caught. Of course, if a fraud had been successfully perpetrated previously, it only emboldens the fraudster to do it again.

In this regard, consider the insight offered by ACFE founder and chairman Dr. Joseph T. Wells. He provides a penetrating analysis of how fraudsters think, using eighteenth-century economist Jeremy Bentham's core ideas. He observes that the likelihood of committing a (white-collar) crime is a function of the perpetrator's perception of the risks and rewards—that is, those who assess the probability of getting caught as high are naturally less inclined to commit fraud. On the effectiveness dimension, fraud risk control activities pale in comparison to the increase in the perception of being apprehended. In this respect, the organization's track record in the handling of past incidents and allegations also matters.[18]

From a behavioral standpoint, this raises the possibility of creating an anticipation effect (i.e., the anticipation of being audited), including unannounced surprise checks, as part of fraud prevention and deterrence controls. Both independent outside auditors and internal auditors, through creative and imaginative approaches to their work using technology (e.g., continuous controls monitoring) or advances in statistics (e.g., discovery sampling approaches, Benford's Law, predictive analytics) or even active brainstorming about the ways fraud could be perpetrated can put up strong deterrents and defenses to fraud, all the while improving fraud detection capabilities. Management must act decisively and swiftly against fraud perpetrators when they are identified as a result of a fraud investigation. Such swift and decisive action can go a long way in cementing fraud deterrence efforts.[19]

As with *Inside the Fraudster's Mind,* it seems worthwhile to learn how fraudsters think, as well as learn about their "thinking errors." Seeing the interviews on film deepens the questions and further underscores the need to understand the mind. In the last several decades, psychologists have developed two major explanations of crime, one using psychoanalytic theory and the other using learning theory. According to the psychoanalytic theory of Sigmund Freud, an individual's sickness or maladjustment can be caused by two possible malfunctions in personal development:

1. Failure to keep the uninhibited impulses of the id in check.
2. Failure of the superego, or lack of conscience.

According to Freud, the psyche has three parts: the *id*, which strives to satisfy basic needs and desires; the *ego*, our normal consciousness; and the *superego*, or the conscience. Psychological problems result from an imbalance of these forces. The id strives to satisfy basic needs and desires. Thus, lying, stealing, and committing other crimes becomes the path of least resistance, and the most convenient means of fulfilling the uncontrolled impulses of the id. Because the source of the id's influence can be tracked back to the unconscious, fraud perpetrators are themselves seldom aware of the real influences on or causes of their criminal activity.

The superego, better known as the conscience, is the motivational force that inhibits people from engaging in illegal, antisocial behavior. When a person has a weak superego, or an underdeveloped conscience, probably from lack of parental identification and social training, he or she does not feel guilty when committing antisocial acts. Because "their acts of dishonesty do not create feelings of guilt or remorse, they can be expected to commit fraud whenever there is an opportunity to do so with little chance of being caught."[20]

The learning theory explanation for white-collar crime is that, like all other human behavior, it is learned and greatly influenced by the environment. According to behaviorist B. F. Skinner's theory of operant conditioning, people do things for which they are reinforced, or rewarded. If dishonesty is in vogue, it should come as no surprise that those caught up in such an environment will be dishonest, too.

Criminal behavior is also encouraged by the benefits from ill-gotten gains, such as the elimination of one's debt or the support of a lavish lifestyle. The learning can occur vicariously; learning by imitation occurs quite naturally. Thus, witnessing others' get-rich-quick schemes can motivate the observer to desire the same.

Sociological explanations for fraud follow the logic of learning theory quite strikingly. Edwin Sutherland's differential association theory posits that criminal behavior is inexorably linked to a personal association with a criminal environment. Thus, in a criminogenic culture, such as an organized crime syndicate or a gang or a cult, the members' social interactions are overwhelmingly, if not exclusively, with others exhibiting criminal tendencies, so they have a high likelihood of becoming criminals themselves. In summary, commenting on Sutherland's theory, W. Steve Albrecht and his colleagues stated the following:

The essence of Sutherland's argument is that criminal behavior is engaged in by persons who have accumulated enough feelings and rationalizations in favor of law violations to outweigh their pro-social definitions. Criminal behavior is learned and will occur when the perceived rewards for criminal behavior exceed the rewards for lawful behavior.[21]

Thus, as part of an attitude of professional skepticism, whenever they perceive a heightened risk of fraud, auditors may consider reevaluating their approach to an audit. Auditors are not supposed to take things and people at face value but are to obtain sufficient competent evidence to support representations made in the financial statements. Although they should surely gather the facts and do an analysis before doing an interview, they might want to make additional inquiries of accounting and finance personnel first, and get a better appreciation of the context, before going straight to the financial statements. After all, the surrounding context in which the financials are produced is as important as the numbers themselves. This may require auditors to develop and hone their inquiry and interviewing skills and require more face time with client personnel. In other words, at the audit planning stage itself, the audit approach must be carefully evaluated. In particular, consideration should be given to the idea that rather than proceeding from the numbers to the people, they might proceed from the people to the numbers.[22] In other words, focus on the architects of the financial statements and their motivations carefully.

A.B.C. Theory: A New Fraud Taxonomy

The rogue trader is a guy at a desk with a romantic vision: He finds a hole in the system and "makes it rain" for his company while secretly knowing it is based on an illusion. Consider the following:

- In July 1995, Daiwa Bank discovered that its head of bond trading in New York, Toshihide Iguchi, had lost $1.1 billion in unauthorized trading. Iguchi had concealed his losses for more than a decade before confessing to the bank's top brass.
- Senior management at Credit Suisse's London office suspended a number of its traders on the collateralized debt

obligation desk in February 2008 after discovering pricing discrepancies in their holdings. What was initially thought to have been human error was, upon investigation, revealed to have been a calculated fraud—with the traders using old data to inflate the apparent value of their positions. The Swiss bank was forced to write down its assets by $2.65 billion.

- Nick Leeson, a Singapore-based trader affiliated with Barings Bank, a 232-year-old venerable British bank, was initially very successful in speculative trades, making huge profits for Barings and getting promoted. In the early 1990s, he was hiding losses from bad trades in a secret account. Leeson was able to accomplish this because of a management flaw in Barings that gave him the responsibility of double-checking his own trades rather than having him report to a superior (even though this internal control weakness had been highlighted by the auditors, Price Waterhouse). Ironically, the trade that undid Leeson was one of his more conservative transactions. Normally, he would have been safe in such a position, but an earthquake in Kobe caused a sharp drop in the Nikkei and other Asian markets and exposed his position to huge losses—more than $1 billion—causing Barings Bank to collapse.

- Brian Hunter was a 32-year-old star trader for Amaranth Advisors, an American hedge fund founded by Nicholas Maounis in 2000 and based in Greenwich, Connecticut. At its peak, Amaranth Advisors managed approximately $9 billion in assets. In September 2006, after suffering from colossal losses of roughly $6 billion from Hunter's trades, Amaranth Advisors collapsed, marking one of history's largest known trading losses and hedge fund collapses.

Perhaps the most famous case of all is that of Jérôme Kerviel, who was employed as an options trader working on Société Générale's Delta One desk in Paris. When his schemes were revealed, he had set a record: a $7.3 billion loss. The bank was satisfied, at least publicly, that Kerviel was the sole perpetrator.

Yet questions remained in Kerviel's case: Was he truly operating alone—the one rotten apple—or was he the fall guy? Were there any others who colluded but successfully remained in the shadows? Were there teammates who were recruited, like the Credit Suisse band of rogue traders? Or was an entire organization involved, such as in the state of Illinois fraud discussed in Chapter 2?

Although the numbers may be small or large in terms of rogue traders, from the behavioral forensics perspective, these are not the same phenomena, and distinguishing how they differ is where we must start. The units of analysis are different.

The A.B.C. (apple, bushel, crop) theory posits moving from the individual to a colluding group to an entire culture or environmental factor when considering fraud. The idea of one bad apple spoiling the whole bunch goes back to at least Chaucer and Shakespeare, who thought of it in terms of "one bad apple can spoil its neighbors."

However, the meaning of this proverb has changed slightly from the early nineteenth century, when it was first used. It originally meant that one bad apple actually spoiled the rest of the apples in the barrel. In other words, it was impossible for good to exist for long when even the slightest rot was present. This actually has a scientific explanation. When the plant hormone ethylene, which stimulates growth and helps fruit to ripen, is prematurely released, it has the ability to overactivate all of the fruit around it and can indeed ruin the entire lot.

Only in recent times have we begun to use the proverb to mean that there can be a few bad apples while the rest of the lot remains good. When we analyze how corporations have evolved, this is truly the manner in which we describe our organizations. We now believe that it is quite possible to have a few rogue employees in the midst of an otherwise sound workforce.

In writing this book, we are using the term *bad apple* in the more recent sense: that a few bad apples can coexist with healthy, thriving apples.[23] However, we do recommend identifying the few bad apples as quickly as possible so as to keep the organizational culture uncorrupted in the long run.

A.B.C. theory anticipates the need for a multilevel analysis of a phenomenon as complex as fraud. There is also a clear expectation that different units of analysis corresponding to the level of fraud perpetration (i.e., apple, bushel, and crop) may be called for. For instance, at the level of a single rogue executive (the bad apple), organizations must invest heavily in their human resources function so that background checks are done on potential employees and current employees are offered extensive ethics training. The culture and ethos of the organization should be such that rogue employees would voluntarily quit the organization because their behaviors would not be tolerated.

The case of collusion within organizations (the bad bushel) is a huge problem, however. First, internal controls such as segregation of duties are at risk of being completely ineffective against collusion, especially when the collusion occurs at the highest levels.[24] Second, because many key employees are in on the act, there may be no one left to blow the whistle. Management fraud involving deeply laid schemes of collusion is more challenging to prevent or even detect, whether by external or internal auditors when they occur at the top levels.[25]

Finally, we have the case of the bad crop, a fraud that permeates the entire organization. Whenever there is an opportunity for reaping an unfair advantage and the risk of being caught is extremely low, even when the fraud starts out small, word will quickly spread, and those activities will continue until detected (and potentially outlawed). The recent book *Liquidated: An Ethnography of Wall Street*, by Karen Ho, an anthropologist, allows us a window into how culturally driven factors influence business behavior (presumably including fraud perpetration).

This is what may actually have happened with the stock-option backdating scandal in the early years of this century. One or two Silicon Valley companies, giving large stock option grants, may have chanced upon the backdating idea. Once it was successfully put in motion and nobody noticed, the word spread, and very soon a whole host of companies was engaging in this palpably illegal accounting of stock options. The cases of United Healthcare, Brocade Communications, and RIM-BlackBerry were the most egregious, but there was a shadow cast even over Apple CEO Steve Jobs for whether he had received backdated stock options. (He was cleared.)

Consider the idea that the few (influential) bad apples at the top or in the middle of the mortgage-lending market at the beginning of this century spoiled the barrel (with Alt-A or liars' loans, predatory lending, robo signing, and so on). The plant hormone ethylene, which stimulates growth and helps fruit to ripen, can, in such a context, be an analogy for how collusion can grow to such an extent that internal policies and controls become overridden or completely ineffective in an organization. When the entire culture (or ethos) is poisoned, the whole barrel is at risk to be or has been spoiled. It may be interesting to explore what the tipping point is in these circumstances.

Conclusion

Although the white-collar criminal is not violent, he or she disregards the rights of others. By disregarding etiquette, civility, and the need for basic trust in others, the violent criminal and each category of fraudster—bad apple, bad bushel, or bad crop—are similar. In Part II, as we examine human behavior, we will explore the roles of psychopathy, antisocial personality, narcissism, and mental illness and their roles in fraud.

Notes

1. See "Greed Takes the Blame" in Appendix B.
2. G. J. Bologna and R. J. Lindquist, *Fraud Auditing and Forensic Accounting*, 2nd ed. (New York: John Wiley & Sons, 1995), 36–37. Technically speaking, based on physical volume, only one-ninth (or about 11 percent) of an iceberg shows up above the waterline, so these authors obviously took some liberties in using one-third (almost three times the feasible actual physical volume) for their analogy.
3. Tracy Coenen, "How to Detect Behavioral Red Flags," Sequence Inc., December 30, 2007, www.sequenceinc.com/index.php?option=com_content&view=article&id=185:how-to-detect-behavioral-red-flags-of-fraud.
4. Stanton E. Samenow, *Inside the Criminal Mind* (New York: Times Books, 1984), book jacket.
5. Tonia Cooke with Gilbert Geis, *Inside the Fraudster's Mind* (video). Interviews with white-collar felons, Association of Certified Fraud Examiners, Austin, TX, 2011.
6. Quoted in Walt Pavlo Jr. and Neil Weinberg, *Stolen without a Gun: Confessions from Inside History's Biggest Accounting Fraud—the Collapse of MCI WorldCom* (Tampa, FL: Etika Books, 2007).
7. Henry Campbell Black, *Black's Law Dictionary*, 5th ed. (St. Paul, MN: West Publishing Company, 1979), 468.
8. U.S. Department of Justice, Federal Bureau of Investigation, *White Collar Crime: A Report to the Public* (Washington, DC: Government Printing Office, 1989), 3.
9. Committee of Sponsoring Organizations (COSO). Internal Control–Integrated Framework, 1992, and updated in 2013. See www.coso.org. Sponsoring organizations: American Accounting Association, American Institute of CPAs, Institute of Internal Auditors, Institute of Management Accountants, and Financial Executives International. May 14, 2013.
10. Public Law No. 107–204—JULY 30, 2002 116 STAT. 745, "Sarbanes-Oxley Act of 2002." Accessible from www.gpo.gov/fdsys/pkg/PLAW-107publ204/pdf/PLAW-107publ204.pdf.
11. Grace Duffield and Peter Grabosky, *The Psychology of Fraud: Trends and Issues in Crime and Criminal Justice* (Canberra, Australia: Australian Institute of Criminology, 2001).

12. L. Cohen and M. Felson, "Social Change and Crime Rate Trends: A Routine Activity Approach." *American Sociological Review* 44 (1979): 588–608.
13. For more on the fraud triangle and to understand fraud as a human act, see Appendix A.
14. Donald R. Cressey, *Other People's Money: The Social Psychology of Embezzlement* (New York: Free Press, 1953). Cressey was affiliated with the University of California, Santa Barbara. He was an assistant to Professor Edwin Sutherland, a past president of the American Sociological Association, who introduced the term *white-collar crime.*
15. See American Institute of Certified Public Accountants Statement on Auditing Standards 99, "Consideration of Fraud in a Financial Statement Audit." Another useful resource is the joint IIA/AICPA/ACFE publication, "Managing the Business Risk of Fraud: A Practical Guide." www.acfe.com/uploadedFiles/ACFE_Website/Content/documents/managing-business-risk.pdf.
16. D. T. Wolfe and D. R. Hermanson, "The Fraud Diamond: Considering the Four Elements of Fraud," *CPA Journal* 74 (December 2004).
17. For an empirical test of alternative fraud models, see D. M. Boyle, F. T. DeZoort, and D. R. Hermanson, *The Impact of Alternative Fraud Model Use on Auditors' Fraud Risk Judgments and Confidence.* Unpublished working paper, 2012.
18. Joseph T. Wells, "Let Them Know Someone's Watching," *Journal of Accountancy,* May 2002.
19. Harry Cendrowski, James P. Martin, and Louis W. Petro, *The Handbook of Fraud Deterrence* (Hoboken, NJ: John Wiley & Sons, 2007).
20. W. S. Albrecht, M. B. Romney, D. J. Cherrington, I. R. Payne, and A. V. Roe. *How to Detect and Prevent Business Fraud* (Englewood Cliffs, NJ: Prentice Hall, 1982), 32.
21. Ibid.
22. With the advent of global communications technology, face-to-face interactions have decreased. This is a challenge for the auditing profession, since, lacking face-to-face interactions, e-mails and phone conversations may simply not permit the reading of emotions. As we will see, emotions are a significant driver of decision making, including the decision to commit fraud (e.g., lying and covering up). "Oh, what a tangled web we weave / When first we practice to deceive" (from the epic poem "Marmion" by Sir Walter Scott).
23. Our view is echoed by Jonathan Macey of Yale Law School, who has observed that clients increasingly value the individuals more than the firms they are affiliated with. Thus, select employees remain valuable even when the firms they work for implode, as happened with certain partners of Arthur Andersen. See J. Macey, *The Death of Corporate Reputation: How Integrity Has Been Destroyed on Wall Street* (Upper Saddle River, NJ: FT Press, 2013).
24. The CEO and/or the CFO was found to be involved in 89 percent of the cases, according to a 2010 COSO fraud study. Because of the requirements of the roles, it is inferred that a larger majority of these cases involved collusion.
25. A May 2011 Conference Board study also shows how a domineering CEO could, through coercion, get a CFO to "cook" the books. Another study indicates that a CEO might even "sweet-talk" a CFO into doing the same thing.

PART

II

THE FOUNDATIONS OF BEHAVIORAL FORENSICS: WHY GOOD PEOPLE DO BAD THINGS

In the many investigations and experiences with fraud that our team has explored, one of the more challenging aspects of the people dimension, the human side of fraud, is this: Where does one start?

Fraud is perplexing. When we explore the human side of the crimes of fraud cases after the fact, we are left wondering about many things, such as the motivations and the seeming absence of concern about the harm done to the trust inherent in human relationships. It is legitimate to ask the following:

- Where is the shame in the bad apple?
- Why did the victims not see the signs?
- How does a leader who ruins his organization sleep at night?

We see the human stories in the headlines. From the fanciful Internet deception that led to Notre Dame's star linebacker Manti Te'o believing that he was having a relationship with a beautiful woman to the hard-hearted deception of the ratings agencies during the run-up to the housing market collapse, fraudulent schemes are limited only by the creativity of the human mind.

Bizarre tales like Te'o's are not as troubling as those that disrupt our trust of the markets and of business in general, of course. The latter leave us cold, distrustful, and cynical. In particular, our concern is deepest about those who seemed beyond reproach (e.g., Tour de France champion Lance Armstrong).

We explore how the mind works to allow for such deception. The unconscious, our defenses, and our emotions correlate directly to the well-accepted model of the fraud triangle (opportunity, pressure or incentive, and rationalization). We expand our understanding of what happens between fraudster and victim. Delving deeper, we explore how drawing a distinction between predatory and accidental fraudsters can help us understand the victims and the environments that support fraud. Everyday people who are honest frequently find themselves on the wrong side of the line. For example, Diann Cattani, who embezzled more than $500,000 from a boutique consulting firm in Atlanta, started small. Her stealing started innocently enough with her travel agent accidentally charging a vacation Cattani was taking to Cattani's corporate credit card.

"It wasn't a check for $500,000," said Cattani, whose rap sheet prevents her from ever again working for a public company or obtaining a professional license. "It was a little bit here, a little bit there. It was an incremental descent into destruction."[1]

Through cases like hers, as well as others featuring more complex organizational factors, we highlight what happens when a person stumbles into fraud and then decides to sustain a fraud. Proven psychological models of motivation help us to understand the *fraud triangle* in a new and more nuanced way.

Applying the models to fraud in a novel way provides a foundation for the transition of small, relatively immaterial frauds to larger, more expensive frauds. As the individual decides to expand, the fraud requires recruiting others. Thus we can begin to understand the transition from the individual bad apple to the bad bushel and bad crop (sometimes referred to as spillover effects).[2] We can also understand the role of "toxic" leadership and other factors that allow for an environment that can lead to fraud. One can discover new insights that allow risk managers, internal auditors, and compliance professionals to be aware of what to avoid and what to support in organizations.

We explore what happens in leadership. There are fundamental characteristics of senior leaders, some that stem from their role as leaders and some that stem from their individual personalities, that can increase the risk of fraud.

We also explore what role deviance or even madness plays:

- Are these acts of derangement or mental illness?
- Are bad apples simply narcissists, profoundly faulted characters who are invested only in attending to their own needs?
- Are they psychopaths, reckless with the law and the feelings of others?

We explore the unconscious, the defenses, and emotions such as shame and pride, which play a key role in decision making.[3] We introduce psychologist Michael J. Apter's reversal theory and demonstrate how it can be a tremendously useful way of organizing our understanding of why rule followers become rule breakers, or why otherwise good people seem to do bad things on occasion (e.g., deliberately play with fire and invite danger).[4] Subsequently, we present ideas on how to utilize these insights from psychology to understand, address, anticipate, and respond to fraud risk in a meaningful and substantive way.

Finally, we offer information on the following:

- The predator-prey dynamic
- The mind of the accidental fraudster (bad apple)
- Behavioral science insights into C-suite fraud behavior
- How to smell a rat and avoid becoming a victim of fraud
- How auditors and forensic accountants can add to their forensic tool kit by using concepts and ideas from the emerging field of behavioral forensics.

Notes

1. Michelle Goodman, "The Embezzler Next Door," ABC News, April 15, 2010.
2. See Will Felps, Terrence R. Mitchell, and Eliza Byington, "How, When, and Why Bad Apples Spoil the Barrel: Negative Group Members and Dysfunctional Groups," *Research in Organizational Behavior* 27 (2006): 175–222.
3. Dr. Antonio Damasio, a distinguished neurologist, persuasively demonstrates how emotions and feelings contribute to reason and to adaptive social behavior and how the absence of emotion and feeling can break down rationality. Antonio R. Damasio, *Descartes' Error: Emotion, Reason, and the Human Brain* (New York: G. P. Putnam's Sons, 1994).
4. Michael J. Apter, *Danger: Our Quest for Excitement* (Oxford, UK: One World Publications, 2007).

4

Beyond the Fraud Triangle and into the Mind

THE BUILDING BLOCKS OF BEHAVIORAL FORENSICS—UNDERSTANDING HOW THE BASICS OF HUMAN BEHAVIOR TIE INTO FRAUD

Despite our best wishes, fraud is not going away; it is here to stay. Human beings are creative, determined, artistic, charming, and intelligent. In many ways these traits serve us very well. They provide us with music, literature, movies, and creative solutions in our day-to-day lives. The smartphone is an example of all of these wonderful human traits coming together into something quite remarkable, delightful, and useful.

Yet these same traits are a double-edged sword, and they can also be instruments of harm. Fraud is one of many ways that human beings tear others down and betray trust. But we are not alone among living creatures in this ability.

Deception Is a Natural Phenomenon

Fraud is theft, but not by force. There is perhaps no aspect of fraud more important than this. There is no robbery at gunpoint, no direct threat of harm to the victim or the victim's loved ones. Rather, the victim willingly gives away money or something of value.

Fraud is a deception, and deception is natural. Many living creatures, both animal and plant, survive and thrive because of their methods of deception. From the viceroy butterfly, which looks like the bitter and mildly poisonous monarch butterfly, to the king snake, which closely mirrors the very deadly coral snake, to the cuckoo, which brazenly lays her egg in a crow's nest and abdicates maternal responsibility, deception is adaptive and thriving in nature. Camouflage and mimicry are also quite common features of the animal kingdom, and both involve some kind of deception, covert or overt.[1]

Year after year and in every possible organization, fraud perpetrators deceive their victims. How does the fraudster pull this off, and why do the victims succumb time and again? To understand this dynamic requires being curious about the working of not just the human brain but also of something even more complex: the human mind.[2]

Understanding the role of the mind, particularly the mind of a person who commits fraud, requires some fundamentals and a clarification. First, the clarification: This book seeks to "bring Freud to fraud," not in the literal sense but rather with the assumption that a basic understanding of the mind will aid those who want to mitigate fraud risk. It will also help the potential victims to successfully resist the fraudster's charm offensive by understanding the fraudster's *modus operandi* better. We have all heard the maxim "Forewarned is forearmed."

When those charged with governance understand the human mind, their understanding can complement other solutions, thus expanding the capacity to comprehend, deter, and even preempt fraud.

The Mind and the Fraud Triangle

Forensic investigators have long relied on the fraud triangle as a basic conceptual framework for understanding the act of fraud. As described earlier, there are three elements that are required for someone to commit fraud: opportunity, pressure or incentive, and rationalization.

Consider the following report about Rita Crundwell, the former CFO of the city of Dixon, Illinois. This case is a fairly recent example of a long-running fraud and a classic violation of trust. A straightforward analysis of this case uses the concepts underlying the fraud triangle.

Kathe Swanson, a Dixon, Illinois, city clerk, had accidentally discovered a curious bank statement from an even more curious bank account and alerted the mayor. Mayor Jim Burke had been helping the feds unravel an embezzlement scheme in which tens of millions of dollars had been siphoned from the city's operating budget.

According to reporter Bryan Smith, "The money was being dumped into a mysterious account and allegedly spent on everything but city business: jewelry, fancy clothes, a custom motor coach, boats, property in Florida, luxury cars, hundreds of the finest horses this side of Amarillo." All evidence gathered seemed to point to Rita Crundwell, Dixon's city comptroller for three decades. Crundwell's hobby was exhibiting her stable of horses at championship events, many of which she won. Smith portrays her Jekyll-Hyde personality as follows: "By day, she was a modest municipal worker with a high school education; by night, she was a diamond-bedazzled high roller, the doyenne of a world that was a million miles in glamour and several million dollars in wealth from the cornfields and cattle farms of Illinois."[3]

Being the Dixon city comptroller obviously gave Crundwell a position of trust and the opportunity and access to the city's funds. The pressure she felt was to maintain her horse-racing hobby and other lavish lifestyle needs. But the rationalization she used to convince herself that she was doing nothing wrong is not obvious.

She clearly did not live up to her professional obligations, but where was the shame? This was not good judgment, but rather fairly impulsive when it all started, so what role did emotion play in this scenario? Over the years Crundwell must have become emboldened and perhaps more brazen in increasing the amount of the embezzlement. What happens in the human mind to allow these ethical compromises? How did she come to believe that she would escape being caught? Perhaps she thought she was smarter than others and therefore invincible.

These answers will unfold over the next several chapters. For now, we start with the basics about the human mind. As with the fundamentals of accounting, and the "debits and credits" vocabulary that characterizes bookkeeping entries, we will systematically introduce new concepts that lay out the territory for understanding the mind of the fraudster.

The "Balance Sheet Basics" of the Mind: The Unconscious, the Symptoms, and the Defenses

Sigmund Freud (1856–1939), who began his medical career as a neurologist in Vienna, Austria, was a pioneer in the importance and complexity of human thought. Our focus will be on the many levels of the mind, something Freud would have appreciated as he was greatly enamored of the human mind's workings.

Erich Fromm persuasively argued that "the theory of the unconscious is one of the most decisive steps in our knowledge of man and in our capacity to distinguish appearance from reality in human behavior." By founding the "science of the irrational," Fromm said, Freud boldly "attacked the last fortress that had been left untouched—man's consciousness as the ultimate datum of psychic experience." Fromm then delivered the ultimate accolade to Freud for his most creative and radical achievement: "[Freud] showed that most of what we are conscious of is not real and that most of what is real is not in our consciousness."[4]

As a result of Freud's brilliant contributions, the eponymous term *Freudian* is often used to refer to the following:

- A focus on unconscious processes as motivators of behavior.
- An abiding concern with the cognitive and the symbolic.
- An affiliation with the basic biological progenitors of human behavior, especially the sexual and the aggressive.
- A strong presumption that early experiences are the causes of later behaviors.
- A penchant for deep interpretation, for rummaging down through the layers of the psyche to seek understanding and explanation.
- The elaboration of the methods of psychoanalytic therapy as a means of producing changes in behavior, thought, and feeling.[5]

As a neurologist, Freud was very interested in how the nervous system worked. He did not, as a young professional, set out to explore the mind. It was his colleague and friend Josef Breuer who altered his career path and led Freud to the formulation of an influential model of the mind.[6] Freud's early attempts to understand the case of "Anna O" (the patient's real name was Bertha Pappenheim) was the beginning of his exploration of the mind and led to his more formal description of the methods of psychoanalysis. He was intrigued not only by the severity of the symptoms but by the symptoms themselves. He found their ability to quickly morph into other symptoms intriguing and perplexing.

This book will follow a similar original case, the case of Aaron Beam ("Aaron B"), which like the case of "Anna O" illustrates the complexities and fundamentals of an entire genre, an entire class of things studied that show similarities in form, style, or subject matter (in this case, fraud rather than hysteria).

To understand the A.B.C. theory of behavioral forensics requires an exploration of what actually happens in the real world. An actual case brings clarity to our understanding and refines our model. For the bad apple, we will explore how the typical e-mail scam or phisher-man uses emotions and a false sense of relationship.

Also in examining relationships, we explore the methods used by Bernie Madoff in recruiting investors. Further on, we move into a larger fraud dynamic. As we enter the world of bad bushels and then bad crops, we outline how an organization's desire to dominate the marketplace through fraudulent financial reporting had such devastating ripple effects. To illustrate this, we have chosen the case of HealthSouth, an outpatient treatment care company, of which Aaron Beam was a cofounder.

The case of HealthSouth is intriguing because it outlines clearly the evolution of a bad apple, the dance between the victim and the bad apple, the methods by which the bad apple recruits (un)will-ing accomplices, and the extent of the damage when it involves the C-suite.[7] Thus, the case of "Aaron B" serves as a backbone case.

Established in 1984, HealthSouth grew to become the largest U.S. provider of outpatient surgery and diagnostic and rehabilita-tive healthcare services. By the end of 2001, the New York Stock Exchange–listed company, through an "acquisitions strategy," came to own or operate more than 1,800 facilities in the United States and abroad. The company's financials grew increasingly complex, and in 2003, the SEC charged HealthSouth with having engaged in fraudulent accounting schemes between 1999 and 2002. Accord-ing to the SEC and Aaron Beam, the cofounder and former CFO of HealthSouth, Richard Scrushy, the company's cofounder and CEO, instructed the company's accounting personnel to materially inflate the company's earnings according to the expectations of Wall Street analysts. Here are some fundamentals about the fraudulent case at HealthSouth.

- By swallowing acquisitions, HealthSouth grew rapidly and was very profitable.
- Richard Scrushy had a vision for profits that began to drift from what was possible and began to put significant pressure on the accounting function to show this profit.

- Tension grew and played out between the cofounders of HealthSouth, Richard Scrushy and Aaron Beam.
- The CEO stayed on as multiple CFOs failed and left or were removed.
- Fraudulent reports grew to replace actual reports as a routine matter.
- The losses were massive and historic.

"Aaron B": The Case of HealthSouth CFO Aaron Beam Aaron Beam left HealthSouth when forced to participate in falsely inflating Medicare reimbursements to make HealthSouth's earnings targets. How did this happen?

As cofounder, Beam had been with HealthSouth since its inception and was proud of the organization. As it grew, he felt excited about the company's potential. In fact, he realized very early that with a modest investment of a few thousand dollars, he could expect a more than handsome payoff of between a hundredfold and a thousandfold. He would be wealthier than anyone in his family had ever been. The opportunity was there as long as the stock kept climbing.

The pressure for company performance to meet or beat Wall Street expectations, however, went hand in hand with this opportunity. As the pressure from CEO Richard Scrushy mounted, Beam began to feel trapped, and soon he found himself on a path to commit fraud.

Beam stated that he knew that "fabricating numbers and inflating Medicare reimbursements" was wrong, but did not feel comfortable challenging Scrushy. "I did not really talk to [Scrushy] or challenge him about this. I had learned from working with him for [years] that he didn't like to be told that he couldn't do something."[8] But those earnings targets had to be met somehow. There was no other way, he believed, and once he got on that slippery slope of "cooking" the books, there was no way out. At about the same time, he started having significant psychologically generated symptoms: extreme distress and physical sickness. This is not uncommon in stories of fraud. However, what happened next to Beam is not as common, and it shines a light on the role of the mind in fraud.

Beam's case is impressive because of the level to which his compromise, the psychological bind of his rationalization, affected him. As he himself noted, he was becoming extremely distressed. As his coping mechanisms became more and more overwhelmed, he became physically sick.

For Beam, becoming ill was the last straw, so he decided to leave the organization. As soon as he had made the decision to leave, his symptoms started to disappear and his health improved. By the time he left, he was significantly better. What finally gave him closure was to come out of retirement and help prosecute the fraud that had been disclosed in the media with what he knew at HealthSouth. Yet even today he does not feel fully recovered.

The level of distress, the physical symptoms, and the subsequent disappearance of the symptoms all highlight the power of the mind. There were no toxins in the air, his food was not poisoned, there was no flu epidemic, and he had not developed a rare genetic illness that suddenly erupted in his late 40s. His symptoms were of his own creation. How did this happen?[9]

Freudian Insights   Freud was one of the first practitioners to explain how neuroses often emerge into our consciousness, and his methods and insights are the best-known to the modern world. A pioneer like Charles Darwin and Albert Einstein, Freud had a drive to systematically explore the human mind and build a model for it that forever changed how we think about people. Thus it has relevance to all human behavior, including fraud.

Freud's models and methods evolved over time, but they remain essentially the same for all who study psychoanalysis. A patient is required to do only three things:

1. Attend the appointment every day at a consistent time.
2. Say whatever comes to mind.
3. Pay the bill.

Freud's (the analyst's) role is also simple:

- Explore all the content in the session for meaning.
- Explore the meaning behind the failure of the patient to fulfill one of his or her requirements.

All in all, this is pretty straightforward. But as with many simple things, it can be very difficult to actually do.

Examples of the required tasks that a psychoanalysis patient might not do are many, but some of the more common are familiar to anyone who has been part of a process like therapy. Perhaps the patient is late; that must be explored. Perhaps the bill is not paid; that must be explored.

In the deception that is fraud, it is often the absence of something that allows for the perpetration. In the case of Bernie Madoff, for example, many professional risk managers recognized that the auditing firm he had retained was not at the scale required for the assets under management. A quick scan indicated that all the checks and balances were in order, but a deeper and more skeptical review made it obvious that the accounting firm was retained because it was toothless.

Our unconscious minds can work this way, too. We can find ways to not do what is required to be adaptive. This can relate to situations beyond breaking the law: being healthy, being a good neighbor, or being a good citizen. The new discipline Freud pioneered was set up to analyze without judgment in order for the unconscious to show itself and reveal how it worked. A patient's noncompliance with the very simple tasks of analysis was in itself a way to highlight the workings of the unconscious. A strategy of looking at spontaneous behaviors using unobtrusive procedures was called for.

It does not always require a process like psychoanalysis to make symptoms go away. Although symptoms are typically viewed as manifestations of a physical illness, in psychological illness and distressed people, the symptoms are the illness. The causes of Aaron Beam's illness (his symptoms) went away as he rallied himself enough to recognize that something was wrong and to change his circumstances. In a sense, he was forced to change because his psychological defenses were failing.

Rationalizations: Compromises We Make within Ourselves

The defenses human beings employ that are maladaptive and create symptoms are generally well understood now, but they were not understood in depth by Sigmund Freud. It was his daughter, Anna Freud, who deepened the understanding of the functions of the psychological defenses.

What Sigmund Freud discovered, and Anna Freud spent a large part of her career defining and describing, are internal compromises to keep certain contents of the unconscious out of awareness. The symptoms Freud saw in his original cases were scary and confusing to him as a neurologist. What he saw in Anna O and in other cases is a window into the hidden part of all of us: the unconscious.

The information in the unconscious is not known for a specific adaptive reason. Primitive urges, emotions, and thoughts are kept out of our awareness so we can adapt to our world and get along with others.

How do psychological defenses work, and where do they come from? As all human beings grow and develop, they build defenses. Defenses are learned in childhood and utilized as a way to deal with the world when it is bewildering and overwhelming. Everyone feels bewildered and overwhelmed as a child and thus vulnerable. In a solution that works at the time, the defense takes hold instantly and becomes an unconscious habit. Strong negative feelings are managed in a compromise. At the time that defenses are generated, they make sense and work for an individual at that point in life. As we grow older, however, some of our defenses have to be refined or dropped; for instance, having a temper tantrum in the grocery store doesn't work for long. The hissy fit[10] in an adult is like an adult frog keeping a tadpole's tail.

Defenses explain why it is so difficult for the perpetrators of fraud to discuss what they did. As criminologist Gil Geis noted, white-collar criminals "may have felt very badly that they were a bunch of crooks, but that wasn't what they told us. You know, it was somebody else's fault. *You know, people want to keep their self-esteem*" (emphasis added).[11] As Anna Freud discovered, the defenses are there for a reason. As all human beings grow and develop, they build defenses. At the time they are generated they make sense and the defenses work for that person at that point in the person's life. But like kid-size clothes, what fit in the past no longer works for us, so we change.

The more powerful the defenses are, the more difficult they are to change, and the most difficult ones allow us to avoid seeing ourselves as bad or guilty. Being seen as bad or guilty happens to everyone at some point, but most of us have not committed crimes. It may not make rational sense to the rest of us that criminals have a hard time talking about their crimes, because most people have not been convicted of a felony.

To understand the power of the unconscious defenses in fraud and to understand the agony of admitting to the crime, a critical part of the mind must be added to the picture: the role of emotions.

Emotions: The Power behind Psychological Defenses

The case of HealthSouth allows us to see many of the human dynamics of fraud. Understanding the emotions and the role they played in Beam's fraud triangle is essential to our general understanding of the behavioral forensics approach to fraud. Clearly evident in Beam's discussion of the reasons that he and the leaders of HealthSouth "cooked the books" is the role of his feelings. These are not minor aspects of the story, nor are they part of an insignificant crime. In a sense they lie at the heart of one of the most destructive frauds in the history of American health care.

The following excerpt from his interview shows how his emotions motivated him to make compromises that disturbed him:

> So in 1996 when we didn't make our numbers we had to report a bad quarter. Richard [Scrushy, the CEO], in essence, asked Bill Owens and me to cook the books. And because I was intimidated by Richard—he had begun carrying a gun, he had bodyguards. He was a very scary person. And I wanted to keep the dream alive, too. I'm not going to say Richard literally held a gun to my head and made me commit fraud, but he's very persuasive in a cult type kind of way. He's very persuasive with what he can get you to do. And I was proud of the company. I wanted the dream to keep going. I didn't want to disappoint Wall Street, either, and I went along. Bill Owens, the chief accountant, made entries on the books. Literally credits to revenue that didn't exist and debit to assets that didn't exist. And in the summer of 1996 we began cooking the books.[12]

Reading Beam's comments, one can sense the trap that had been laid for what the larger business community perceived as a very powerful CFO. To the outside world he was a man to be reckoned with, but inside the organization he cofounded, he lived in fear. He mentioned specifically that he felt intimidated by Scrushy, who was armed and "scary," yet he also was caught in a bind because he was proud of his company and "wanted the dream to keep going."

Other parts of his interview contain emotional weight, too (e.g., later his relationship with Scrushy is reviewed, and he again mentioned the emotional pull of Scrushy's strong personality). The selection here highlights the pressure he felt as well as the reasons— or rather, the rationalizations—for what he did. Beam's story provides insight into the role of emotions in fraud, the first of three critical factors influencing the mind and thus the behavior of the fraudster. How does one understand emotions?

Emotions as a Threat to Understanding the Rational World of Accounting

As previously noted, we recognize the primacy of professional accountants' ability to work with numbers. Indeed, understanding how financial statements work is at the heart of accounting and highlights the special ability of accounting professionals. A facility with quantitative approaches and modeling numerical data is also at the heart of other hard sciences like physics, chemistry, and genetics, which are valued for their objectivity and rational consistency. Consider the frequently quoted observation of physicist Lord Kelvin: "In physical science the first essential step in the direction of learning any subject is to find principles of numerical reckoning and practicable methods for measuring some quality connected with it. I often say that when you can measure what you are speaking about, and express it in numbers, you know something about it; but when you cannot measure it, when you cannot express it in numbers, your knowledge is of a meagre and unsatisfactory kind; it may be the beginning of knowledge, but you have scarcely in your thoughts advanced to the state of Science, whatever the matter may be."[13]

However, William Cameron questioned whether "calculation and reckoning" should be put on such a high pedestal. He wrote, "It would be nice if all of the data which sociologists require could be enumerated because then we could run them through IBM machines and draw charts as the economists do. *However, not everything that can be counted counts, and not everything that counts can be counted*" (emphasis added).[14]

We should remember that despite the success of mathematical models in accounting, finance, and economics, all of these disciplines fall squarely into the domain of the social sciences, not the physical and mathematical sciences. Consequently, in many instances, and depending on context, perceptions tend to matter more than reality in these disciplines. Emotions are contextually rich concepts and challenging to understand, especially when they do not easily lend themselves to quantitative approaches and data-based modeling; they are often considered to be subjective or irrational. However, like a good computer algorithm or a heuristic problem-solving approach, a complex emotion can be broken down into smaller parts, analyzed, and mastered. There are several problems to address in emotions that relate to fraud:

1. The aspect of emotion that is common to all human beings
2. The function of emotions themselves
3. The critical emotion(s) that play a role in our defenses

Understanding emotion is not easy. In fact, in the last century, psychoanalysis itself has found it challenging to determine what role emotion plays and how best to understand its relative primacy in motivation and behavior. Donald Nathanson has summarized what gets in the way of appreciating the study of emotion:

> Many of us treat emotion as something that interferes with thinking. We demean arguments by calling them emotional, discredit people who seem emotionally involved in whatever bothers them, [and] trust feelings less than we trust cognition. Our culture even has code words that allow us to pretend we are talking about thinking rather than feeling. Rather than admit that our concern is emotional, we will say, "I have a problem with that" or "Don't bother me with such ideas" or "That upsets me!"[15]

The reality is that, as with politics, we pretty much take for granted that emotion exists, for better or worse, and that we have to live with it.

Most people know that the function of the heart is to move oxygenated blood out of the tissues and that the function of the lungs is to get oxygen in the blood. Many people understand the dangers of smoking and the risk of high cholesterol. Yet many people don't know the function of emotions. Are they as essential as the heart and the lungs, or are they unnecessary, like the appendix? Are emotions just something left over from our animal past that no longer serves us?

Emotion is actually helpful—not just something to live with, but a tool to help us adapt to our world. Charles Darwin and more recent researchers have made it clear that emotion provides children with a way to communicate their needs before they can speak.[16] A caregiver can respond to the needs of a child for nourishment, warmth, or safety just from the emotional signals the child sends.

Using emotion to communicate our needs without language extends into adulthood, though in a moderated way.

When we are little, before we have the capacity to speak any language, we can communicate our needs. By age one or slightly thereafter, we are able to tell those who are caring for us whether we are okay or whether we are in trouble. We have multiple ways of expressing unmet needs that only get more precise and refined as we grow older and mature, but there are a set of hardwired emotions that are common to all human beings.

Imagine a child, not a newborn or yet speaking in full sentences. He or she is an excellent communicator with the ability to tell his or her caregivers relatively complex messages about whether the environment is meeting his or her needs. Caregivers can adjust the temperature, ensure safety, satisfy the need for a drink or food, depending on the emotional signals the child sends.

Emotions interact with social rules, defined as "those guidelines, norms, requirements, expectations, customs, and laws, written and unwritten, spoken and unspoken, that reflect society's attitudes, values, prejudices, and fears, and determine the roles we play and the actions we take, as we interact with other people in society as individuals and as groups."[17] Unlike developmentally normal adults in a particular society or culture, people with autism have a very hard time mastering how to manage their emotions surrounding these day-to-day interactions deriving from "said and unsaid" cultural assumptions and social norms. Assimilation into the business world requires high levels of mastery of many of these soft skills, drawing upon the human emotions.

Exhibit 4.1 shows visual examples of the core, biologically hardwired emotions from childhood to adulthood in both sexes.

These emotions remain with us as adults (and as risk managers and fraud investigators) every day, to some degree. An astute observer can anticipate them if one knows how they work. Thus, we will extensively explore the best possible models for understanding emotions. It is probably true that adults learn how to control, even hide, their emotions, unlike children, who are far more uninhibited and expressive.

The deceptive dynamics of fraud between the bad apple and the victim utilize the emotions—in particular, excitement and fear in the short run and shame in the long run, especially with those who commit fraud in a predatory way. We can speculate that "hardened

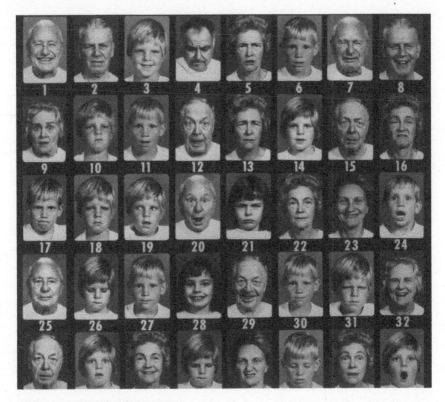

Exhibit 4.1   The Spectrum of Emotions

Source: © Tomkins Institute. Used with permission.

Human beings are capable of a wide range of expressions, yet since the worldwide explorations of Darwin, there has been an appreciation of a core set of meaningful faces common to all races, both genders, and any culture. Here is a set from the noted authority on affect, Silvan Tomkins. The viewer can see enjoyment, fear, surprise, contempt (dissmell), and other emotions.

criminals" have become hardened or desensitized to the accompanying affect and hence show little empathy or sympathy when becoming aware of the plight of their victims.

In the moments of rationalization, which are, in a way "moments of truth," emotion plays a key role in the person who becomes an accidental fraudster by switching his or her attitudes about following the rules (i.e., a motivational reversal). Emotions also relate to narcissism and personal values and the role they play in committing fraud.

Affect's Two Ties to Fraud: Motivation and Communication

Hardwired emotion is called *affect*. Affect is essential for getting by
in the world. It allows us to be motivated to take action, and it also
serves us by communicating to others.

Affect enables us to tell others whether our needs are being met.
It is a very old system, present in other animals in a more primitive
form. It is inborn in humans and is lacking only if a person has brain
damage or has been diagnosed with psychopathy or sociopathy.[18]
When we see someone who is scared, that message comes through
loud and clear. This is also true of the other hardwired emotions,
such as distress, anger, or enjoyment.

Silvan Tomkins, a psychologist most famous for his affect theory and
script theory, has collaborated with other mental health professionals
to develop a finite set of affects common to all human beings. His work
was an important source of insight for Michael Basch, who was able
through his clinical experience as a psychiatrist and psychoanalyst to
make the connection to motivation. The collective work of Tomkins,
Ekman, Damasio, Le Doux, and others have also demonstrated how
important affect is to motivation. Without affect, there is no action.[19]
Without affect, therefore, there is no fraud. This is an extremely important
observation relevant to everyone who studies the fraud phenomenon
or is an antifraud or risk management professional.

The following are considered to be innate emotions:

- Enjoyment
- Interest
- Surprise
- Anger
- Fear
- Distress
- Disgust
- Contempt
- Shame[20]

With this model, emotions are no longer infinite and subjective
but finite, objective, and quite specific (and therefore predictable).
Because these affects are common to all human beings, their universal existence helps an investigator of fraud to get past issues of gender,
age, culture, and other factors.

The Tomkins concept of emotion is a construct grounded in observation of the human face. As such, it enables fraud to be studied scientifically. The nine affects listed have been found around the world and revealed to be universal. We are capable of experiencing others' emotions, especially if we are able to see one another.[21] This is again very important for the understanding of fraud.

Being in the presence of another person highlights the power of emotion. There is clear evidence that when we are in the presence of someone, our brains, and thus our internal experiences, resonate with the internal experience of the other. One of the most interesting developments in neuroscience in recent years is the discovery of the "mirror neuron system" in human beings. The implications are summarized in a fascinating book by Marco Iacoboni on "the new science of how we connect with others."[22]

For example, if Sheila and Stephanie are in the same room and are having an animated conversation, their respective tones will influence each other. If they are arguing, the emotional tone can escalate and increase the intensity. If they are enjoying the subject, it can lead to a fun and delightful conversation. Anyone who has had a great conversation and then realized that the time has flown by can appreciate this. University of Chicago psychologist Mihaly Csikszentmihalyi identified these kinds of experiences and described them as "flow," a state in which work is done effortlessly.[23]

In terms of the affect dynamics, Sheila and Stephanie's conversation looks like the image in Exhibit 4.2.

In our fictional scenario, if Stephanie is expressing the high end of interest, which is excitement, then Sheila will experience excitement as well. This is known as *contagion*. Fraudsters actively encourage this emotional state. We will return to this scenario of Sheila and Stephanie later to highlight what the fraudster does.

A shared emotional tone can readily be seen in movie theaters, where people who see a film together reflect the overall affect or mood of the show. Infants in nurseries are also known to share affect: If one baby in a nursery begins to cry, others will as well. Similarly, the laughter of an infant can be contagious.

With fraud, this sense of fun and excitement causes a person to let his or her guard down, as we will see later when we discuss Bernie Madoff's Ponzi scheme.

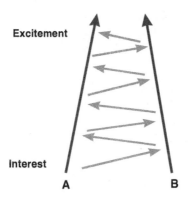

Exhibit 4.2   Affect Dynamics: Mutual Interest-Excitement

Source: © Morrison Associates Ltd. Used with permission.

Human beings naturally will reflect back another's interest as in this case between person A and person B. If there is a shared interest, this moves both A and B from a low level of interest to a higher level that transitions to excitement. This is the dance of a shared conversation on a captivating subject, the dance of courtship or the discussion of making profits.

Psychologist Paul Ekman's work on facial expressions had its starting point in the work of Tomkins. Ekman's projects included developing techniques for measuring facial muscular movement while also developing theories about emotion and deception. Building on the work of Tomkins and even Darwin, Ekman showed that facial expressions of emotion are not culturally determined but are universal across human cultures and thus biological in origin.

The expressions he found to be universal are anger, disgust, fear, shame, joy, sadness, and surprise. The findings on contempt are less clear, although there is at least some preliminary evidence that this emotion and its expression are also universal. Ekman developed the facial action coding system (FACS) to classify every human facial expression. He conducted and published research on a wide range of topics in the area of nonverbal behavior. His work on lying, for example, was not limited to the face but included observation of the rest of the body. Ekman has contributed to the study of the social aspects of lying, why we lie, and why we are often unconcerned with detecting lies.[24]

One of the problems of this line of pursuit of deception is the use of a single affect to determine a lie. Ekman noted one of the problems of assessing fear in relation to lying: Is the person afraid of being caught in a lie or afraid of not being believed?

Although Ekman's FACS instrument is commonly cited as essential for understanding liars, his model has some limits. Tomkins is considered by some to understand human beings in a more complex and dynamic way.

Ekman wanted to assist the layperson in reading people. He has taken a deep interest in spotting liars for decades. For example, he has highlighted the ability of the Secret Service to outperform other professions (including psychiatry) in recognizing deception.[25]

In this book we attempt to understand the emotional interplay of the fraudster and the victim. For that reason we will limit our analysis and use the biologically based affects of Tomkins. As we move into the interplay of the bad apple, bushel, and victim(s), we will see that the affects move beyond their function as communication and play a clear role in motivation.[26]

Conclusion

As noted earlier, fraud is not a theft by force, but by deception. The dance of fraud, therefore, is a dance of deception. As such, it requires the cooperation of the victim. The victim too must be influenced by emotions, and therefore the entire dance depends on the following fundamentals:

- Emotions—to distract and persuade
- Defenses—to rationalize (both fraudster and victim)

Without this set of fundamentals, the dance of the fraud is a confusing mess that could always be summed up too simply as being caused by greed.

The model we are building here promotes an understanding of human behavior. A white-collar crime requires both a criminal and a victim to play along—it is a deception, not a threat or theft in the middle of the night. Both players are human beings. In the bigger picture, the dynamic can escalate to include the bad bushel and the bad crop, but for now, to set the foundation, we will focus only on the two individuals and how the interplay between them allows fraud to take place.

Both the fraudster and the victim are going to relate and respond to the world based on the models presented so far. Having a straightforward model of how people work helps to decrease the "white noise" of all the unique factors in a fraud investigation or in a program designed to minimize risk. These can include many important factors that are also uniquely human: the culture of the organization, the personalities of the people involved, the point in time, the decision context and the high stakes involved for the inter-acting parties, and all the unique human contexts (holidays, illness, Mother Nature) that can confuse the picture for the investigator or the person responsible for risk management.

Many forensic and risk models and solutions start out at the macro level, which is a legitimate line of inquiry. Most forensic solutions that rely on computers start there, and they work. We offer a different line of thought, however, and start at the core of what happens between two people. This is where we will now turn our attention:

- How does the fraudster attract his victim? If there are human beings involved, emotions must be present, along with defenses to keep the emotions from becoming overwhelming.
- What role do the emotions play in the deception? There are only a finite number of core, biologically wired emotions, or affects.
- What affects are critical in the dance of fraud? For the answers, we will look into the basic mechanics of a simple fraud attempt via e-mail and then proceed to more complex frauds, such as Bernie Madoff's scam and the case of HealthSouth.

Notes

1. Peter Forbes, *Dazzled and Deceived: Mimicry and Camouflage.* (New Haven, CT: Yale University Press, 2009).
2. J. M. Schwartz and S. Begley, *The Mind and the Brain: Neuroplasticity and the Power of Mental Force* (New York: HarperCollins, 2003), 365. The authors explain, "The brain . . . is indeed the physical embodiment of the mind, the organ through which the mind finds expression and through which it acts in the world." However, the opposite view is taken in V. Paquette and J. Levesque et al., "'Change the Mind and You Change the Brain': Effects of Cognitive-Behavioral Therapy on the Neural Correlates of Spider Phobia." *Neuroimage* 18, no. 2 (2003): 401–409.
3. Bryan Smith, "Rita Crundwell and the Dixon Embezzlement," *Chicago,* December 2012, www.chicagomag.com/Chicago-Magazine/December-2012/Rita-Crundwell-and-the-Dixon-Embezzlement.

4. Erich Fromm, *The Crisis of Psychoanalysis: Essays on Freud, Marx, and Social Psychology* (Greenwich, CT: Fawcett, 1970), 5.

5. A. S. Reber, R. Allen, and E. S. Reber, *Penguin Dictionary of Psychology* (London: Penguin, 2009), 311.

6. Breuer, a physician who used the "talking cure" to treat hysteria, was perplexed and at times overwhelmed by a complex and shifting set of symptoms that motivated him to ask for help. Seeing the young Dr. Freud as a reasonable resource, he had asked for his consultation.

7. The involvement of the C-suite is significant because it reflects the fourth element of *capability* as postulated in the fraud diamond characterization.

8. Self-Study Guide to *Inside the Fraudster's Mind* video (Austin, TX: Association of Certified Fraud Examiners, 2013), 78.

9. It is reasonable to conjecture that Aaron Beam was experiencing the effects of psychosomatic illness or disease. Psychosomatic: pertaining to the interrelations of mind and body; having bodily symptoms of psychic, emotional, or mental origin. A psychosomatic disorder is one in which the physical symptoms are caused or exacerbated by psychological factors, such as migraine headache, lower back pain, or irritable bowel syndrome. It is now recognized that emotional factors, including psychological and cultural contexts, play a role in the development of nearly all organic illnesses. Each person responds in a unique way to stress; emotions affect one's sensitivity to trauma and to irritating elements in the environment, susceptibility to infection, and ability to recover from the effects of illness. Adapted from *Miller-Keane Encyclopedia and Dictionary of Medicine, Nursing, and Allied Health*, 7th ed. (Philadelphia: Elsevier, 2003).

10. *Hissy fit*, a term that originated in the American South in the twentieth century, refers to an emotional or temperamental outburst. It is probably a contraction of *hysterical fit*, but the sounds of hissing and spluttering when throwing such fit may also have contributed to the prefix *hissy*.

11. Gil Geis, *Inside the Fraudster's Mind*, video transcript, 2013, 141.

12. Aaron Beam, in Kelly R. Pope, *Crossing the Line: Ordinary People Committing Extraordinary Crimes* (documentary) (Chicago: DePaul University, 2011).

13. W. Thomson, *Popular Lectures and Addresses*, vol. I (London: MacMillan, 1891), 80.

14. William Bruce Cameron, *Informal Sociology: A Casual Introduction to Sociological Thinking* (New York: Random House, 1963), 13.

15. Donald L. Nathanson, *Shame and Pride: Affect, Sex, and the Birth of the Self* (New York: W. W. Norton, 1992), 23.

16. Charles Darwin, Paul Ekman, and Phillip Prodger, *The Expression of the Emotions in Man and Animals*, 3rd ed. (London: HarperCollins, 1998). See also Paul C. Hollinger and Kalia Doner, *What Babies Say Before They Can Talk*. (New York: Simon & Schuster, 2003).

17. Temple Grandin and Sean Barron, *Unwritten Rules of Social Relationships: Decoding Social Mysteries through the Unique Perspectives of Autism* (Arlington, TX: Future Horizons, 2005), ix.

18. Martha Stout, *The Sociopath Next Door* (New York: MJF Books, 2005), 125. Stout mentions studies that "indicate that sociopathy involves an altered processing

of emotional stimuli at the level of the cerebral cortex." Further, she notes that "sociopaths trying to complete an assignment based on emotional words, a task that would be almost neurologically instantaneous for normal people, reacted physiologically more or less as if they had been asked to work out an algebra problem."

19. M. F. Basch, *Affect: The Gateway to Action* (New York: Basic Books, 1988), 65–99.

20. Silvan S. Tomkins, and Robert McCarter, "What and Where Are the Primary Affects?" *Perceptual and Motor Skills* 18, no. S1 (1964).

21. M. F. Basch, "Psychoanalysis and Communication Science," *Annual of Psychoanalysis*, no. 4 (1976).

22. See Marco Iacoboni, *Mirroring People: The New Science of How We Connect with Others* (New York: Farrar, Straus & Giroux, 2008).

23. Mihaly, Csikszentmihalyi, *Flow: The Psychology of Optimal Experience* (New York: Harper & Row, 1990).

24. The TV series *Lie to Me* that ran on the Fox channel from January 2009 to January 2011 was inspired by the work of Paul Ekman, regarded by many as the world's foremost expert on facial expressions and a professor emeritus of psychology at the University of California, San Francisco School of Medicine. Dr. Ekman has served as an adviser to police departments and antiterrorism groups (including the Transportation Security Administration) and acted as a scientific consultant in the production of the TV series.

25. Paul Ekman, Maureen O'Sullivan, and M. Frank, "A Few Can Catch a Liar," *Psychological Science* 10 (1999): 263–66.

26. See also Will Felps, Terrence R. Mitchell, and Eliza Byington, "How, When, and Why Bad Apples Spoil the Barrel: Negative Group Members and Dysfunctional Groups," *Research in Organizational Behavior* 27 (2006): 175–222.

CHAPTER 5

"Said the Spider to the Fly . . ."[1]

THE PREDATOR-PREY DANCE—PUTTING BEHAVIORAL SCIENCE FUNDAMENTALS INTO MOTION

Sam Antar is the former CFO of Crazy Eddie, a consumer electronics chain, and a convicted felon. Antar is a felon because he and the Crazy Eddie chain bilked investors and creditors out of millions of dollars in the 1980s. Now he works professionally speaking about fraud; he is an expert from the wrong side of the law. He still makes a living through his understanding of fraud in the corporate world. He does so by shorting suspicious companies. He recently said, "If I was out of retirement today, I would be bigger than Bernie Madoff. . . . Nothing has changed."[2]

Fraud, as we said before, is not an act of computers. It is a human act in which the mind plays a crucially important role. The psychological concepts of the unconscious, the defenses, and emotions constitute a strange, unfamiliar stew for the gatekeepers of financial integrity, viz. accountants, auditors, finance directors, risk managers, and regulators. Former HealthSouth CFO, Aaron Beam—the "Case of Aaron B"—is an excellent example of what happens when these psychological factors combine in an unpleasant way: he became physically sick. However, although his department created the false accounts, and he was complicit in the cooked books at HealthSouth, he was not the (predatory or malignant) bad apple.

Emotions, Unconscious, Defenses—Oh My!

What does the unholy and potent combination of emotions, the unconscious, and the defenses mean for the people who are managing risk in an organization and for those who are investigating fraud? People in accounting or engineering often don't like the subjective side of human nature, and for that reason they may have even actively avoided studying the arts and the humanities in school.

In the previous chapter we looked at several lists to make an elusive and complex subject, emotions, finite and manageable. This is significant. For fraud investigators or managers of a financial function to be able to see a list of common emotions is very pragmatic. It can greatly help them get into the mind of the fraudster. Japanese swordsman Saito Yakuro brilliantly observed, "The hands manipulate the sword, the mind manipulates the hands. Cultivate the mind and do not be deceived by tricks, feints, and schemes. They are the properties of a magician, not of the samurai."[3]

Both fraudsters and acts of fraud are uniquely human; thus, what can be said about them applies to all people—a critical fact for understanding fraud as a human act. For the manager, it is often reassuring and supportive to have a theory that is common to all people. Like the fundamental laws of physics or Mendeleev's periodic table of chemical elements, the model we propose has established, well-understood scientific applications. But most important, because it helps us to understand fraudster motivation, it provides insight into the deception.

Each of the nine biologically innate emotions, or affects, listed in the previous chapter has its own unique function; each motivates us to act in a particular way. Affects set in motion the motivations of fraud. Thus the hard wired emotions play a critical role in the deception and trust violation of fraud. Their critical role is in the communication and motivations of the individuals involved in the theft.

Relationships: Where Fraud Is Set in Motion

The behavior that we know as a fraud has at least two aspects: the perpetrator and the victim. As Tony Stark, or Ironman, said in the movie *The Avengers*, "We can't solve the problem unless we know all the variables."[4] We have to consider the mind of the fraud victims and the mind of the fraud perpetrator as well as those of the auditors, the regulators, and other overseers. The fraudster certainly does. If we can arm the victim, the fraudster will lose a considerable amount of power.

Therefore, we need to evaluate the relationship between the fraudster and the victims, which requires communication and motivation. This brings us back to affect, our innate biologically wired emotion system, and the role it plays in deception and trust violation.

The affects are the language that exists beneath the surface, and they betray the victim and often the fraudster. They are the inherent connective tissue that allows a relationship to be close or that makes it distant. Fraudsters can take advantage of either a close relationship or a distant relationship. For instance, many interpersonal exchanges happen on the ubiquitous spreadsheet—especially with an auditor or some other control function. Another example is fraud perpetrated by phishermen who use the Internet to create a false sense of closeness.

Phishing: The Affective Dance of Fraudster and Victim

For the sake of simplicity, let's start with a common fraudulent scheme that is familiar to all: the e-mail "phishing" attempt. The following case is an example that arrived in people's in-boxes shortly before New Year's Day 2012.[5] The targets were people who had high bills from the holidays and needed money. Typical of this type of phishing, the email originates in Nigeria, and as foreigners they have poor knowledge of American English and of American culture. The phisherman promised credibility and set the reward the reader would get for accepting the offer. The mechanics of fraud requires at least one deception of one human being by another. This is the basic dynamic of the entire crime. Not all frauds will work exactly this way, but many forms will follow this process. We will explore this "elemental" fraud that arrives on a regular basis in all of our inboxes, and then search for applications in white-collar crimes and in particular the C-suite. The similarities in many cases are intriguing.[6]

In the first step one finds the "spider's" welcome:

> I, Ted Turner, UN Foundation Chairman, wish to inform you of your selection as one of the Beneficiary of 2.8 Million Great British Pounds Sterling, for the ongoing 2011 Financial Empowerment Program worldwide. So, this letter is to officially inform you that your benefited funds has been accredited into Visa/ATM CARD in your favor, with ATM Card Number (4080 2010 1765 5501); Your Personal Identification Number is 343.

Then, step two, the e-mail tells you what to do to get your money. Requiring the victim to ignore risk is at the heart of phishing fraud, because it requests the reader to turn over valuable personal information. The larger purpose distracts from the risk by implying the security of grand organizations and people, which in this case were highlighted in the introduction:

> On behalf of UNITED NATION'S Secretary-General Ban Ki-moon and Mr. Jean-Pierre Gonnot, Acting Director, Division for Social Policy and Development, we wish to inform you of your selection as one of our Beneficiary for ongoing Financial Empowerment Program, according to the meeting held on Commission for Social Development, on 48th session (UN Headquarters, 22nd of June 2011) in collaboration with Barack Hussein Obama's Foundation in United State of America. All participants/beneficiaries were selected randomly from Worldwide online networks Directories.

In step three, the phishing e-mail makes a threat. In this case, the phisherman warns that the relationship being initiated between sender and receiver is secret and special:

> Take note that you are warned to stop further communications with any other person(s) or office(s) different from the staff of UN Foundation West Africa, Abuja Nigeria, to avoid impersonation or hitches in receiving your Empowerment Funds.

What affects does this e-mail intend to provoke? The predominant affect that the e-mailer wants to exploit is the excitement of found money. Sending such an e-mail just when there are concerns about paying for holiday excesses is a smart tactic for the phisherman (or phisherwoman).

At the same time, the phisherman must minimize or eliminate any concerns that this might be a fraud. He must extinguish the e-mail recipient's fear of being a victim of theft. There is no actual request for funds at this point in the interchange, only information for delivering the money to the randomly chosen "lucky" recipients. The target emotion is excitement, and the author wants to create a contagion of excitement while ignoring any fear of risk.

The phisherman pursues the strategy of distracting from fear in several ways. First, he wants the reader to relax, feel safe, and trust the e-mail. He uses enjoyment, an affect that allows us to be able to relax and trust, to engender credibility. Who is more credible than CNN founder Ted Turner, UN Secretary General Ban Ki-Moon, and President Obama?

Second, it is helpful that the gift is for a noble cause. What is more noble than financial empowerment? The third tactic is the sense of specialness that is conveyed. The note explicitly states that the recipient is not to correspond with anyone about the note, he or she is sworn to secrecy, or the found money will go away. If you betray the secret, all is lost. This creates a specific target for fear: the fear of losing the relationship. As the relationship progresses by e-mail, and over time, the affect provoked by the threat of loss of a relationship is distress. Shame will be experienced if the relationship is questioned, disrupted, or ruptured. The introduction of shame—a powerful human emotion—is the fourth and final step.

The Fraudster, the Victim, and Emotional Seduction

In this phishing case, the e-mailer has, in a one-page e-mail, utilized common affects, our core human emotions, by doing the following:

- **Excitement.** Instilling excitement through unexpected money, thus solving the holiday debt problem.
- **Enjoyment.** Proffering enjoyment (even joy) through credibility, nobility, and specialness and decreasing fear of risk while doing so.
- **Fear.** Using veiled threats to instill fear of the disruption of the special relationship.
- **Shame.** Adding a sense of shame from disappointing a powerful person (the e-mailer is only an emissary).

Most phishing attempts fail, and there are many reasons for this one to do so, too. The limited understanding of English is one reason as well as a poor comprehension of how Ted Turner, President Obama, and the United Nations are related is another that raises one's skepticism in a healthy way. Most people who use e-mail are familiar with these types of seductions. It seems ridiculous that anyone would fall for something as transparently deceptive as this, but all it takes is one or two gullible, trusting respondents.

The classic e-mail fraud comes in many forms, but the strategy of exploiting basic emotions has a great deal in common with other kinds of fraud. An excellent resource is the AARP's so-called scam alert expert, Sid Kirchheimer, who has written an extremely helpful book for older U.S. citizens.[7]

The process in the "phishing expedition" is, in fact, the same process that occurs in frauds committed in the C-suite. Like a pickpocket, the fraudster must distract the victim from being aware of the deception. Fraud, as we have stated, is a crime in which the victim (inadvertently) allows him- or herself to be a victim. It requires some semblance of a relationship, typically that of an employee and employer or a client and an expert (e.g., a personal financial advisor).

Thus, one reason this e-mail could fail is that the sense of emotional closeness is weak. As much as the phisherman is phishing for money, he is first phishing for a suitably gullible person, and thus he must be emotionally competent to sustain his deception. The deception is generally not easy, especially when there is no history of a relationship and there is no face-to-face contact, as with Sheila and Stephanie in the previous chapter.

Yet this simple fraud has fooled many, including executives at Archer Daniels Midland (ADM). These are known as "advance fee frauds or "Nigerian 419" scams, based on the Nigerian law that makes them illegal. But they are not tied to small thefts. In fact, this scam was the initial trigger for a major series of embezzlements by ADM whistleblower Mark Whitacre. Although relatively small losses of several thousands of dollars were incurred by ADM executives who fell prey to the Nigerian 419 scam, the final tally as ADM became the victim was $9.5M. Here is Whitacre's version in his own words: "We made a decision that we were going to reimburse ourselves fraudulently from the company and basically embezzle from the company to make up for those losses." He had invested with three other ADM executives.[8]

In order to appreciate the difference between this example and what happened at HealthSouth, it is critical to note the power that Richard Scrushy had over Aaron Beam, in Beam's mind. Scrushy was not dealing with Beam for the first time, as the phisherman was with his victims. Scrushy was not only in a long relationship with Beam, he was also often in the room with him. It is likely that the third step noted about phishing scams, using veiled threats to instill fear, was communicated with particular force to Beam.

Let's look at some of the emotions in Beam's situation. First, there was excitement in easy money:

> Before long the stock was $10 a share, and it was easy to do the math (100,000 shares × $10 = $1,000,000). The $5,000 I paid for my 100,000 shares in 1984 was now worth $1,000,000![9]

Second, there was enjoyment in what the money provided:

> Once the lock-up agreement period was completed, we all sold some of our stock. I think I sold 10,000 shares. I never had $100,000 in cash before. I never even came close to having that kind of money. In fact, I am sure I had never had $10,000 in cash before. This kind of money can change your life.[10]

But the relationship with his boss started out ominous:

> We went to his [Scrushy's] boss's office, and Richard introduced us. We sat, and Richard said, "Aaron and I stayed up late last night working on these numbers, and we think we need to sign this contract. . . . I was stunned. I hadn't worked with Richard 30 minutes and he'd already told a lie. It wasn't a huge lie, but the brazen way in which he told it made me wonder. Later, as the years went by, I often reflected on this first lie told by Richard. I always wondered if he tested me that first morning on the job— to see if I would go along with him.[11]

We can now understand how it is possible to get seduced by the cycle of excitement-enjoyment-fear-distress/shame.

The story worsened at this point for Beam. The roles personal growth, narcissism, and his life's dream played in his downfall will be discussed subsequently. He was trapped within a system and in a CEO relationship that was beyond his capacity to manage. Interestingly, a 2011 Conference Board study found that CFOs often succumb to CEO pressure rather than seek immediate financial benefit.[12]

The Relationship as an End in Itself: Bernie Madoff

Bernie Madoff has become one of the symbols of the economic crisis of 2007–2009. The collapse of his Ponzi scheme peddled as a hedge fund is well-known to those who have followed the financial crises of the past decade. What does his story tell us about the relationships that support fraud?

Successive articles in the *New York Times* reported the following:

- Madoff was charged with 11 felony counts, including securities fraud, money laundering, and perjury. Under federal sentencing guidelines, those crimes would yield a life sentence for the 70-year-old trader. On June 29, 2009, he received a 150-year sentence.
- The federal investigation into Madoff's $65 billion Ponzi scheme included the arrest of an accountant who had audited Madoff's investment advisory business for more than a decade. The accountant, David G. Friehling, who operated from a tiny storefront office in Rockland County, was charged with securities fraud and with aiding the investment advisor fraud committed by Madoff. Friehling, 49, is facing one count of securities fraud, one count of aiding and abetting investment advisor fraud, and four counts of making false SEC filings. If convicted on all six counts, he faced up to 105 years in prison. In addition to citing the deceptive audits, the civil complaint by the SEC accused Friehling of collecting "ill-gotten gains" in the form of substantial audit fees—about $186,000 a year.
- Two computer programmers who worked for Madoff's brokerage firm were arrested and charged with helping Madoff to sustain his long-running Ponzi scheme. The programmers were accused of designing the software that generated thousands of fake customer account statements as well as fraudulent trading confirmations from the London Stock Exchange and fictitious clearinghouse records showing transactions that never occurred.[13]

It is quite clear that Madoff's fraud was deliberate, designed from his experience working with both the New York Stock Exchange and NASDAQ as well as from his understanding of market regulations. His initial fund targets were the very wealthy and those in his social circle, which included predominantly Jewish social clubs and philanthropies. Until the end, because of his financial performance for those deemed worthy of his fund, he was seen as a mensch, the Yiddish word for a good-willed person of integrity and honor. Yet the financial losses of his clients have been estimated by the court-appointed trustee to approximate $18 billion. The repercussions spread from exclusive financial networks on the East Coast to more well-known institutions, and ultimately there was a panicked dash around the world.

How did Madoff's fraud ensnare so many people?[14] There were at least three factors that Madoff used to defraud his investors. These are what appeared on the outside of the deception:

1. **Sustained financial performance.** Solid positive results were standard.
2. **Exclusivity.** Only select clients were invited.
3. **One of us.** He is our "kin."

The first factor was his ability to create a demand by consistently reporting a steady and modest sustained growth, which was essential in tricking the rational part of the minds of others.

The other two factors related to the power of his relationship with his investors and involved their wanting to be part of his magic. One factor was the perception that his fund was exclusive. The other factor, perhaps most important for early recruitment, was the sense that Madoff was "one of us."

The artificially created modest growth combined with two relationship factors compounded the greed of others (the investors) while deepening their trust and increasing their gullibility. The excitement of specialness and the enjoyment of being part of a safe and exclusive protected group were key affects, which we also saw in the phishing scheme.

The combination of these factors was so successful that Madoff essentially never had to do any marketing of his investment fund. In fact, only a select few knew about his fund and who he was. The exception to the need for marketing his product came at the end, with a panic, as he raced around the globe searching for investors while the financial crisis threatened to expose his fraud.

Therefore, to understand the mind of Bernie Madoff is to appreciate how well he understood the minds of his victims and their need to be related to. An article that documented the role of his wife, Ruth, raised questions about how much she knew and whether she played a role in pulling people into the fund. Within the dance of seduction into the Madoff fund where many stories. Those early to join the fund benefitted while those who got in late where harmed when it failed. As the Ponzi scheme was being prosecuted, questions arose related to whether the family of Madoff was involved.

One noteworthy investigation revealed an important dynamic: A classmate from high school of Madoff, Don Rosenzweig, knew the couple then and even had dated Ruth. He had a chance to ask Mr. Madoff for financial advice, but was even more curious about being able to invest in the famous fund. When Rosenzweig asked about getting into the fund, he was disappointed to find the threshold of $2 million was more than he could afford. He was able to meet the requirement by inviting several of his close family members. Reflecting on the conversation about entering the fund he was impressed with Madoff's charm.

To Rosenzweig, "at no time did it feel like he was pulling me in," in fact, it seemed as if Madoff "was doing me a favor."[15] Rosenzweig was deceived and defrauded by Madoff as any one of us might be: He was deceived by someone who was immensely special. The "pulling me in" that he describes is the danger of what law enforcement calls an *affinity fraud*. But it never would have worked had Madoff not been perceived as great and powerful.

To Rosenzweig, Madoff's magic over him was a result of the fact that Madoff was selective. Madoff was top in his field and immensely successful. No one but the very elite had a chance to be "blessed" by him and have access to the potentially easy and secure wealth that he had.

Yet there was one exception, a unique aspect of Madoff that unfortunately led to the losses of many like Rosenzwieg. Madoff was part of a larger community, defined by his faith, that had close ties to him and his family. The effects of distress, fear, enjoyment (acceptance), and excitement (secure wealth) run through his story like bright yellow lines. These were also the basic affects used by the phisherman. But in the Madoff case and the other cases we will explore, there was a substantive, meaningful, and powerful relationship.

By definition, the crime that is fraud requires the cooperation of a victim. Thus there must be a relationship. It is natural for human beings to be drawn into relationships with others who can support their mental and physical health. Rozenzweig's story of investing with Madoff is compelling. One can imagine being drawn into the scheme as he was. The Madoff example demonstrates how powerful the pull of a promising relationship can be even when the relationship is new. The reality as well as the fantasy of a relationship is powerful in fraud.

Lance Armstrong and His Accomplices

The story of the associates of bicycling champion Lance Armstrong illustrates that if the relationship has become important enough and is threatened, some very unpleasant results can occur. And if the important relationship is with a powerful and influential person (as Beam's was with Scrushy), there is a danger behind the threat of losing the relationship and all that it implies. In recent years, Lance Armstrong has been perhaps the best example of a man who was a popular hero in public who created fear with his anger and threats in private.

In 2001 he made a commercial in which he said, "What am I on? I'm on my bike, busting my ass 16 hours a day. What are you on?" Well, by now we know that he was "on" something and thus was defrauding an international and highly lucrative sport, among other things. And it was not easy for the U.S. Anti-Doping Agency to pursue Armstrong: It determined his guilt only by breaking through the code of silence in cycling and getting those who had made bad choices to confess them.

Armstrong's fiefdom was highly complex, far-reaching, and, over many years, similar to the worst financial frauds. His money-making machine was only loosely tied into, but it very publicly promoted, the beneficent goal of treating cancer, thus deepening the extent of the hurt in those he betrayed. And all along he bullied his fellow racers into colluding, so he reinforced a bad crop, an entire sport of "doping" cheaters. It is well known now that the field was rampant with those who were abusing medications and medical treatments while denying that they were participating in something the sport of competitive cycling had declared illegal. Armstrong and his team of colluders were competing with other teams who were also using pharmacological performance enhancers illegally. Several bad bushels were at work in this sport. It was as if the entire generation was routinely doping while participating in competitive sports cycling. Certainly, a bad crop scenario.

Armstrong was known to be using a doping agent designed to enhance the oxygen-carrying capacity of the blood to abnormal ranges. This drug, erythropoietin ("epo"), was commonly used by those who were doping in competitive cycling, and the sport was tainted by it. Fraudulent denials that it was not being used kept the illusion of a clean sport for a long time. More and more evidence was uncovered that Armstrong was not just a bad apple. The collusion even went beyond a bad bushel, because the fraud had extended itself to the whole crop. Armstrong's personality and the machine behind him were sustaining the crop.

Testosterone was the other drug used in the cheating. Armstrong and others used a combination of epo and testosterone to enhance their endurance, and testosterone in particular improves the capacity to repair and grow muscle. This most likely played an important role in Armstrong's ability to brazenly carry on the fraud for so long and to attain such a great series of falsely gained victories in the Tour de France. Testosterone is a hormone found in both men and women. When used as an additive, it has the same results as steroids, and as happens with steroids, testosterone can make a person aggressive, potentially hostile, and even paranoid.

The epo made Armstrong perform better, and the testosterone made him aggressive and intimidating. The challenge for his team-mates for the better part of two decades was to get past his intimidation. This empire of fear and aggression ran throughout his world and affected all of those he was capable of influencing.

In his 2003 memoir on battling cancer, *Every Second Counts* (written relatively early in his cheating and denials), Armstrong wrote, "Michele Ferrari was a friend, and I went to him for occasional advice on training . . . he wasn't one of my major advisors." But this was not true. Armstrong had introduced Ferrari to 15 cyclists, and financial records showed that Armstrong had paid him $1 million in consulting fees through the period of his Tour de France victories.[16] Perhaps Armstrong's surviving cancer left him with feelings of indomitability and invincibility and a sense that he could beat anything, even doping investigations. Thus he misjudged the risk. Yet, to his credit, he almost got away with it.

Underneath Armstrong's charming exterior was his practice of intimidation and threats. When a former low-level assistant to the cycling team worked for Armstrong and his teammates, she was exposed to the entire operation. At first her responsibilities included booking hotel rooms, massaging sore muscles, and doing the laundry. Soon, however, her responsibilities grew and became much less contractually defined as she was drawn into a sport she admired, working with a team that was on the rise:

> Ms. O'Reilly, then not yet 30, said she wound up transport-
> ing doping material across borders, disposing of drugs and

syringes when the authorities were lurking, and distributing performance-enhancing substances to the team's riders whenever they needed them.[17]

Despite her admiration for the team and the sport, she decided to share what she knew out of an internal obligation to be honorable, a sense of loyalty to her supervisors, and a feeling of betrayal. Unfortunately, once she came forward, Armstrong threatened her in many ways in an attempt to silence her:

> Ms. O'Reilly said Mr. Armstrong demonized her as a prostitute with a drinking problem, and had her hauled into court in England. . . . "He was suing me for more than I was worth," Ms. O'Reilly said. "I was worried he would bankrupt me."[18]

This leaves one wondering about the absence of Armstrong's self-perspective. Clearly he was caught up in the bad crop and sustaining it with all of his efforts. How could one man be so brazen and proud? How could he be so lacking in humility that he would harm those he was dependent on?

Where Is the Humility?

The financial collapse of 2007–2009 affected many people worldwide. The financial centers of the world were the focus of our attention for many months; so were the financial institutions, some of which are very powerful. Outside observers have been angered and distressed by how impervious the industry seems to be to what happened to the economy. Regulators, insurance companies, banks, and investment firms collectively failed, and no one apologized, much less paid any consequences. Why was there no shame on Wall Street for what happened on Main Street? The anger extends from the largest of the crimes to the smallest. We want to see that those who caused harm are contrite and regret their actions.

> [Sen. Carl Levin's] subcommittee investigation concluded in 2010 that Goldman sold risky mortgage backed securities even as it was quietly betting its own money that those securities would fail. . . . The Goldman executives, including CEO Lloyd Blankfein, said they didn't do anything irresponsible. "Regret

to me means something you feel you did wrong—I don't have that," said Daniel Sparks, the former head of Goldman's mortgage department.

This may be a smart legal argument in court, but it is unsatisfactory on a human level. We are dumbfounded when investigators find malfeasance but the perpetrators are indignant. In a similarly shameless way, Armstrong claimed not to know what *cheating* meant when he was interviewed by Oprah Winfrey. He noted that he had to look it up in the dictionary. This may be one of many things: ignorance, playing coy, or looking for a way to justify that what he did was not cheating. None of these bode well for his character.

What is confusing to someone who is not caught in the fraud dance, as either victim or perpetrator, is "Why didn't the people act differently once they realized what was happening?" In Aaron Beam's case, he was intimidated and shamed into complying because the relationship had developed so far, and the threat of being cut off from the power and the wealth, as well as the implicit threat of violence, caused him to believe he had no other option.

The Power of Shame

The experience of the core emotions is common to all humans, and these affects are powerful. Shame in particular is powerful. When Beam realized that his job had stopped being fun, he was beginning to reject what he thought he had wanted. His bind and his compromise then turned on him, and we can see the human side of his story and even feel sympathy for him. As he began to want to leave his situation, an important affect that he had ignored, in his excitement about the wealth, came to the surface: disgust. It was a harbinger of the shame that he had been defending himself against but that he would soon feel.

As noted in the previous chapter, assessments, interpretations, perceptions, and higher levels of understanding occur in different levels of our brains. As they do so, the potential always exists for each emotion to find expression in our bodies. Sigmund Freud noted this in his work, and Anna Freud further explored how hard the mind works to manage strong affects in order to prevent negative feelings from overwhelming the person.

Many others in the medical and mental health fields have noted the price our bodies pay when our defenses are ineffective. The migraines

from work stress; the heart attacks from hard-driving, aggressive personalities; and the joint, back, or other pain that is a psychological
substitute for loss are just a few examples. When someone has compromised his or her values, and especially if this has caused harm to
others, there is a price to pay. In fact, for the person who becomes
conscious of what he or she has done, it is agony, and others can see it
written on the face and in the body language of the person.

A conflict with our values is, at its very core, a conflict with how
we would like to be—in other words, our real selves versus our ideal
selves, a profoundly personal and existential question. Everyone has
an internal image that is an ideal version of the self. Affect-based
ideals drive our values and encourage us to act in a way that fits our
ideals. Given the importance of our values, we all work hard to live
up to them, but the realities of life can highlight our imperfections,
and confronting these is painful.

The following vignette that appeared in the *New Yorker* from
singer and poet Patti Smith illustrates the power of affect-based values when reality confronts us with our imperfections. It highlights
the effect of disgust and the visceral response that occurs when we
recognize we've acted contrary to our values:

> When I was ten years old, I lived with my family in a small ranch
> house in rural South Jersey. I often accompanied my mother to
> the A&P to buy groceries. We did not have a car, so we walked,
> and I would help her carry the bags.
>
> My mother had to shop very carefully, as my father was on
> strike. She was a waitress, and her paycheck and tips barely
> sustained us. One day, while she was weighing prices, a promo-
> tional display for the *World Book Encyclopedia* caught my eye. The
> volumes were cream-colored, with forest-green spines stamped in
> gold. Volume I was ninety-nine cents with a ten-dollar purchase.
>
> All I could think of, as we combed the aisles for creamed
> corn, dry milk, cans of Spam, and shredded wheat, was the
> book, which I coveted with all my being. I stood at the register
> with my mother, holding my breath as the cashier rang up the
> items. It came to over eleven dollars. My mother produced a
> five, some singles, and a handful of change. As she was count-
> ing out the money, I somehow found the courage to ask for
> the encyclopedia. "Could we get one?" I said, showing her the
> display. "It's only ninety-nine cents."

I did not understand my mother's mounting anxiety; she did not have enough change and had to sacrifice a large can of Le Sueur peas to pay the amount. "Not now, Patricia," she said sternly. "Today is not a good day." I packed the groceries and followed her home, crestfallen.

The next Saturday, my mother gave me a dollar and sent me to the A&P alone. Two quarts of milk and a loaf of bread: that's what a dollar bought in 1957. I went straight to the *World Book* display. There was only one first volume left, which I placed in my cart. I didn't need a cart, but I took one so I could read as I went up and down the aisles. A lot of time went by, but I had little concept of time, a fact that often got me in trouble. I knew I had to leave, but I couldn't bear to part with the book. Impulsively I put it inside my shirt and zipped up my plaid windbreaker. I was a tall, skinny kid, and I'm certain every contour of the book was conspicuous.

I strolled the aisles for several more minutes, then went through the checkout, paid my dollar, swiftly bagged the three items, and headed home with my heart pounding.

Suddenly I felt a heavy tap on my shoulder and turned to find the biggest man I had ever seen. He was the store detective, and he asked me to hand it over. I just stood in silence. "We know you stole something—you will have to be searched." Horrified, I slid the heavy book out from the bottom of my shirt.

He looked at it quizzically. "This is what you stole, an encyclopedia?"

"Yes," I whispered, trembling.

"Why didn't you ask your parents?"

"I did," I said, "but they didn't have the money."

"Do you know it's wrong?"

"Yes."

"Do you go to church?"

"Yes, twice a week."

"Well, you're going to have to tell your parents what you did."

"No, please."

"Then I will do it. What's the address?"

I was silent.

"Well, I'll have to walk you home."

"No, please, I will tell them."

"Do you swear?"

"Yes, yes, sir."

My mother was agitated when I arrived home. "Where were you? I needed the bread for your father's sandwiches. I told you to come right home."

And suddenly everything went green, like right before a tornado. My ears were ringing, I felt dizzy, and I threw up.

My mother tended to me immediately, as she always did. She had me lie on the couch and got a cold towel for my head and sat by me with her anxious expression.

"What is it, Patricia?" she asked. "Did something bad happen?"

"Yes," I whispered. "I stole something." I told her about my lust for the book, my wrongdoing, the big detective. My mother was a good mother, but she could be explosive, and I tensed, waiting for the barrage of verbal punishment, the sentencing that always seemed to outweigh the crime. But she said nothing. She told me that she would call the store and tell the detective I had confessed, and that I should sleep.

When I awoke, sometime later, the house was silent. My mother had taken my siblings to the field to play. I sat up and noticed a brown-paper bag with my name on it. I opened it and inside was the *World Book Encyclopedia*, Volume I.[19]

Shame is biologically wired, and so is the green nauseated feeling Smith described. The setting and context of the story make the dynamics of shame and disgust very vivid. The visceral feeling she had is disgust, not shame. At the most basic level, her mind wanted to spit out the dishonest side of her that she did not see as ideal. Her disgust was a response to shame. In the nervous system, there are myriad connections between the body and the brain, and our gut and our mind in particular so when we reach a psychologically meaningful understanding, there are physiological effects.

In this case, the effect of disgust, the embedded visceral response that occurs when one experiences shame and then recognizes the actions, was contrary to Smith's values. Her response highlighted the power of her relationship with her mother and how important it was.

This elegant story relates directly to fraud and the ties Aaron Beam felt to Richard Scrushy. In his autobiography of his career at HealthSouth, when Beam discovered the path was set to commit fraud, he felt miserable about the trap he was in. He was unable to avoid the emotional and physical repercussions, and eventually he realized that the fraud had been discovered. The defenses shored him up unconsciously until he heard that the fraud was discovered. His experience was similar to Smith's; he too became physically ill:

> I was relaxing and watching the evening news at my recently finished sprawling retirement home at Beam Acres in Fairhope, Alabama, when the [television] announcer said, "We open tonight's broadcast with a breaking story from Birmingham, Alabama. A massive accounting fraud at HealthSouth Corporation has [been] revealed. . . . Early reports indicate that the fraud has been going on for several years and may exceed $2 billion." I immediately felt as sick as I did helpless.[20]

Several CFOs succeeded Beam at HealthSouth. Many of them left very quickly after they arrived; the last one, Weston Smith, was the fourth in a relatively short time span. Just as stealing a book made Patti Smith feel real physical pain, the tremendous pressures that Weston Smith experienced in the accounting and finance division of HealthSouth undoubtedly made his HealthSouth world turn green "like right before a tornado," too. The seduction of the crime and the agony of the consequences of committing it can be seen in many well-known media photos, which portray the effects of distress, shame, and excitement on celebrities' faces. In the educational DVD *Inside the Fraudster's Mind* there is an excellent example of this look of contrition in the film of the convicted fraudster Steve Comisar.[21]

Shame has a function. When it works right, it stops inappropriately felt positive emotions, which can get people into trouble.[22] Thus, tolerating and understanding shame can be helpful.

In large groups, in terms of the business requirements of marketing and sales, the management of shame is relevant in the challenges of distinguishing persuasion from manipulation. This will be explained subsequently. Within organizations in a game of one-upmanship, calling those in the accounting department "bean counters" or the human resources development department training "charm school" is inherently a childish put down, and in an important way it is. As we grow up, we are expected to show a certain level of maturity throughout childhood. All of us had a stage that was relatively hard for us. When we fail to meet the level others expect to see in us, we can feel shame. Specifically, as we grow up, shame plays a role in eight key areas:

1. Size and strength
2. Dexterity and physical skill
3. Dependence versus independence
4. Cognitive ability
5. Communication
6. Sense of self
7. Gender identity and sexuality
8. Interpersonal skills[23]

What often happens in childhood and continues into adulthood is that we are strong in some areas and delayed in others, so we minimize and poke fun at our areas of weakness and highlight our areas of strength as the greatest. Thus, high school terms like *jocks* and *geeks* are echoed in the *quants* and *empty suits* of organizations.

A healthy experience of shame actually correlates with a healthy sense of pride. As we grow up and have normal experiences of shame in the milder forms of self-consciousness and embarrassment, we also learn the unique pleasure of mastery. For example, when one achieves mastery learning to ski, ride a bike, play a musical instrument, or a sport, it feels delightful. In fact, there is evidence that mastery is one of the earliest pleasurable experiences in infants.[24]

Those who study shame note that pride moves in lockstep with mastery. A person wishes for something, acts on it, and, with successful completion or fulfillment, experiences the positive affects of enjoyment and excitement.[25] How pride gets out of whack and, in particular, how humiliation and narcissism enter the dynamics of fraud will be discussed in the next chapter.

Good to Evil: How a Hardwired Emotion Is Ignored and Manipulated

Emotions, particularly shame and pride, are important in relationships and can create a healthy give-and-take among employees within an organization. We have seen how emotions play a critical role in our values, and when these are compromised, such as in committing fraud, it can affect our physical and mental health. The predatory fraudster who wants to hook a victim exploits emotions to create the sense of a special relationship and then uses an implicit threat of losing that special relationship.

In the case of Patti Smith's theft of a book, we saw the power of the compromise that is made when we break our moral code with those we care about. In the case of Bernie Madoff, we learned about the power, and even the blinding pull, of a strong relationship. And in the simple case of the phishing e-mail we saw how all of these factors can be brought together to exploit our basic human emotions and fool us into being defrauded.

What happens in internal predatory fraud? How do shame and other emotional dynamics tied to the interplay of fraudster and victim come together between a bad apple and a victim who are in the same organization?

In the rest of this chapter we will explore the dynamics behind the emotions that lead the fraudster to ignore his own internal warning signals, and we will examine how this core dynamic of emotion also plays a role in recruiting others to be part of the crime or at least keep it hidden. Finally, we will try to understand the fraudster's mind-set once the crime is committed and the role of mental illness.

Shame as an Inborn Tool for Learning and the Interpersonal Engine for Fraud

As little children, human beings are intrinsically wired to be curious. However, there are many things in the world that are dangerous if explored without some caution. Electrical outlets and hot stoves are two examples that most parents will recognize. As we get older, the dangers that face us are less about physical harm and more about social harm that must be minimized (think of the Hippocratic oath that doctors take: "First, do no harm"). Thus, we learn how to navigate critical relationships at work, in the family, and in the community. Mastering the building of relationships is an essential part of a happy and healthy adulthood.

The role of shame evolves to guide us socially so that we avoid embarrassing others or ourselves. As young children, we learn not to say or do certain things in public, such as discussing the voiding of bodily wastes at the dinner table or pointing to a stranger's disfigurement or deformity.

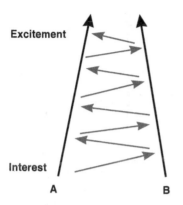

Exhibit 5.1   The Interesting Conversation That Is at Risk of Being Derailed by Shame
(A) Stephanie; (B) Sheila
Source: © Morrison Associates, Ltd. Used with permission.

As we become adults, we are taught more about what is permitted and what is not. Once again, shame shapes our behavior with our elders, the opposite sex, and at religious ceremonies. Shame is a powerful and adaptive tool for this reason.

Imagine our two hypothetical individuals from the previous chapter, Stephanie and Sheila, having a conversation about something they both find interesting. Stephanie says something that Sheila finds interesting, then Sheila says something that Stephanie finds exciting. They start out with a modest amount of interest, but as they explore the subject, the stimulation increases, and the effect of excitement rises. This is the dance not only of great conversation but also presages meaningful artistic collaboration. See Exhibit 5.1.

Because of shame, certain subjects are not discussed openly but are kept hidden and may simply be assumed. Thus, the dance of seduction becomes riskier the further it progresses. And the greater the excitement expressed about the subject, the greater the risk for embarrassment.

When interest or excitement is not reflected back, the dynamic is different. See Exhibit 5.2.

Shame as a Healthy and Adaptive Function in the Workplace

Shame is a very effective, direct, and conscious instrument for reinforcing norms in the workplace. It is used by every function

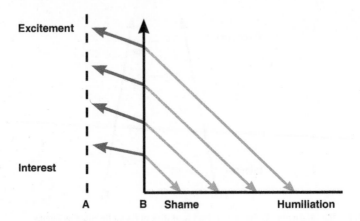

Exhibit 5.2   Lack of Mutual Interest

Source: © Morrison Associates, Ltd. Used with permission.

in an organization, and in general it is the affective instrument of those who are seeking to manage both performance and risk.[26] Most organizations understand the role of shame at some level and use it in policies and procedures related to compensation and other benefits. It is a powerful force in performance management. Within a sales force it drives the desire to not be beaten by the competition, to avoid being outperformed by peers, and to win business across the entire organization. To manage risk, for example, by declaring directly what the consequences are for certain behavior (e.g., sexual harassment), the organization's intent is to help employees manage themselves by avoiding the shame of transgressing the rules.

As accountants and auditors know only too well, there are always exceptions to rules. Motivations for shame change as we make up new rules, yet we also break rules at times for a variety of reasons. Consider the following observations made by some cultural anthropologists: "No two people do things exactly alike, and no one lives by the rules all the time. . . . Thus, there are various levels of rules or systems: things people say they do; things they say they should do; things they really do; ways they bend the rules without actually breaking them; ways they break the rules and get away with it; and the ways they feel about all this."[27] For example, in certain situations and with critical motivations that relate to fraud, people can

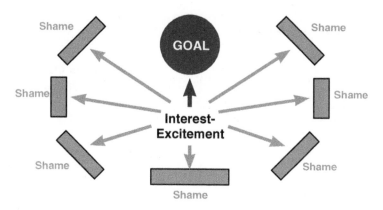

Exhibit 5.3   Shame-Based Consequences
Source: © Morrison Associates, Ltd. Used with permission.

be motivated to break the rules because they find it fun. This will be discussed in a subsequent section on why we change our minds.

In general, however, shame is adaptive in the workplace, because it keeps the workers focused on and emotionally interested in the immediate task at hand. Most checks and balances, such as blocking Internet sites or making employees punch a time clock, are designed to shame all work activities that are not tied directly to the goals of the organization. If an activity does not relate to the stated goals, shame-based consequences are implemented to realign the people in the workplace. See Exhibit 5.3.

Shame is unpleasant, but like thirst or hunger, it is merely a stimulation to action. In this way, like the other affects, it motivates. However, it is generally more difficult to discuss than other affects.

As Donald Nathanson has noted, "There is shame merely about the word *shame*."[28]

Shame as a Driver for Better Performance

Most of us have, at some point, addressed a group, made a presentation, or given a speech. This common experience can help us to understand how to use shame. Fred Harburg, a former president of Motorola University in Illinois was virtual and a professor of leadership at the Air Force Academy in Colorado Springs, recognizes the adaptive use of shame and ties it to the experience of making a

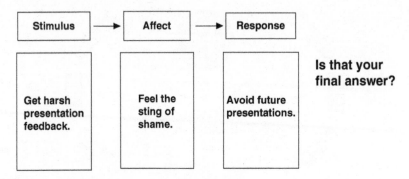

Stimulus	⟶	Affect	⟶	Response
Get harsh presentation feedback.		Feel the sting of shame.		Avoid future presentations.

Is that your final answer?

Exhibit 5.4   A Pavlovian Response

Source: © Fred Harburg and Morrison Associates, Ltd. Used with permission.

presentation. When shame is used well, he says, it is "Pavlovian," or reflexive. The reflexive and the adaptive functions of shame (when it works well) are shown in Exhibits 5.4 and 5.5, respectively.

When Shame Is Maladaptive at Work

We have explored the role shame plays in reinforcing our values and when we do not live up to our ideal selves. The emotion thus plays an essential role when a rule is broken, especially when that rule is

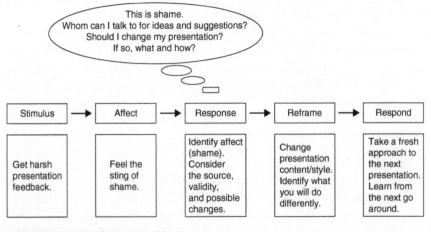

Exhibit 5.5   Adaptive Response to Stimuli

Source: © Fred Harburg and Morrison Associates, Ltd. Used with permission.

a law and thus a crime has been committed. This section describes how shame plays a role in fraud at work.

Shame works in the unspoken rules and roles of the workplace the same way it works between individuals. The same dynamics are involved. The social threat of being cut off from the group, being unpopular, or even just being seen as "not çool" is the primary motivational pressure of shame.

Wherever there are employees—on the assembly line, in cubicles, or in the boardroom—shame exists to reinforce the rules as well as the hierarchy. Messages about the rules of the workplace are reinforced with shame in many ways. From gentle teasing or self-deprecating jokes to more hostile acts such as cruel pranks or even bullying, shame is the motivator for what is tolerated and what is not. In addition, shame is a cause of sabotage and violence in the workplace, at any level of an organization. Shame can even be found in the interpersonal dynamics of the C-suite.

Shame is a powerful and dangerous motivator that weighs heavily on those who have felt it and who seek revenge. In November 1995 the federal government was shut down in a battle between Congress and the White House. Incredibly, Speaker of the House Newt Gingrich noted in a speech in the middle of the crisis that he did so intentionally because he had felt shunned by President Bill Clinton on Air Force One earlier that month while traveling to Israel. Although Gingrich noted that the physical separation interfered with his and the president's ability to work together on a budget over the long flight (more than 24 hours), he also noted his complaint was "petty." His main concern was that they were in the back of the airplane and had to depart from the plane's rear exit.[29]

Their dramatic battle underscored what the behavioral sciences have seen played out in families in terms of shame. Parents are known to induce shame with specific behaviors and often with facial expressions of contempt or disgust to reinforce the message.[30] The behaviors parents use are often seen at work in the C-suite, too:

- Power assertion
- Overt disgust or contempt
- Sadistic teasing
- Silent treatment
- Love (in the form of attention or resources) withdrawal[31]

What happened with Clinton and Gingrich was a steadily increasing mismanagement of shame. Each man felt big and powerful but thought that the other had tried to make him small and weak. Because shame quickly turned into humiliation for both of them, maladaptive coping mechanisms kicked in, and shame lost its value to inform and educate.

How this works in relation to the C-suite and to the accounting and auditing functions will be explored subsequently.

Think of shame as a compass with four points: avoidance, attack self, attack other, and withdrawal. These points are common unconscious shame defenses to ward off the experience of being embarrassed. They drive the effect of shame to an unconscious level and inhibit its conscious experience.[32]

Powerful people use shame tactics, in particular, *attack other*, as a way to distract attention from the fraud. It appears from the record that Richard Scrushy used this tactic at every turn. He was an intimidator, a person who covered up his trail with threats. Andrew Fastow, the former CFO of Enron, was known to tell investment bankers and others wanting business with Enron that they would have to accede to his demands, or else he would cut them off from having anything to do with Enron.

Here is how this tactic fit the two personalities of Aaron Beam and Richard Scrushy:

> Richard was absolutely at his best at investor conferences. When he spoke, the room was always packed. . . . Wall Street loved Richard's brashness and hard-driving salesmanship. . . . Richard's brashness, of course, showed in his management style. Richard managed by intimidation. It's tough to put into words just how brutally nasty Richard could be. . . . One of the misconceptions that many have about Richard is that he is a big man. He is not. To compensate for his shortness, Richard had lifts put into all of his designed shoes. . . . But instead of stature, Richard used his facial expressions, his voice, and his demeanor to intimidate others.[33]

The actual interchanges with Scrushy could be humiliating:

> During our regular Monday morning meeting, one of the accountants who reported to me started talking about how he

had gone fishing over the weekend, and, like Richard, had caught a big fish. He described the fish and how it was huge. Richard did not like this. He had to be the center of attention— it always had to be about him and no one else. Richard jumped all over the poor guy. Veins popped out of his neck and on his forehead. He was irate. He aggressively admonished the guy. "Shut up! Nobody wants to hear about your damn fish!" Richard yelled, shaking his finger at the fellow. The guy became silent. Richard continued with his barrage, "If you keep that up you'll find yourself doing accounting in the basement!"[34]

In a very vivid scene, the cruelty of the CEO is recreated. His need to be seen as good at fishing is nonsensical. He has the power. Yet his actions indicate that for others to be as competent or even better than he at fishing is immensely threatening. The reasons are unclear, but they do reflect a poor sense of self-awareness. He is obviously incompetent in managing shame. His inability to allow someone else to have the attention is immature and harms an organization. It does not fit the example from Figures 5.4 and 5.5 regarding critical presentation feedback. In that situation the person experienced the shame and made the connections via self-reflection to adapt the behavior to fit the feedback.

Yet although Scrushy's skills in self-perception are poor, so, unfortunately, are those of his coworkers, for they are unable to walk away or give him the shaming feedback he needs to hear. But this is understandable, since it would surely put their jobs on the line.

False Pride: With the Threat of Shame Comes Hubris

Hubris is a problem of shame mismanagement or even incompetence. When discussing the challenges of hubris as a cause for problems in professional accounting and leadership in general, Duane Kullberg, the managing partner of the Arthur Andersen accounting firm, once wrote, "I always knew when a partner was about to get in trouble . . . it was when they started to believe their own bull***t."[35] Kullberg led Arthur Andersen through challenging periods of growth and success, overseeing the emergence of Andersen Consulting (which later became Accenture).

The dynamics around HealthSouth at the senior levels is an elegant series of examples of the compass of shame. A person may use alcohol consumption to dilute the feeling and thus avoid the experience of shame. Beam did this.[36] When a person threatens another, as Scrushy did to Beam, he is attacking that person. The one who is attacked may feel helpless and powerless, become depressed, feel trapped and betrayed, turn the resulting anger inward onto oneself, and thus attack oneself in the process. Finally, the person may withdraw, which is what Beam did by resigning at what appeared to the outside world to be the peak of his career.

The English novelist and physicist C. P. Snow observed presciently, "Far more, and far more hideous, crimes have been committed in the name of obedience than have ever been committed in the name of rebellion." Similarly, basing their inferences on Wall Street scandals, D. S. Beu and M. R. Buckley have noted that in the corporate world, leaders and their subordinates "morally disengage" from bad actions by denying personal responsibility, minimizing the consequences, and dehumanizing their victims.[37]

This may also occur in many fraud cases, especially when the CFO is not strong enough to confront the CEO, but it is not the only important dynamic to consider. But what of the Enron executives themselves? What of the motivations of leaders like Scrushy or other individuals who commit fraud and co-opt others into cooperation and compliance? Motivation is complex and is worthy to consider the motivation of all participants of a fraud, including even the "mastermind" himself or herself.

The Predator Bullies the Professionals

The dynamics that intimidated Aaron Beam work for others, too; those on the outside might expect to be strong enough to refuse, but they can fall victim to the "spider" as well. Any professional—physician, lawyer, regulator—can be coerced, but most relevant to our discussion are the accounting and finance professions. The intimidation that disempowers the profession can happen in many forms. Clients often shame professional accounting firms by emphasizing their own supposed greatness: "We are a great client, we have tremendous revenues, and others admire us, so who are you to question us?" Thus there are risks: The accounting profession is at risk of not addressing the bullying behavior and of being submissive to the client.[38] And the broader public is at risk of market failures when the house of cards collapses, as in the mortgage scandal. One idea is to match the personalities of the client CEO and/or CFO with the personality of the audient engagement partner and second partner, so that they are able to stand up to such pressures. This harks back to the famous, often-repeated story of Mr. Arthur Andersen. A Norwegian-American, Andersen originally started his firm in 1913 in Chicago by putting reputation over profit. As the *Wall Street Journal* reported, "In 1914, months after the 28-year-old Northwestern University accounting professor founded his tiny company, the president of a local railroad demanded that he approve a peculiar transaction that would have lowered the company's expenses and boosted earnings. Mr. Andersen, who at the time was worried about meeting his next payroll, told the president that there was 'not enough money in the city of Chicago' to make him do it. . . . The client promptly fired the accountant, but Mr. Andersen was vindicated months later when the company filed for bankruptcy."[39]

Leonard Spacek, who succeeded Arthur Andersen and led the firm from 1947 to 1963, continued this proud tradition of an accounting firm famous for its independence and integrity. Once he accused Bethlehem Steel of overstating its profits in 1964 by more than 60 percent. He called the SEC to account for failing to crack down on companies that cooked their books and become more aggressive in its enforcement, commenting that at its best, the SEC has been "a brake on the rate of retrogression in the quality of accounting."[40]

Speaking truth to power requires moral courage in addition to professional and technical competence. It is a tall order but extremely important in the training of future generations of accountants to equip them to deal with the bullying aspect of clients and other market participants.

Let us now look at some examples of bullying behavior that have been reported in the context of the Wall Street financial crisis and before. Bethany McLean and Joe Nocera's account of the "hidden history of the financial crisis" is a rich treasure trove of anecdotes and conversations that highlight how shaming others and exhibiting excessive pride are characteristic behaviors of bullies, some of whom may be predators.[41]

Joseph Cassano, head of the financial products division at insurance giant AIG, has been described as follows: "His temper. That's what AIG-FP traders always mentioned whenever they talked about their old boss, Joe Cassano. . . . It was brutal and indiscriminate—terrifying when unleashed," said a trader. "Sometimes he could seem uncontrollable." Cassano would rage at traders who were making the company a fortune and traders who were on a losing streak. He would go out of his way to embarrass executives in front of their peers and blow up over the most inconsequential things. "Talking to him was like walking on eggshells," said another former FP executive. "You were always worried about what would set him off."

Once he got mad because a trader wore a V-neck sweater over a T-shirt. From two desks over, he loudly berated the man and then sent him home to change into a collared shirt. A new hire, speaking to Cassano for the first time, told him that the firm was making 50 basis points on a certain $1 billion transaction. "I said that was $5 million a year," recalled the trader. "Cassano erupted, 'How dare you do the math on me?' He was a bully. It was his fatal flaw."[42]

After the Enron bankruptcy in December 2001, possibly to fend off regulation, Moody's adopted a code of conduct that stated in part that the "determination of a credit rating will be influenced only by factors relevant to the credit assessment . . . not . . . by the existence of, or potential for, a business relationship between Moody's and the issuer." Yet in a lawsuit, the state of Connecticut alleged that shortly after two experienced compliance officers were fired and replaced by employees from the structured finance department. The head of the department later complained, "My guidance was routinely ignored if that guidance meant making less money." Investigators also allege that during a dinner party after a board meeting, the president of Moody's walked by the head of compliance and said, quite loudly, "Hey, how much revenue did Compliance bring in this year?"[43]

A former physicist, John Breit of Merrill Lynch, had earned a reputation of being one of the best risk managers on Wall Street. In 2001, he reported directly to Merrill's CFO and had access to the board of directors. But by 2007, he had been effectively stripped of his authority. He had to report to a newly promoted risk officer and was exiled to a small office on a different floor, far away from the trading desks. As if to suggest that the Merrill Lynch CEO was perhaps out of touch with how his most trusted lieutenants were being treated, McLean and Nocera asked, "Did Stan O'Neal know any of this history?" In other words, shaming strategies can be effective in impeding information flow for decision making.[44]

Clearly, putdowns are ways that the predator tries to shame his or her victims into submission. There is even a fertile area of research on micro-gestures and micro-inequities.[45] It is the classic "attack the other" strategy, which works most of the time because people are simply too polite and decent to challenge the attacker.

Nowhere in this process is there movement away from reality because of derangement or illness. These are all high-functioning people who, if they showed signs of delusional thinking or being out of touch with reality, would be asked to not come into work anymore. What role, then, does mental illness play in fraud?

The Role of Mental Illness

Fraud is not like kleptomania. This is a very important clarification. Given the fact that fraud is a crime and that many of the news stories about it are outrageous and beyond the average person's ability to imagine himself or herself committing such acts, it is natural to wonder if those who commit fraud are mentally ill. Is there a compulsion or derangement of some kind that is beyond the control of the fraudster?

In kleptomania, the thief doesn't desire what he or she steals. The items have very little value and provide no satisfaction to the thief other than a sense of relief after committing the act of stealing. Fraud, however, involves stealing things that clearly have value. For instance, the phisherman wants the money; the e-mail scam is not being done for a compulsive, obsessive, or unconscious reason.

Fraud may be consciously committed by a predator who sets out to steal by deception. In the public perception, this is what a bad apple is. But there is another path.

In many cases the fraud doesn't start out being intentional. A hole in the accounting system is exposed by accident, and the accidental fraudster gains from it. Over time, the fraudster becomes dependent on it and others are co-opted. The deception occurs after a cover-up of the initial cheating. This is the rationalization of the crime, but it is done in a rash and impulsive way.

As the fraud persists, its ongoing nature is evidence that the commission of it is willful and the person is conscious of the illegality. This long-term, consistent lawbreaking, with clear evidence of covering up the fraud, aligns with the Association of Certified Fraud Examiners *Report to the Nations* survey data. The cover-up confirms that this is not due to a mental illness, for there is an awareness that fraud is wrong. At this point it is not predatory toward anyone other than the organization.

Thus, there is no mental illness in fraud, only a criminal mind-set. Within that mind-set, there are two categories of people who commit frauds: the accidental fraudster and the predator.

Bernie Madoff, Richard Scrushy, and the phisherman are clearly predators. However, to understand the dynamics of rationalization and the ongoing quiet fraud of the accidental bad apple, we need to consider another category: the psychopath. Although *psychopath* is not technically a medical word, it is often associated with mental illness. Narcissism, which is not considered a mental illness, will be explored in Chapter 7.

Monsters in the Nursery

Psychopath is a common term in criminology. The label is typically assigned in response to a pattern of cruel actions. The concept of psychopathy is entering the discussion of fraud. In the 1960s the term was softened to *sociopath* to highlight the suspected societal causes of criminality. The term has been softened further in cases associated with prejudice, particularly when used to describe children.

Those who study truly malignant behavior find it quite disturbing. When malignant behavior is seen in children, it can be haunting. Yet adults who have criminal records usually didn't start out as angels. The stories of these "monsters in the nursery" are unpleasant to hear. How that behavior relates to fraud is important to understand.

Most people learn to have a healthy sense of trust in others. When that trust is lost (or never developed), the world is a dark place. The greatest betrayal of trust occurs when someone shows no sense of concern for others (i.e., lacks empathy) and even takes pleasure in harming others. This is what we all find disturbing about serial killers like the BTK of Wichita or genocidal dictators like Joseph Stalin and Augusto Pinochet. Such people and their actions are deeply troubling.

The 1986 movie *Stand by Me* portrayed this type of character. Chris could have been on his way to becoming a psychopath. Coming from a troubled family, he was a problem child in school. As his friendships with other characters deepened and he worked to change (and show a capacity for empathy), he told a poignant story in which he confessed that he stole milk money from the class. Once he confessed, his teacher then stole more of the milk money and used it to purchase a new dress. Counting on the fact that she would be believed over Chris, a "bad seed," she decided to cross the line. It is easy to imagine her rationalizations:

- He's going to steal again, anyway.
- He would have spent the money on bad stuff, and what if he had?
- There is no harm done to take it. The money would have been gone, anyway, lost to the school and never to be recovered.
- I deserve a reward for catching him, and the school would never let me keep the money.
- I've been good and have always played by the rules.
- The school doesn't pay me enough for all the work I do.
- No one would ever believe him over me.
- Well, what they don't know won't hurt them.

This teacher is in the same mind-set as fraudsters (at least those who intend to pay back what they've stolen). She is somewhere between an accidental fraudster, who finds a hole in the system, and a predatory fraudster, who decides to take advantage of someone.

Imagine an individual who speeds down a deserted highway at night. No one catches her, and no harm is done. Is she a monster of the nursery? No, she's not; she's more likely a person like you or me.

Now imagine a group of people from these three categories: a political dictator, a fraudster, and you, the reader. We will imagine this group in order to think about psychopathy on a continuum.

The Role of Subclinical Psychopathy in Recruiting or Small-Time Frauds

The concept of subclinical psychopathy has been implicated as a root cause of some of the callous or destructive behavior of Wall Street. *Subclinical* means a set of clinical findings that do not qualify for a formal diagnosis. Qualities and skills that are actively sought during the hiring process for high-paying and competitive jobs might actually predispose those who get the jobs to psychopathic behavior. Ronald Schouten, a Harvard forensic psychiatrist, argues specifically that the following traits might serve someone well in an interview:

- Glibness and superficial charm
- Lack of empathy
- Consistent decisions in their self-interest, even where it is ethically questionable
- Chronic, sometimes transparent lies, even with regard to minor things
- Lack of remorse
- Failure to take responsibility for their actions, and instead blaming others
- Shallow emotions
- Ignoring responsibilities
- Persistent focus on gratifying their own needs at the expense of others
- Conning and manipulative behavior[46]

This list may not seem that odd as it relates to the workplace. In fact, many of these items might be strengths in certain situations. Being skilled in these ways could enable individuals to fool interviewers and get ahead. Exhibiting any of these traits does not mean that one is a psychopath. Nor does anything on this list imply that a crime is inevitable. A person could exhibit all of these traits and never cross the line and break the law.[47] Yet convicted fraudster Justin Paperny's comments reveal a shocking lack of compassion: "People are saying that their lives have been ruined because of me. . . . I'm so disgusted to admit it but I said to my brother I've never seen these people before. Even at that time, at my sentencing, I was still so caught up in my own life that I didn't think I really had played a significant role at these people's lives being worse."[48]

Those who study psychopaths report that true psychopaths score in the top quartile of the measurement known as the Hare Scale.[49] What about those who just miss making this rank? What about the fictional schoolteacher, who cheated "just this once"—is she a psychopath? The subclinical concept may be adequate to explain the accidental fraudster.

Along this line of thinking about psychopathy and fraud, another way to conceptualize fraud and psychopathy is to put the traits of psychopathy on a continuum from low to high, or none to excessive.

Exhibit 5.6   Alcohol Continuum—Extremes

The odds are that there is no one who does not at some time do something on that list. Seeing psychopathy in this way adds perspective. One can imagine not being on either end of the continuum.

To understand this, imagine the extremes of behavior related to alcohol consumption: Some people never consume anything alcoholic, even over-the-counter medications that contain alcohol. Other people have serious problems with alcohol. They ruin their health, their careers, or their important relationships because of their abuse of alcohol. This continuum is shown in Exhibit 5.6.

Most individuals, however, do not fall at either extreme. Most people consume alcohol and lie somewhere in the middle. We all know people who are neither teetotalers nor destructive alcoholics. The reality looks more like Exhibit 5.7.

In this conceptualization, alcoholism is not something only for state troopers and emergency room doctors to be concerned about, but all of us. The problem of fraud has similar, broader implications for society as a whole.

As with the alcohol continuum one can imagine a similar one for psychopathy. In one model of psychopathy there exists a subclinical form. Thus on the lower end is no evidence of psychopathy. See Exhibit 5.8.

Assuming that there is a continuum of psychopathic traits can help to put fraud in perspective. There are times when all of us are unempathetic, are driven by self-interest, are insensitive to social rules, and take advantage of others to some degree. To do so in all

Exhibit 5.7   Alcohol Continuum—Reality

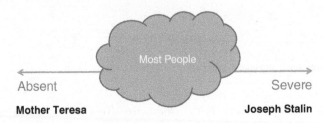

Absent   Severe

Mother Teresa   **Joseph Stalin**

Exhibit 5.8   Psychopathic Traits Continuum

circumstances and with significant harm to others is to be a hardened psychopath. See Exhibit 5.9.

Fraudsters move along the continuum and gradually increase the damage they do. How they move along the continuum and cross over into the realm of the illegal will be explored in the next chapter.

None   Fraudster   Tyrannical Murderer
                                                    (Joseph Stalin)

Exhibit 5.9   The Place of the Fraudster on the Psychopathic Traits Continuum

Conclusion

Given fraud's many possible reasons, methods, and environments, it is bound to be a problem for all of us at one time or another. As with alcoholism, the challenge is to catch it early and to create environments that minimize the temptation.

We do not see mental illness as a cause of fraud, and neither does the typical fraud court. Not guilty by reason of insanity is an extremely rare form of defense used by bad apples and their lawyers. Yet mental health does play a role in the harm done to others. And although the cases of Scrushy and Madoff are compelling and intriguing because of their scale and audacity, most frauds do not reach that level, so organizations would do well to consider how to stop the more typical frauds.

In the typical fraud, there is a tendency to change one's motivation around the rules. This pull to reverse motivation and disregard the rules is at the heart of most frauds that become financially lucrative.

The next chapters explore what happens when things go wrong and fraud is committed.

Notes

1. Mary Howitt, "The Spider and the Fly," 1829. (The full poem is in Appendix II.)
2. Laton McCartney, "Where There's Smoke There's Fraud," *CFO*, March 2011.
3. http://www.roughzen.com/blogzen.
4. *Marvel's The Avengers*, directed by Josh Whedon, Disney Studios, 2012.
5. For the complete e-mail, see "Sample Phishing E-Mail—the Case from the In-Box," in Appendix B.
6. The phisherman's tactics are so basic that no one except the most gullible would be fooled (the spelling mistakes and all are dead giveaways). We use the phisherman example as the biologist uses the fruit fly (drosophila). We regard the "Nigerian" phisherman as the equivalent of the drosophila for studying the mind of the human fraudster at the most elementary level, before proceeding to apply our understanding to more sophisticated cases.
7. Sid Kirchheimer, *Scam-Proof Your Life: 377 Smart Ways to Protect You and Your Family from Ripoffs, Bogus Deals, and Other Consumer Headaches* (New York: Sterling, 2006), 301–323. Note: AARP is the acronym for the American Association of Retired Persons.
8. Association of Certified Fraud Examiners, *Inside the Fraudster's Mind*, DVD, part 1.
9. Aaron Beam, with C. Warner, *HealthSouth: The Wagon to Disaster* (Fairhope, AL: Wagon, 2009), 50.
10. Ibid.
11. Ibid., 19.
12. Mei Feng, Weili Ge, Shuqing Luo, and Terry Shevlin's book, *The Role of CFOs in Material Accounting Manipulations* (New York: Conference Board, 2011), investigated the factors that may lead a CFO to engage in accounting manipulations. It found that CFOs often succumb to CEO pressure rather than seek immediate financial benefit. The analysis draws on instances of corporate fraud and a comprehensive sample of accounting and auditing enforcement releases issued by the SEC from 1982 to 2005.
13. Diana B. Henriques, "Madoff Will Plead Guilty; Faces Life for Swindle," *New York Times*, March 11, 2009; William B. Rashbaum and Diana B. Henriques, "Accountant for Madoff Is Arrested and Charged with Securities Fraud," *New York Times*, March 19, 2009; and Diana B. Henriques, "Two Are Charged with Helping Madoff Falsify Records," *New York Times*, November 14, 2009.
14. See also the book by Madoff victim, psychologist Stephen Greenspan, *Annals of Gullibility: Why We Are Duped and How to Avoid It* (Westport, CT: Praeger, 2009).
15. David Segal and Alison Leigh Cowan, "Madoffs Shared Much; Question Is How Much," *New York Times*, January 15, 2009.
16. Alexander Wolf and David Epstein, "A Massive Fraud Now More Fully Exposed," *SI Vault*, October 22, 2012.
17. Mary Pilon, "Armstrong Aide Talks of Doping and Price Paid," *New York Times*, October 12, 2012.
18. Ibid.
19. Patti Smith, "Off the Shelf," *New Yorker*, October 10, 2011, http://www.newyorker.com/reporting/2011/10/10/111010fa_fact_smith#ixzz1hxMK6n7e.

20. Beam, *HealthSouth*, 9.
21. Association of Certifed Fraud Examiners, *Inside the Fraudster's Mind*, DVD, part 1.
22. Virginia Demos, *Exploring Affect: The Selected Writings of Silvan S. Tomkins* (Cambridge, UK: Paris, 1995), 392.
23. Donald Nathanson, *Shame and Pride: Affect, Sex, and the Birth of the Self* (New York: W. W. Norton, 1992), 159.
24. Michael Basch, *Affect: The Gateway to Action* (New York: Basic Books, 1988).
25. Nathanson, *Shame and Pride*, 160.
26. Because the result of shame is something more potent than what even economic disincentives produce, we could call shame a most effective instrument for influencing human behavior. In other words, shame is both an affective instrument and an effective instrument!
27. Beryl Benderly, Mary Gallagher, and John Young, *Discovering Culture: An Introduction to Anthropology* (New York: D. Van Nostrand, 1977), 22–23.
28. Nathanson, *Shame and Pride*.
29. "Gingrich Comment on Shutdown Labeled 'Bizarre' by White House," CNN, November 16, 1995, www.cnn.com/US/9511/debt_limit/11-16/budget_gingrich.
30. Melvin R. Lansky and Andrew P. Morrison, *The Widening Scope of Shame* (Hillsdale, NJ: Analytic Press, 1997).
31. M. Lewis, *Shame: The Exposed Self* (New York: Free Press, 1992).
32. These four shame defenses, proposed by Donald Nathanson, mirror several of those identified by Anna Freud. The mechanisms she identified are regression, repression, reaction formation, isolation, undoing, projection, introjection, turning against the self, reversal, and sublimation. A thorough explanation of all of these technical terms is beyond the scope of this book.
33. Beam, *HealthSouth*, 68–69.
34. Ibid, 69.
35. Personal communication with coauthor Daven Morrison.
36. Ibid, 66. Beam also mentioned engaging in excessive spending and gambling.
37. D. S. Beu and M. R. Buckley, "This Is War: How the Politically Astute Achieve Crimes of Obedience through the Use of Moral Disengagement," *Leadership Quarterly* 15 (2004): 551–68.
38. The AICPA professional standards specifically state: "In the performance of any professional service, a member shall maintain objectivity and integrity, shall be free of conflicts of interest, and shall not knowingly misrepresent facts or subordinate his or her judgment to others." AICPA, Professional Standards, ET Section, Rule 102, Integrity and Objectivity, adopted 1988.
39. Ken Brown and Ianthe Jeanne Dugan, "Arthur Andersen's Fall From Grace Is a Sad Tale of Greed and Miscues," *Wall Street Journal*, June 7, 2002.
40. Ibid.
41. Bethany McLean and Joe Nocera, *All The Devils Are Here: The Hidden History of the Financial Crisis* (New York: Penguin Books, 2010).
42. Ibid., 187.
43. Ibid., 119–120.
44. Ibid., 1.

45. See Mary Rowe, "Micro-affirmations and Micro-inequities," *Journal of the International Ombudsman Association* 1(1): 2008.

46. Ron Schouten, "Psychopaths on Wall Street," n.d., http://blogs.hbr.org/cs/2012/03/psychopaths_on_wall_street.html.

47. Ron Schouten and J. Silver, *Almost a Psychopath: Do I (or Does Someone I Know) Have a Problem with Manipulation and Lack of Empathy?* (Center City, MN: Hazelden, in press).

48. ACFE Self-Study CPE Guide accompanying *Inside the Fraudster's Mind* (video), 2013, 141.

49. Hare, R. "A Research Scale for the Assessment of Psychopathy in Criminal Populations," *Personality and Individual Differences* 1(1980): 111–119.

The Accidental Fraudster (Bad Apple)[1]

WHEN THE APPLE TURNS AND HONESTY REVERSES COURSE

We believe that the model for distinguishing between accidental and predatory fraudsters is a useful one. The predatory bad apple (described in Chapter 5) decides to coerce and harm others with intimidation and hostility. In contrast, this chapter will focus on the accidental fraudster (bad apple), who finds a hole in the system and decides to perpetrate a fraud. Then, realizing the low likelihood of being caught and becoming enamored of the risk-free payoffs, he or she continues the fraud over a long period.

The situation thus works differently for the accidental fraudster than for the predatory fraudster. Opportunities to steal present themselves, and if the workplace environment allows it, such as weak or non-existent controls, these opportunities can be exploited. This type of fraud can be expensive in terms of cost and damage to the reputation of the organization. Such frauds remain unmanaged risks and can be sustained often as the perpetrators are poorly supervised and unlikely to be detected because they are usually highly trusted individuals.

Committing the Crime

In the previous section, we gave an example in which we outlined the role of emotions in a general fraud and then explored a case in which one powerful emotion, shame, was manipulated by a corrupt CEO in order to coerce a CFO to commit fraud. This was a predatory act, premeditated to steal from those who did not know they were being deceived. What about the less notorious but more common fraud? This chapter will explore the dynamics behind accidental frauds.

The ACFE *Reports to the Nations* indicate that the typical fraudster is a middle-aged man, but increasing numbers of women are also now committing white-collar crime. A disproportionately large percentage of fraud perpetrators are first-time offenders with no prior criminal record, according to the ACFE. One case in particular highlights how an average person can end up convicted of fraud despite being a model citizen. A classic description of the accidental fraudster follows.

Before committing fraud, Diann Cattani was known as a resourceful, hardworking student athlete: she played softball, basketball, and volleyball and ran track, and she was skilled enough to earn an athletic scholarship to Brigham Young University. A member of a stable and law-abiding Mormon family, she wanted to work hard and succeed when she became employed at a specialized human resources organization based in Atlanta, Georgia. She started as an all-purpose assistant, and her hard work, her sense of responsibility, and the fact that she was likable and outgoing led to more and more access to larger and larger funds and spending.[2]

The company grew phenomenally, and the resourceful and opportunistic Cattani was right in the center of it all. As her career progressed, she realized she had access to an open checkbook from the company. She was able to personally gain from the organization at just about every turn.

How did this happen? How did Cattani move from being a law-abiding person to one who was breaking many laws and stealing in all possible ways? Is this merely greed on steroids? If so, what caused the switch?

Beyond Greed

As we have noted before, fraud perpetration can be traced to many motivations other than greed. In this chapter, we are most interested in the motivational switches that lead otherwise law-abiding, decent people to commit white-collar crime. To better understand what causes motivational switches or reversals, we need to delve into the workings of the human mind. The ACFE video *Inside the*

Fraudster's Mind offers 10 clues to understanding a fraudster's thinking:

1. Sense of entitlement
2. Excessive optimism
3. Rationalization
4. Peer or financial pressure
5. Instant gratification
6. Diffusion of harm
7. Lack of remorse
8. Inadequate fear of punishment
9. Egoism
10. Disregard for authority and rule

Note that none of the 10 clues is greed (although instant gratification and sense of entitlement come close). We now proceed to take a look at a variety of psychological factors that may cause a person to engage in fraud.

Once committed to sustaining a fraud, an individual will settle into a consistent frame of mind. Affect provides the model for the raw fraud behavior with a finite set of hardwired emotions—in a sense, the fuel—so we need a finite set of motivations to explain why some people commit fraud and others do not. The model discussed below provides such a list. It argues for the underlying value *in the moment* as the driver of the motivation behind any action. We can therefore begin to see variations in behavior that in the past has simply been reduced to greed.[3] After a point, labeling fraudulent behavior as the result of excessive greed is not that helpful in advancing our understanding of why fraud occurs.

Exploiting a Weakness: A Motivational Theory of the Accidental Fraudster (Bad Apple)

The underlying motivation of fraud has thus far been traced to our biologically wired emotions. The emotions provide the impetus to get over any inertia in order to take action. How we choose to direct that action has infinite possibilities. The groundbreaking work of psychologist Michael J. Apter has the potential to expand our thinking beyond greed and understand why people choose to disregard the rules. He called it *reversal theory.*[4]

Reversal Theory: Choosing to Ignore Rules

Apter argued that there are four basic motivational questions that orient the direction of an action:

- **Taking action.** Is the action about a transaction or a relationship?
- **The role of play.** Am I most interested in enjoying the journey or getting to the destination?
- **Who benefits?** For whom am I doing it: myself or another person?
- **Obedience.** How do I feel about rules?

Regarding the last question, we all have ambivalence about the rules, perhaps because many rules appear arbitrary and *ad hoc*. Most people will admit to ignoring speed limits or other safety measures (e.g., motorcyle helmets or seat belts) when they judge them to be irrelevant or unnecessary. Reversal theory applies to the fraudster's mind at the point when there is a switch from wanting to obey a law to wanting to break it.

When a person who normally respects the rules abruptly reverses this behavior and ignores the rules, this perplexes those who study fraud. Apter's basic premise was that a person may, at any point and for any reason, be motivated to switch and act from the opposite motivation.

If switching can happen at any time for many different reasons, then this model is ideal for understanding the question of why good people do bad things.

Apter's reversal theory provides new insights into the heart of the question of *why*.

Before expanding on this model, it is important to revisit the case on fraud behavior to this point. We have identified several aspects of motivation common to all human beings in the previous two chapters:

- Affects (our innate human emotions) provide energy for taking action.
- The affects can be seen in all people in ways that are hardwired.
- One of the key affects is shame.
- Shame keeps us from harming others but is also a powerful motivator for revenge or for intimidating others (especially when used by a predator).
- Mental illness most likely does not play a role in fraud.

The conceptual fraud triangle consists of opportunities, pressures and incentives, and rationalizations (see Exhibit 6.1). As rationalizations, or thoughts, are added to the affects, motivations become more complex. Thoughts can be powerful motivators behind shame. With reversal theory we have a finite list of motivations as parameters for exploring why people choose to commit fraud.

Apter notes that affects play an important role in the motivational switch, and there is also often social pressure. For example, most people find themselves switching their motivations in these situations (and are subsequently surprised at themselves when it is pointed out to them, suggesting unconscious motivations rising to the surface):

- Telling a dirty joke during a solemn occasion.
- Correcting a friend's English during a casual and fun get-together.
- Beating a child in a board game.
- Telling about one's own volunteer efforts when a friend wants to share his or hers.[5]

This motivation model can be used to examine oneself and others for relative dominance and the capacity to change from one motivation to another. It is particularly helpful for determining what behavior executives need to change or for other leadership

Opportunity: *Find a hole in accounting process*

FRAUD

Pressure/Incentives:
Knowingly commit fraud for a perceived need

Rationalize:
Justify theft to self

Exhibit 6.1   The Fraud Triangle

Source: Adapted from Ramamoorti (2008) with permission.

development processes. This changing behavior has an intriguing application to fraud. Reversals can explain the multiple faces of the greed seen with fraud.

The Four Polarities and Eight States of Motivation

In reversal theory, motivation can be divided into four polarities, and the two poles of each polarity offer a choice:

1. **Rules.** Do I conform or rebel?
2. **The task.** Do I get the job done or enjoy the journey as the task gets done?
3. **Who benefits?** Is this for me, or do I focus on helping others?
4. **Who grows?** Do I feel more mastery, or do I help others gain theirs?

These eight choices create eight motivational states or values that show how Apter sees fraud might arise; they are explained in Exhibit 6.2 and the list that follows.

1. **Serious.** A desperate need for money to avoid bankruptcy.
2. **Playful.** The fun of the risk.

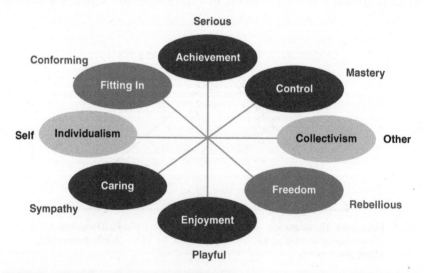

Exhibit 6.2   The Values of the Eight Motivational States
Source: © Apter International. Used with permission.

3. **Conforming.** Everyone in the company is doing it.
4. **Rebellious.** The pleasure of doing something wrong.
5. **Mastery.** Beating the system.
6. **Sympathy.** A form of self-indulgence.
7. **Self.** Personal gain.
8. **Other.** Using the money for one's family.[6]

Others have considered the various motivations behind deception. Ekman, in fact, alluded to reversal theory. Not every deceit, of course, involves concealing emotions, but even those that do not may still generate emotion-based behavioral clues to deceit if the liar has strong emotional reactions about engaging in the lie, such as being fearful of being caught, guilty about lying, or excited by the challenge.

The reversal theory model is an elegant tool for the investigator who is not as interested in psychology or human behavior but wants to be paying heed to risk factors that might indicate fraud or a potential for fraud. It is important to stop and inventory the new insights.[7]

New Insights in Behavioral Forensics

We assume that employees who commit fraud were originally motivated to obey the rules, and we do so because of the following findings from ACFE's *Report to the Nations*:

- Employees who commit fraud are long-standing; that is, they most likely obeyed other rules to stay employed.
- Employees commit fraud successfully over long periods, and by doing so they commit very costly acts of fraud; that is, they were also obeying other rules in order to sustain the fraud.
- At some point, the person who had followed the rules stopped doing so.
- Reversal theory shows that human beings switch motivations for any reason at any time. Affect theory says that no one is amotivational (i.e., an emotional vacuum); thus, one motivation must be replaced or compensated for by another.
- Many employees who commit fraud must reverse their motivations at some time.

If this set of conclusions is true, we have four new insights:

1. The set of eight states of motivation provides a template for moving beyond greed to subcategories.
2. Reversal theory goes deeper in providing an understanding of the dynamics of the pressure and rationalization points of the fraud triangle.
3. Simply making threats of punishment only tantalizes those who are in a playful mode, which is enhanced the greater the person finds himself or herself in a mind-set in which they feel protected. Excitement and arousal can serve as fuel to be playful like oxygen to a fire. It can also intensify the desire for mastery, in terms of beating the opponent in a game.[8]
4. We now see how an average person can break the law and commit fraud.

The implications of these new insights are significant. By understanding a broader set of motivations, managers can assess behavioral and integrity risks more effectively, and control systems can be more responsively designed to deal with such people rather than process-oriented risks. Individuals like Aaron Beam and Diann Cattani can be supervised in a manner that helps them not to cross the line and perhaps also to cross back over the line to the good side at less personal cost and to the organization's overall benefit. In this regard, the insightful book *Project Management AS IF People Mattered* by Robert Graham is worth reading. Early in his book, Graham observes: "So the project manager must be part planner, part psychiatrist, and part masterful organizational politician."[9]

Most important, with a more comprehensive set of ideas and fundamentals in the affects and the reversals, organizations can catch frauds earlier and with less of a financial cost. Ties between the organization and its employees can grow deeper, and the employees can be vigilant on behalf of the organization rather than being in conflict and feeling taken advantage of by the employer.

Convicted felon Diann Cattani approached federal investigator Oliver Halle in Atlanta, after he had retired from the FBI. Although he was never involved with her case, Halle mentioned later in an interview that he found Cattani's responses quite striking:

> Through all of it, he was listening for phrases like "sweat equity,"
> "they short-changed me," or "they never paid me what I was

worth." Instead, there were phrases like "they treated me like
family and I stabbed them in the back," "I stole this money," and
"I'm the one to blame."[10]

So Halle never heard the typical motivations for fraud, directly
or indirectly associated with selfishness or greed. Cattani's case is
uncommon yet remains a costly lesson for society, and it is, perhaps,
more intriguing to understand than cases like Madoff's. The core
question of what happens when a rule-following person like Cattani
decides to commit fraud is important. It is essential to understand
cases like hers in which there has been a change of mind (and
possibly a change of heart, too).

Seeing the Insights

How does this change of mind play out over time and with the known
fraud triangle? The next few exhibits highlight how a fraud is perpetrated and show a possible scenario in which law-abiding people find
themselves on the wrong side of the "unofficial" line of legality. The
dynamics are important, since in a typical crime the act is committed once. In fraud it is often committed multiple times, and *thus the
importance of how the person manages the theft internally in his or her own
mind is very important.*

We get some appreciation of what goes on in a white-collar criminal's mind by reading the following description from a repeat offender:

> There's no doubt about it, every part of the criminal lifestyle is a
> tremendous adrenaline buzz. Coming home with twenty thousand
> pounds in the car. The excitement of reliving what you've done.
> Also, the fear itself which is part of it. Then having a shower, putting
> on a smart suit, nice jewelery, going out, talking to other criminals,
> it never ends. Then next morning it all starts again. Sometimes
> you don't go, and you try to find other ways of substituting the
> adrenaline. Gambling comes close, but it isn't the same.[11]

First come the fundamentals from the fraud triangle
(see Exhibit 6.3): opportunity, pressure, and rationalization. The
employee (often accidentally) finds a hole in the oversight process and
realizes that money can be taken out of the system unnoticed. He or
she rationalizes that the rules, in the case of the reversal, do not matter.
The longer the experience of pressure (or pleasure and excitement)

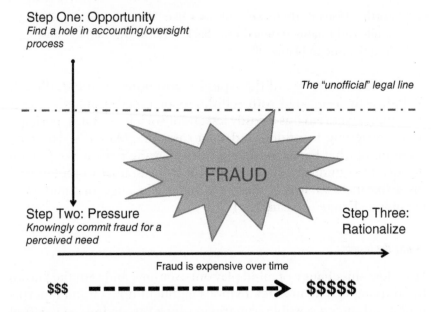

Exhibit 6.3   The Fraud Triangle in Motion
Source: © Morrison Associates, Ltd. Used with permission.

persists, and the longer the rationalization works, the more money can be taken out. Thus the little dollar signs become bigger ones over time.

Next (see Exhibit 6.4), Apter's reversal motivation model of disregarding the rules is highlighted as it relates to being on the wrong side of what is legal and in terms of the rationalizing and the pressure of the fraud triangle. Here the person needs to find a reason to repeat the deception over time. In this case, the person asks the question: "Do I keep the money?" And the answer with the reversal is "Yes!" and then a reason or rationalization must be created around disobeying the rules.

Now comes the critical aspect of how to change motivation and disobey the rules; in other words, what motivation is the foundation for sustaining the fraud and financially harming the organization? Exhibit 6.5 notes that there are eight broad categories and highlights four.

The final motivation is what evolves over time as the sustained rationalization, and the pressure comes from the dependency on what the money provides the person in terms of this rationalization—for instance, "I am getting what I deserve," "This is all for my family," "They are not as smart as I am," and "It's fun to trick them."

How Honesty Reverses

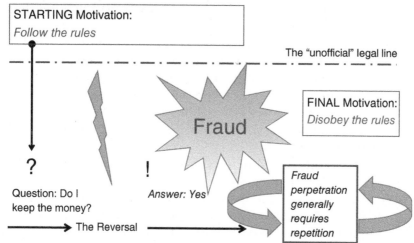

Exhibit 6.4   The Fraud "Reversal" Process

© Morrison Associates, Ltd. Used with permission.

Sustaining Large Scale Fraud Is Sustaining the Reversal

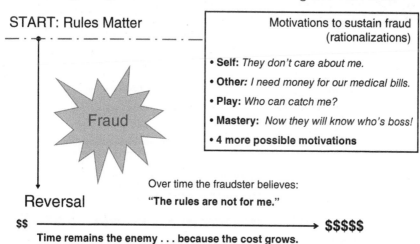

Exhibit 6.5   Sustaining the Reversal in Motivation

Source: © Morrison Associates, Ltd. Used with permission.

What is also likely related is how large frauds are sustained with more than one person involved. In really large-scale frauds, in which co-conspirators are recruited, the dynamics are similar, but the rationalizations are no longer private and personal but rather created for recruiting. Exhibit 6.6 summarizes how this might happen.

Accidental bad apples settle into mind-sets that allow them to be comfortable emotionally. This is the purpose of the rationalization. The underlying mind-sets of reversal theory allow for investigators to listen for rationalizations that may be thinly veiled by larger motivations of Apter's eight states.

It must be emphasized that fraudsters are not out of touch with reality. Like the young Patti Smith who tried to steal the book at the grocery store, they are not mentally ill or delusional, and they know that what they did was wrong. They are no longer uneasy, as they were at first, but have now settled into a homeostasis with their fraud behavior, and the environment they work in does not upset this stability.[12] Cattani was motivated to turn herself in when she saw Oprah

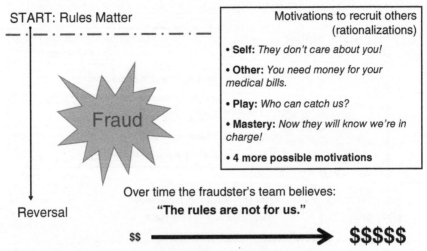

Sustaining Large Frauds Requires Getting Accomplices (Others) to Reverse Motivation

Exhibit 6.6   Sustaining Large Frauds: The "Reversal" of Others

Source: © Morrison Associates, Ltd. Used with permission.

Winfrey on television asking probing reflective questions of a person who was not dealing with her guilt.

Examples of Accidental Bad Apples Reversing

Up to this point Aaron Beam and Diann Cattani have been discussed. A third fraudster, investment adviser and convicted felon Justin Paperny, exaggerated the relative wealth of one of his clients in order to be seen as bigger player in his organization. He had been a professional baseball player and had just missed out on becoming an athlete in the major leagues. And so he longed for the cheers of adoring baseball fans and desperately wanted to be at the top of whatever game he was playing.

How do the cases of these three individuals fit reversal theory? The new motivations are shown in Exhibit 6.7.

Exhibit 6.7   Motivations after Reversal

	Justin Paperny	Aaron Beam	Diann Cattani
Apter Motivation	Play: It's a game. I've played in big games before. I can ignore the rules, because this won't apply to me.	Other (person): My CEO is threatening and terrifies me. I cannot cross him.	Self: The organization is getting so big and moving so fast. I am not sure it cares what I am doing.

Disregarding Risk: The Thrill of Being Close to, but Not in, Danger

Despite these tantalizing tales of egregiously unethical or illegal behavior, most people who feel shame or have other reasons to reverse their motivations don't change their behavior. Why this is so helps us to understand one aspect of fraud that played a significant role at Enron. It is the final concept for understanding reversal theory and fraud.

It's Only a Game: The Role of a Protective Frame of Mind in Making Rules and Repercussions Disappear

Apter's reversal theory has a long-standing tie to fraud that may explain why an accidental fraudster persists beyond what is reasonable. Apter and his father, K. C. P. Smith, began building the model while working on a similar problem to fraud: how to deal with delinquent boys. They found that the boys were not intimidated by possible consequences; in fact, they grew more motivated with bigger and more threatening consequences. To these delinquent boys, breaking the rules and not getting caught was a game.

This mirrors what was discovered in *The Smartest Guys in the Room,* the story of Enron recounted by Bethany McLean and Peter Elkind, and *Catch Me If You Can,* the story of impersonator Frank Abagnale that was made into a movie in 2002. The Enron executives were motivated not by the ethical laws of providing energy services to citizens but rather by the "game" of manipulating the energy grid. Their winnings were huge profits from the California energy system, and the manipulation enraged the citizens of California. In the documentary film about Enron (of the same title as the book), one can hear the very obvious glee of the traders at Enron. The motivational effects of excitement and joy, which are at the high end of the positive emotions, and the relative lack of shame, distress, or any of the negative emotions are unsettling to hear.

Apter developed a concept that explains what is happening and why risk is either not considered or minimized. His central analogy is to a tiger in a cage. Human beings, he noted, will not go up to something lethal like a tiger, much less consider provoking one, yet if the tiger is in a cage, people are much more likely to be curious or even provocative. People seek out risk when they perceive that they are safe, such as at a sporting event. Some fans will be much louder and more argumentative in the stands than if they were actually playing in the game itself. Apter called this state of mind the *protective frame.* A protective frame provides safety from social harm (the effect of shame).

Reversal theory explains another reason for risk taking or even denial. In one state of motivation, being in a playful mind-set (thinking about the journey rather than the destination) can allow a person to be unrealistic toward risk. When playfulness fits the context, it is the right motivational state to be in, but in the wrong context, playfulness can be dangerous.

A movie like *Jaws,* which provokes fear and the thrill of being scared at the same time, creates a combination of affects, which is more complex and has a specific effect on each person. Emotions have a unique blend when they are at odds in this way. Apter has a special term to describe them: *parapathic emotion.*[13] And, according to reversal theory, one finds it easy to leave the emotion behind as part of the fantasy when he or she leaves the movie theater.

Here is another example of how parapathic emotions work. A veteran who has suffered trauma relives its physical sensations—accelerated heart-rate, sweaty palms, and overall high stimulation—differently depending on his play mind-sets. He could have the same sensations while driving a snowmobile across a semi-frozen lake during a spring thaw and feel exhilarated, despite the potential danger. But he might experience group therapy as very unpleasant, despite the fact that he is sitting safely with others and there is no threat of physical harm. In the case of fraud, the fraudster leaves the sympathetic feelings behind for the thrill of making money.

The protective frame and the playful frame of mind have direct ties to the case of Enron. In the documentary, the excesses of Enron's energy traders are tied to the Milgram experiment, which studied experimental participants' readiness to obey authority even when they were ordered to give someone an electric shock against their will.[14] Both the authorities and the "victims" were actors. Over the course of the experiment, the supervisors directed the subjects to administer high and higher levels of electrical shocks, and the "victims," were prerecorded and their cries were played depending on the level of voltage. Seen in the light of the protective frame, an alternative explanation can be reached and thus the Milgram experiment is the wrong analogy for the Enron fraud.

Although the experiment applies to the power company supervisors who were manipulating the power grid on site in California, it does not pertain to the people working at Enron. They were not being instructed to be cruel; rather, they were motivated to be as cruel as they wanted to be because no one was holding them accountable. The Enron leadership provided a protective frame because of the culture it had allowed to develop. Organizational cultures that encourage or condone fraud can thus provide a protective frame—a context in which fraud can and will flourish. In such environments, fooling the auditors can become a game.

Fraudsters Make and Defend Protective Frames to Avoid Seeing Danger

The protective frame is most likely playing a role in the e-mail phishing frauds coming into the United States from overseas. The phishermen are safe, hidden behind the physical distance between them and their victims lying safe behind the veil of their email, and they are also safe with corrupt governments that will likely not prosecute them for their crimes. Similarly, government officials who move within the protective bubble of high-powered politics are also immune from the affective data that would help them to manage risk. It explains why the call for ethics training and stronger and more effective legislation gets repeated on a regular basis to governments around the world. And the training is essentially toothless.

Financial or other business success does not always come with an element of play for those who are not in the leadership ranks. For many it comes with the expectations of longer hours. Yet, for a senior executive team that becomes highly invested in the most exciting deal, they can get into a playful mode and end up pushing the organization down a hazardous trail when they lose sight of the larger consequences. The deal becomes the end-all. Harry Kraemer, who teaches a course on leadership and has written a book on the subject, discusses how senior leadership teams get in trouble when they ask "Is this legal?" instead of "Is this the right thing to do?"[15] The language of law, the seal of approval from an elite law or consulting firm, can reinforce or create a bubble from reality, much like that of the sports fan in the stands or the veteran racing across a thawing lake. The sense of a bubble outside the threat of risk is increased when government officials are coerced into kowtowing to senior leaders of corporations.

For instance, HealthSouth headquartered in Birmingham, Alabama, was able to have the senator and the governor of Alabama in its offices in a matter of hours, showing CEO Richard Scrushy's influence in political circles. Scrushy specifically created an environment of fear of the leader, similar to that created by political dictators who count on such fear boxing their followers into a forced allegiance.

Here is an observation from Aaron Beam on Scrushy's leadership style:

> Each person had three minutes to tell the important things he or she accomplished during the previous week and what their goals were for the coming week. The intent was to give everyone in the room an understanding of what was going on in the company. . . . He never spoke for only three minutes. He never told us what he accomplished the week prior, and he never told us what he would be doing the following week. It was simply his time to assert absolute control. More specifically, it was Richard's time to belittle, berate, and publicly embarrass employees for

lack of performance, underperformance, or just to scare everyone silly into fully buying into the "Pulling the Wagon" mantra.[16]

Why Now? Understanding Life-Span Issues in Fraud Reversals

The ACFE report notes that the typical age of a fraudster is 45–55,
not 20 or 30. Middle age is a time when trust placed in someone is at
its maximum, often because one's role, influence, and network are
perceived to be at or near their highest points. Americans, for example, are very comfortable with the president being in this age range.
There is a similar perception in the world of corporate leadership.

So why is mid-to-late middle age the most common age of fraudsters? What is happening at this stage of life? Actually, many things
are happening.

In reversal theory, what is most important is the shift from the
journey or play as an end in itself to the task. For a variety of reasons,
tasks take center stage in midlife. For example, a leadership position
at work, and being required to care for an elderly parent can change
the life course of a middle-aged adult and cause reassessment of
motivations into his or her 40s. In addition, the consequences of too
much play—such as unstable relationships, challenges with troubled
children, addictions or abuse, or the inability to stay employed—
become evident at this stage of life.

Middle age is sometimes accompanied by a midlife crisis; this
has been determined by academics to not be very common, yet it
remains a theme in popular culture.

The psychologist Erik Erikson explored this period in his comprehensive examination of how human beings progress through life.
His focus was on the inherent challenges of each phase of life. He
argued that early in life we must navigate the challenges of basic
trust versus mistrust, and at the end of life we must consider an integrated life narrative (what Erikson referred to as ego-integrity versus
despair).

Per Erikson, at midlife the individual is focused on producing,
executing, and making the most of opportunities, skills, and relationships. From ages 40 to 65, Erikson believed, the individual must
confront the challenge of generativity versus stagnation—what will
be my legacy? The push for generativity most likely underlies the
pressure in the fraud triangle, and in particular the reversal of going
from following the rules to rebelling.

The Psychological Conflict of Midlife and Fraud Triangle Pressure

Erikson's midlife challenge of generativity versus stagnation is intriguing in terms of the mind of the fraudster. Above all else, this dilemma motivates people in midlife to focus their efforts on what will outlast them. They are driven to do so as they begin to appreciate their own mortality and the limits of what can be done in one lifetime. If people perceive that they are doing well, they engage more fully with the world; if they feel they have not achieved their goals, they tend to withdraw. (Clearly the effect of shame plays a role in Erikson's model.) If Erikson is correct, then the withdrawal must come from a fear of being stagnant, missing opportunities, and being ineffective.

In the 1988 film *Midnight Run*, Robert De Niro played a former Chicago cop who got burned by the corruption of the police department by the Mafia. He had made a decision to leave formal police work and focus on just being a bounty hunter in order to get the bad guys without any threat of an organization's corruption getting in the way. Focused on maintaining his integrity, with one simple case, he found himself caught in a bigger web of persecution and powerful forces, to the point that he himself was the target of pursuit. Desperate to complete his task and having lost his rental car, he was forced to hot-wire a car and drive it across the Arizona desert. His focus and his own entrapment were revealed as he recklessly drove through the desert, avoiding police cars and helicopters. He gritted his teeth and muttered, "I've come too far! I've come too far!"

This fictional character illuminates the challenge of being focused on work and generating something for a lifetime of work. In the case of fraud, what is more intriguing than the Erikson dilemma is actually the concept of the midlife crisis.

Counterpoints

Academic attempts to document the existence of the midlife crisis are questionable. Interviews have been used to assess the presence of such a crisis, but the method of interviewing is suspect. It is illogical, because many mental functions that follow are rooted in the unconscious and out of our awareness, yet they still motivate our behavior.

Thus, merely asking a person a question does not allow access into his or her unconscious. As we noted earlier, there are powerful and functional defenses that can halt any attack as obvious as a direct question. We need unobtrusive procedures to "pierce" any proffered rationalizations and get at the true motivations.

Lessons from Executives and Managers on the Couch

It is likely, then, that middle age provokes an inherent pressure, as described by the fraud triangle, to take action. It is a critical period for the individuals seen in executive consultations. Along the lines of Erikson's thinking, individuals at this point in their lives can be working hard to avoid some very painful questions. At the heart of all of the questions are concerns about their efforts. They are defending against their shame and may have the following doubts:

- Did I do enough?
- Did I make the wrong choices?
- Is this all I get for my efforts?
- Did I make the most of those who wanted to love me?

Here are some possible rationalizations based on what has been discussed so far:

- This will give me a chance to have what I've been working for all my life.
- I cannot allow my children to not go to a decent college and have a leg up on life.
- I passed on that affair, so I deserve something for myself.
- She [or He] had it so easy, so why can't I get a break?
- I need to meet the expectations I was told I could meet.

Conclusion

Those who are accidental bad apples can be seen as examples of "It didn't have to be that way." Experienced accounting professionals point out the tragedy of the lack of oversight, the naïveté, and the bad luck that create an ecosystem in which fraud can take hold. Sometimes the problem is merely a series of bad turns of fate. The middle-aged (45–55 years old) person who commits fraud reverses motivation from being honest and obeying the rules. This accidental fraudster is not as glamorous as the person who is in the headlines of the newspaper for stealing millions, but through their sustained fraud can still incur significant losses for society. These individuals have lost the respect for the bright line between the money that is theirs and the money that is not theirs. They have a significant challenge when they finally reflect and understand that their psychological defenses have failed them. They had been self-deluded and now realize what they have done.

Now that we have completed an overview of the predatory and accidental bad apples, we will turn attention to the final challenge of the bad apple: when that person is in a position of leadership.

The behavioral sciences have brought us to the threshold of the C-suite. This area of investigation helps behavioral forensics to understand "tone at the top" (which we will explain), other human factor concerns, and related organizational factors that are known to create an environment that is conducive to fraud. Beyond the bad apple and the bad bushel, the bad crop has tremendous importance to the functioning of our markets and to trust in general. Thus, we turn now to what makes senior executives unique.

Notes

1. The so-called "bad apple" comes in two varieties: one that is rotten to the core—the malignant type, the predator we covered in Chapter 5—and the benign type, the accidental fraudster that we take up in this chapter. Both the "case of Aaron B" and Diann Cattani are examples of accidental fraudsters. We owe this typology to the excellent paper "The Evolution of Fraud Theory" by Jack Dorminey, A. Scott Fleming, Mary-Jo Kranacher, and Richard A. Riley, Jr., *Issues in Accounting Education* 27, no. 2 (2012): 555–579.
2. Sara Israelsen-Hartley, "Greed Is No Respecter of Persons; Y Grad., Convicted Felon Shares Her Cautionary Tale," *Deseret News* (Salt Lake City), March 5, 2011.
3. See "Greed Takes the Blame" in Appendix B.
4. Michael J. Apter, *Reversal Theory: The Dynamics of Motivation, Emotion and Personality* (Oxford, UK: One World Publications, 2006).
5. From L. Festinger, "A Theory of Social Comparison Processes," *Human Relations* 7 (1954): 117–40. We know that if people around us achieve more than we do, it adversely affects our own self-esteem. No wonder some people deliberately shy away from class reunions!
6. Michael Apter, in an e-mail to Daven Morrison, July 23, 2008.
7. Paul Ekman, Maureen O'Sullivan, and M. Frank, "A Few Can Catch a Liar," *Psychological Science* 10 (1999): 263–66.
8. Consider the following from online gaming: PWN or PWNED—"Thr styff of lemgendz: Gamer defeats gamer, types in 'I pwn you' rather than I OWN you. 'This word is just an overly used Internet typo. It has been overused to the point that people who play online games are using it in everyday speech.' —Tory Rowley, Corunna, Michigan." Lake Superior University's Banished Words List

for 2007. See Glossary of Online Gaming Acronyms, Abbreviations and Slang, at http://www.lagkills.com/gaming-acronyms.htm.

9. Robert J. Graham, *Project Management AS IF People Mattered* (Bala Cynwyd, PA: Primavera Press, 1989).

10. Israelsen-Hartley, "Greed Is No Respecter of Persons."

11. Quoted in M. J. Apter, *Danger: Our Quest for Excitement* (Oxford, England: One-World Publications, 2007), 159.

12. *Homeostasis* refers to the tendency of the body to regulate its own tempera-ture, blood pressure, and so forth at a constant level. Thus, the human body regulates body temperature in an effort to maintain an internal temperature around 98.6 degrees Fahrenheit by sweating to cool off on hot summer days and shivering to produce heat on cold winter days.

13. Apter uses horror novelist Stephen King's question to make his point: "Why are people willing to pay good money to be made extremely uncomfortable?" Well, it turns out that all emotions are enjoyed—even supposedly negative and unpleasant ones such as fear, anger, horror, grief, and disgust—in the presence of detachment. Apter's special name for the enjoyable forms of negative emo-tions is *parapathic emotions*. See Apter, *Danger*, 73.

14. In the analysis of what happened in the deregulation of the California elec-trical grid, the model of the famous Stanley Milgram psychology experiment is highlighted to explain what happened. In his celebrated book, *Obedience to Authority* (New York: Harper & Row, 1974), Stanley Milgram reports a dramatic series of experiments to show how easily "people follow orders." Specifically the experiment sought to explain why individuals go against their values and harm others. The experiment demonstrated how average people will act against their values not to harm others when they are directed to by perceived authority figures. The experiment was important in helping to understand what had hap-pened in the wars and other atrocities of the last century. It has been argued that analogously, as the Enron traders requested unusual outages in the elec-tricity grid, the orders were accepted because the traders were seen as authori-ties and experts and thus overrode the inherent preference to not harm others.

15. Harry Kraemer, *From Values to Action: The Four Principles of Values-Based Leadership* (San Francisco: Jossey-Bass, 2011).

16. Aaron Beam and C. Warner, *HealthSouth: The Wagon to Disaster* (Fairhope, AL: Wagon, 2009), 76.

CHAPTER

7

The Bad Bushel and Beyond

SEEING THE LARGER CONTEXT OF THE C-SUITE

In Chapter 6, we discussed how the challenges of midlife for senior executives may contribute to the potential rationalizations of those who commit fraud. Personal expectations about what a career will provide and one's perceived sense of value to an organization can lie at the core of the motivation to commit fraud. The emotional, and specifically the shame-driven, motivations to take control and earn a lot of money can cause senior executives to take what is not rightfully theirs but what feels like it.

As an individual moves higher in the organization, his or her relative influence grows. And as it does, so does the relative risk of significant losses—or, in financial terms, the financial materiality. Studies and programs have been designed to address tone at the top. Many headline-grabbing stories of significant financial losses consistently illustrate that the challenges of stopping illegal behavior in the C-suite were not met.[1]

Senior executives are just like the rest of us, aren't they? Not quite! This chapter outlines what is known about senior executives from an organizational psychiatry perspective. This understanding is then contrasted with what is known from the allied field of organizational behavior in order to explain why things go wrong in the boardroom and the C-suite.

Luck and Effort Distinguish Senior Executives

For senior executives in whose health and well-being the company has a vested interest, policies and procedures require a comprehensive, postemployment medical examination annually. However, to have one that includes psychiatry as the main focus is relatively uncommon. Yet a psychiatric exam consisting of interviews, testing, and dialogue would be a good resource for executives who are being stretched or are at risk of derailing.[2] The psychiatric consulting firm Morrison Associates, with a father-and-son team as the principals, has conducted such a program for over 30 years.

For three decades now, they have had the opportunity to understand the narrative of an executive's work life as it is unfolding. The tests executives initially take provide objective data on the executive's capacity to problem-solve. The subsequent interviews provide an autobiographical sketch on what has happened in the executive's career as well as his or her life outside work. The executives have a chance to talk with a team of experts over a couple of days the way they might talk about their physical health at an elite medical program such as the Mayo Clinic. A team of specialists composed of a psychiatrist, an MBA graduate, and professionals from other allied fields are typically available at hand. The discussion about success and balance provides further insight into the executive's values and current pressures beyond what is learned in the interviews. The following is a high-level overview of what is typically found.

Interviewing Executives

In an executive development process, interviews provide insight into the lives of the leaders. Executives' biographies are as unique as their fingerprints. However, there are some distinct aspects commonly seen in the C-suite in three areas:

1. **Personal.** "I learned growing up that if I wanted something it was up to me to get it."

    The tragedies of alcoholism, parental death, mental illness, divorce, and domestic abuse occur in the lives of executives just as they do in the experiences of people who are not in the C-suite. There are biographies that are just as tragic as any heard on a locked psychiatric ward. The executives' drive to achieve, however, is notable. They were often the first in the family to be a college graduate. Many were the first to have a significant career, reaching levels of leadership that their parents had no idea how to advise on or support.

Finally, what is also often unique is the new way of living with wealth as an executive enters middle age and beyond. Living with wealth is generally experienced as pleasant, but it does have consequences for raising children as well as for managing the needs of an extended family. Many struggle with balancing the time they devote to work and the time they are available to the family.

2. **Work.** "I cannot remember a time when I wasn't working."

Work was important to executives from an early age, often to the exclusion of social life and sports. Work was pursued early in order to get what they wanted, whether it was basic needs, gas for the car, or clothes. It is not uncommon that this work was so important because the family was poor and needed supplemental income.

In their careers, executives generally recognized that success came from building relationships, outworking coworkers, and often just having "dumb luck." Because of their work ethic, others recognized their potential and opened doors for them, and they flourished with greater responsibility. Developing or managing people is considered a challenge of work, but for many it is not what is most exciting and motivating about the C-suite.

Generally the "people side" is avoided. Dealing with poor performance or change resistance is not seen as a challenge in the same light as the obstacles to growth, handling a tough client, or doing a major deal. The typical senior leader is not as motivated to address talent development, conflict in the senior leadership team, and other sticky interpersonal problems as they are in dealing with other challenges.

Managing people is not avoided but in general it is seen as something unpleasant. However, one general exception that many cherish is the opportunity to mentor others. In fact, those who are successful often appreciate the chance to pay back the organization for the mentoring and compassion they received. This merits emphasizing. Those who rise to the leadership ranks often attract mentors who look out for them because the mentors value the hard work and the sheer effort expended. The successful young leader as protégé and the mentor have a mutually rewarding relationship, and credit is due to both the mentor and the young hard-driving protégé.

3. **Education.** "I took art history because I had to."

For most successful executives, college was a tool for getting a good job. While in school, for which they were frequently paying the bills, they were often working two or more jobs. It is not uncommon for education to have been postponed because family or other demands pulled the future executive out of school and back into managing a crisis. Thus, there was generally a low tolerance for subjects and degrees that did not immediately lead to a well-paying job. Liberal arts classes were often not taken because they did not support the perceived needs for accounting, finance, or business proficiency. As previously noted, the executives often put themselves through college completely and may have been the first in the family to attend college.

Problem-Solving: Putting Executives through Industrial-Grade Assessments

Executives generally do well on intelligence tests that measure knowledge of how the world works and the ability to make connections at the right level. There is one important exception: the picture arrangement subtest of the Wechsler Adult Intelligence Scale. This test measures the individual's capacity to create a logical story out of a jumble of related drawings. It also requires a recognition of the context and an ability to attend to the emotion (the affect) expressed in the pictures. Executives are not usually asked to be attuned socially to others; rather, they are supposed to deliver results. It is perhaps more common for an elementary schoolteacher or a police officer to need to be skilled in this way.

On other tests, executives' scores fall across a wide range in terms of their ability to perceive relationships or tasks and to use trial and error to learn. Finally, their capacity to tolerate ambiguity is higher than that seen in the general population, and they have a greater than average tendency for perfectionism.

In terms of character or personality, it is very common to find that executives are hypercompetitive. This makes them vulnerable to framing issues in their lives into win-lose scenarios, and because winning is associated with feeling competent, they fear being beaten.

Combining this finding of hypercompetitiveness with the midlife challenges discussed in the previous chapter, it is easy to understand why many wealthy middle-aged entrepreneurs regret selling their businesses for too little. They generally feel emotionally depleted (their batteries are low), and it is not uncommon for executives to show a high need for psychological nurturance and an excessive self-reliance that can border on narcissism (which is common among CEOs). Because of its inherent risk for pathology, narcissism will be discussed in depth subsequently.

In summary, the high-grade quality assessments of executives in the C-suite found the following:

- They have generally accurate perceptions about their world and tolerate ambiguity well.
- They are driven to outwork others (because of their high standards and hypercompetitiveness).
- They exhibit above-average intelligence except in reading emotional cues.
- Narcissistic traits are more common in CEOs.
- Work and life circumstances can deplete their batteries, especially when it comes to dealing with their emotions.

Life as an Executive: Excitement, Vigilance, and Caution

As they describe how they experience their lives, executives recognize that it is not natural for them to be reflective or pay attention to social cues. They note that they are data driven and prefer to have things communicated clearly and concisely; otherwise, we see the MEGO, or "My eyes glaze over," syndrome.[3] When combined with a blindness to the affects, this can lead to an overvaluation of all things positive, such as industry fads that encourage an artificially positive mental attitude and initiatives designed to drive out negativity or naysayers.

This doesn't mean that executives are inattentive or careless. They often, in fact, feel very responsible and at risk. One CEO reflected, "I feel like my job is to be like the radar for the local forecast. I have to constantly be scanning the environment for storms so I can understand them, shut them down before they get going, and minimize any damage."[4] At the same time, the exhilaration of being

seated at the table and involved in the highest levels of decision making is something they readily admit to missing when they step down.

Because of their importance, executives who are self-reflective
have recognized how powerful an influence their support can be.
They are therefore often quite cautious about openly supporting a
decision, lest the action be taken merely out of fear of opposing the
CEO. One CEO, we'll call Steve, related how he had to watch out for
others using "Steve says" as a carte blanche to get something done in
the organization.

Like the proverbial wizardry in *The Sorcerer's Apprentice*, the power
within the C-suite has to be wielded thoughtfully. (As Abraham Lin-
coln once said, "Nearly all men can stand adversity, but if you want
to test a man's character, give him power.") The same power that can
be focused to maximize an organization's effectiveness can also be
undermined if it is wielded by a leader prone to vanity, egocentrism,
or narcissism. Power is a serious behavioral risk factor for fraud.

Trouble in the C-Suite: Overwhelmed, Overpaid, and Overconfident—Narcissism and Beyond

When Aaron Beam tells his story in his own book of how he interviewed to work for Richard Scrushy, he openly admitted that he
ignored emotional data. As part of the team that supported Scrushy
as he rose in the organization, Beam rode his boss's coattails for his
own benefit. He paid $5,000 for 100,000 shares in the company and
ended up a millionaire.

Beam discussed how the world seemed to revolve around the
CEO. This is true in many large organizations. And when that tendency is focused on a person who already believes that the world
revolves around him—someone who is narcissistic—there is the risk
for epic failure. In Beam's story, however, it is not known whether
Richard Scrushy is a narcissist. Despite whatever problems result
from narcissism in the workplace, some people even argue that a
narcissist may be good for an organization.

There's an organizational culture aspect to the perceived importance of the CEO in relation to the board of directors. To demand better
board oversight of the CEO's behavior is disingenuous, for many board
members owe their seats to the CEO. So such oversight is more difficult
than "herding cats." Harvard professor Michael Jensen has insightfully
written, "Board culture is an important component of board failure.

The great emphasis on politeness and courtesy at the expense of truth and frankness in boardrooms is both a symptom and cause of failure in the control system. CEOs have the same insecurities and defense mechanisms as other human beings; few will accept, much less seek, the monitoring and criticism of an active and attentive board."[5]

Narcissism: Beyond Self-Love

Narcissism can be a serious problem in leadership, especially in leaders who are charismatic. But narcissism in itself is not a cause of fraudulent behavior; in fact, at times it can be adaptive. Psychoanalyst and anthropologist Michael Maccoby has noted that narcissism can be helpful to a CEO when it is combined with what he called *strategic intelligence*: an interrelated set of skills that includes foresight, vision, motivation, systems thinking, and partnering.[6] These skills are very helpful in allowing a CEO to take on challenges and directions that others cannot.

Imagine the life of a CEO of a large corporation. He or she does the following:

- Has the final word on virtually all decisions.
- Determines the composition of the senior leadership team.
- Starts and ends meetings.
- Receives gifts from those who hope to receive influence in exchange.
- Has a desired opinion or perspective that is sought by many.
- Is part of a cohort that can "make things happen."

All CEOs are not narcissists, but the question arises: does becoming a CEO make anyone a narcissist? Psychiatrists argue that character is formed early in life and gaining the role of CEO allows the narcissistic aspects of personality to flourish. In Michael Maccoby's clinical experience, CEOs have narcissistic traits at a higher rate than the rest of the population, and they are able to utilize their skills on behalf of their organizations.

This does not mean that narcissistic CEOs do not have weaknesses. Maccoby sees the following traits as the most glaring weaknesses:

- Unwillingness to listen
- Oversensitivity to criticism
- Paranoia

- Anger and condescension
- Overcompetitiveness and overcontrol
- Isolation
- Exaggeration and lying
- Lack of self-knowledge
- Grandiosity[7]

Many of these are weaknesses of shame management, as described in earlier chapters. They are also weaknesses that make one vulnerable to reversals that are inappropriate, especially around rules. Yet this is not the worst of it.

Ironically, these weaknesses may very well be what gets someone into the C-suite: they reflect the potential for a single-mindedness that blinds the person to actions and consequences that would hinder someone with a different personality. What makes this aspect particularly damaging is that the organization suffers and has to learn, too. If such a person is in the C-suite, problems can and will escalate—quickly and rather dramatically—and there soon comes a point when it is simply too late to recover from the fallout of such dysfunctional leadership personalities.

In particular, if this set of weaknesses is coupled with the clinical experience noted by Morrison Associates of a narrow focus on getting tasks done, comfort with ambiguity, and the avoidance of emotional issues (especially those that relate to confrontation), this creates a ticking time bomb. Because of these personality traits, by the time this leader is in the C-suite, an environment of conflict avoidance has been manufactured. Subordinates quickly learn the new rules, sycophants thrive, and critical information is covered up. Fraud and other catastrophically poor decisions lurk ominously in the background.

Yet CEOs who are narcissistic are not inherently vulnerable to dishonesty to the extent that they break the law. Maccoby suspects that Enron's Jeffrey Skilling was narcissistic but that Ken Lay was not. "They can be honest or crooked, brilliant or ordinary, wise or foolish," Maccoby wrote. "What they share is vision or boldness persuading others with their unshakable conviction about the value of their actions."[8] In other words, CEOs can be extremely persuasive and know how to fire up the troops.

Narcissism in the CEO, especially in terms of Maccoby's identified weaknesses, puts the organization at risk, and fraud is one of many possible threats. Several years later, Richard Scrushy used the

"Aw shucks" defense and brazenly claimed in courtroom testimony on May 20, 2009, that he had "no knowledge of any financial fraud at HealthSouth."[9] These weaknesses may push a narcissistic leader over the line, as Maccoby noted: Those who failed "fell prey to unbridled greed and grandiosity, were puffed up by their own vision and initial success, and isolated themselves from advisors who could help them from self-destructing."[10]

Pete Pesce, the former head of human resources at Arthur Andersen, noted that intellect hurts CEOs when they are dismissive of critical voices outside their sphere. At the point that they crawl into a cocoon of gloating self-adulation, they lose touch with reality. This happens because they are smart enough to come up with very useful rationalizations, such as "I could always count on them, and now they aren't helpful anymore. They've lost it." Unfortunately for them, they have lost access to useful information.

In other words, when the trusted advisor gives tough feedback to the narcissistic leader, the leader dismisses the feedback. In an attack-other shame defense, the leader believes that the trusted person is not the resource he or she once was. Now the former confidant is a persona non grata to the CEO; he or she is "out of it, of no more use to me."

The Power of the Narcissistic Leader Turns to Harm

The "case of Aaron B" featured the domineering and egotistical personality of Richard Scrushy. As one experienced CEO and board chairman noted, "Richard Scrushy had an auditorium named after him as well as having a sculpture of himself in the lobby—I had never seen that before!"[11] This individual ended his business affiliation that day. Reflecting on the process he went through, Beam realized that he had ignored Scrushy's conceited and egomaniacal traits at his own peril. Reading the story of Beam, one can feel a certain sadness at the sense of betrayal, not only of Beam by Scrushy but also of Beam by himself. The role of emotions is the same as with the phisherman, as well as the cycle of excitement-enjoyment-fear-distress/shame:

- Instilled excitement through unexpected money.
- Proffered enjoyment (even joy) through credibility, nobility, and specialness.
- Instilled threat of shame if the specialness of the relationship is betrayed.

How did Scrushy manipulate his CFO so facilely? What distinguishes Beam's story from that of the phisherman's victim is the interpersonal nature. The relationship between Beam and Scrushy is much more of a factor in the deception. The power of the personality is significant. This has implications for other CFOs, given the description Beam gave of himself as being more introverted and not as aggressive as Scrushy.

If an average person had been in Beam's shoes, would that person have been charmed, seduced, and ultimately ensnared as well? Most people can appreciate Beam's description of being charmed by somebody charismatic and becoming entrapped in the working relationship. Based on Beam's assessment of Scrushy, the idea of the psychopath is worth considering.

Psychopathy and Antisocial Personality as Related Concepts in a Leader

Beam calls Scrushy a con artist. *Con artist* is a lay term for a psychopath, at least in the small-time version. The realization that psychopaths are in leadership positions is not new. The Hare psychopathy model is developed conceptually in a book entitled *Snakes in Suits*, in which the understanding of the psychopath is compared with observations of executives.[12] It is an intriguing idea.

Here is what Aaron Beam had to say about his CEO:

> As brilliant as Richard was in his business dealings, he was equally diabolical, callous, and cruel in his justification for attaining success. Unbeknownst to me from the onset was the fact that Richard was an egotist of the highest order, a consummate narcissist, likely a sociopath, and one of the biggest liars and fraudsters to ever lead a Fortune 500 company.[13]

This perception of Scrushy by Beam highlights the poor regard Beam had for his CEO and the terrible dilemma he found himself in. Though in a powerful role, he was trapped and not strong enough psychologically to break out of the trap.

With the information available, a diagnosis of psychopathy cannot be made.[14] Yet if a narcissistic leader is prone to making decisions without regard for others or legitimate ethical or even legal cautions, the environment is at great risk for financial fraud.

Given the information available, the potential exists for a diagnosis of pathological narcissism. Psychiatrists who focus their careers on severe personality disorders like narcissism and who are familiar with treatment challenges highlight how the harmful and maladaptive aspects of narcissism take a significant toll on those around them.

Jerrold Post has further developed the research on inherent dangers of pathological narcissism. His research emphasis lies directly in the sweet spot of fraud and the challenges of a pathological narcissist on an organization and its employees. Above all else, Post argues that the lack of restraint by a fully formed conscience, and an extreme self-absorption, creates a dangerous alchemy for virtually no empathy and thus no social or interpersonal "brakes" when there is a risk of harm to others.[15]

Thus, like many of the concepts in this chapter, narcissistic leaders greatly affect the tone at the top. The traps created by narcissists also unfortunately align with another trap for fraud: the protective frame. The potential for isolation can be worsened by the escape from reality that a protective frame creates. Not all people will become narcissists. But if the personality is consistent with narcissism, then beware!

When leaders are narcissists, it is not the role that created the narcissist but rather a personality formation instilled early in life. Post cites the example of the mother of Robert J. Hawke, the prime minister of Australia, who indicated that she looked into the crib and knew that her newborn son would someday be prime minister. Thus she raised him to be special and through the formation of his personality, reinforced her expectations of his rise to greatness.[16]

In the period in which they become leaders, pathological narcissists have serious limitations. "The narcissist feels entitled, and when that sense of entitlement is disappointed, hurt, rage, and retaliation can occur. Underlying the rage are shame and humiliation and a feeling of helplessness to right the perceived wrong. But acting upon the rage converts the sense of helplessness into a sense of mastery."[17] This is the same shame and humiliation described earlier, but it is magnified by the leader's personality and by the power and influence of the leader's position.

The Individual and the Group: Bad Bushels Arise

The capacity to inspire, reassure, and instill confidence in trying times is essential for leadership. Yet there is also the risk of moving out of touch from dangers and threats that may include fraud. When leaders engage with followers, this can create an environment ripe for bad bushels. Rules, ethics, and laws can be run over roughshod when passions are high and a demand for action is in the air. Charisma plays a role at these times and has the potential to play a catastrophic one.

Charisma is part of a potentially destructive dynamic related to narcissism between a leader and his or her followers.[18] This system deepens the tie between what a leader creates as an image and the fit with the followers who are ready to be entranced by the charisma. It is a fitting description for the tie between Steve Jobs and those who followed Apple products as well as for Sam Walton and the employees at Walmart.

Jerrold Post notes that senior leaders and lower level employees can develop a follower and savior relationship that can border on messianic.[19] Seen in this way, as a system, there is a new fraud threat that is less about an individual narcissist and more about the bushel of bad apples that perpetrate a fraud. It is a potentially very dangerous give-and-take between the leader and those who become zealous and fanatic followers.[20]

The charismatic leader-follower dynamic can be very powerful for an organization and can help a group get through a crisis (as with Martin Luther King, for example), but it can also put the organization at risk, because it places the leader in too important a role, psychologically, for the organization. In work, profiling leaders who threaten national security, Post has defined it as a dance between "mirror-hungry" leaders, who crave the stage, and ideal-hungry followers, who want to follow someone they imagine to be faultless. Together they fit like lock and key, per Post.[21]

The first part of the dynamic is the leader. These leaders, whose basic psychological constellation is the grandiose self, hunger for confirming and admiring responses to counteract their poor inner sense of self-worth and lack of self-esteem. To nourish their famished selves, they are compelled to display themselves in order to evoke the attention of others. No matter how positive the response, they cannot be satisfied, and they continue to seek new audiences from whom to elicit the attention and recognition they crave.

The second required feature of this charismatic dynamic is of course the followers, the ideal-hungry personality types who can experience themselves as worthwhile only as long as they are relating to individuals whom they can admire for their prestige, power, beauty, intelligence, or moral stature.[22]

Those who are concerned about fraud recognize that when it is combined with an organization that is vulnerable (e.g., aggressive competitors, a global recession, a crisis in product quality, loss of a key supplier) there is the potential for this dynamic to develop. For example, facing tough competition, economic headwinds, or crisis in the leadership team, the charismatic leader/follower dynamic can hardly solve problems neither the leader nor the employees nor board want to fully address. Leaders who speak with confidence and exhibit no self-doubt during times the organization is wounded can pull those who are ideal-hungry into this dance. Many despots have risen to power in this way. Ken Lay at Enron appears to have played this role, for he sold his stock before it lost value while at the same time promoting a message of confidence to employees and investors in the latter half of 2001.

As with Enron, whether or not this dynamic is temporarily successful, the system is delusional and there is ultimately a catastrophic end for the charismatic relationship between leaders and followers. This is perhaps most vividly described in Rudyard Kipling's classic story "The Man Who Would Be King." In this story of Kafiristan, ambitious British opportunists willingly accept and exploit the mantle of God in order to have access to power and wealth, only to be brought down in front of "their people" when they discover they are very much mortal: "He is neither god nor devil but a man!"[23]

For the narcissist, who is mirror-hungry for praise for financial performance, having followers who are hungry for an ideal leader can easily push him to cross the line and make up fraudulent numbers. The followers, the investors (as in the case of Bernie Madoff), put on blinders to the red flags of risk.

Here is where the tone at the top is critically important. Steven Law was Chief of Staff of the Labor Department investigating what became of the pensions at Enron. From the beginning, his analysis incriminated senior leadership. Here is what he felt happened when the leadership created a toxic culture:

> What we found was a small circle of certifiably bad actors who acted without regard for the law or for anyone else. Surrounding this inner circle was a culture that gave these employees tacit permission to run roughshod over others and break the law.
>
> While lower-level Enron employees did their jobs honorably, senior management cultivated a malignant esprit de corps that

corroded the company's ethics. The C-Suite view was that no one was smarter, faster or more aggressive than these executives. Mortals couldn't possibly understand what they did. That belief created its own closed-system logic, leading to deceptive accounting schemes, self-dealing and, ultimately, a battery of criminal convictions for Enron's top brass.[24]

Enron, as any casual observer of the American and international corporate world recognized before the collapse, was seen as one of the very best organizations in the world. This is fairly alarming as it relates to fraud risk. Is its decline and failure a sign that there are others? Are we at risk of further failures because of a crisis of the tone at the top and charismatic leader-follower dynamics? Not necessarily. There are other stories of good outcomes because of leadership. One positive outcome unfolded nearly contemporaneously as the Enron story was playing out.

Narcissistic-Like Traits: Comparing and Contrasting Three CEOs

Three CEOs sat together at an annual program for several years. Two, Dennis Kozlowski and Ken Lay, are well-known names associated with corporate fraud. The third, Harry Kraemer, is a colleague in the study of leadership and values with one of the authors (Daven Morrison). The program was structured based on the size of the participating organizations, and the individual CEOs sat alphabetically by surname, viz., Kozlowski, Kraemer, and Lay.

The contrast among these leaders helps us to understand the possible mechanisms for what CEOs do or don't do that "inoculate" them against fraud. See Exhibit 7.1.

Here is a tone-at-the-top story about Kraemer's tenure as Baxter's CEO. In 2001, there were reports of death following dialysis in Spain:

> The dialysis filters used in all of the cases had come from a single lot—the same lot as the filters used in Madrid. They had been manufactured by Althin Medical AB, which had been acquired in March 2000 by the American company Baxter International Inc.
>
> The U.S. business press didn't report much on the situation. News of the deaths was soon eclipsed, first by the profound tragedy of September 11 and then by the opening bars of Enron's

Exhibit 7.1   Comparison and Contrast of CEOs

	Dennis Kozlowski	Harry Kraemer	Kenneth Lay
Organization	Tyco	Baxter	Enron
Size of organization	$19 billion	$12 billion	$101 billion
Industry	Security, fire protection, and flow control	Healthcare	Energy (power and natural gas)
Number of employees	106,000	50,000	22,000
Extent of fraud	$100M plus in unauthorized bonuses and purchased art	None	Financial restatements from 1997–2000: additional $591M in losses and additional. $628M in liabilities.
Repercussions	Embarrassment of organization	None (no fraud)	Market capitalization lost (billions), personal fortunes lost, tens of thousands unemployed, California energy grid sabotaged. Disgrace and dissolution of Arthur Andersen, employer of 85,000+ people in 84 countries.
Penalty to CEO	Surrender of wealth, incarceration	None (no fraud)	Found guilty but died before sentencing, so conviction was vacated
Practice of self-reflection, genuine humility	Unclear	Consistently; teaches course and wrote text	No evidence
Ranking in terms of financial losses (Lehman is #1)	Not readily determinable	Not readily determinable	#3 (was #1, then surpassed by WorldCom and Lehman)

opera of greed and deceit. Over the next few weeks, though, a total of 53 deaths in the United States and six other countries would be linked circumstantially to Baxter's filters. It wasn't clear until later that the filters were to blame. To this day, it isn't clear exactly what went wrong.

But what was certain was this: Baxter and its CEO, Harry M. Jansen Kraemer Jr., faced a moment of truth. How Baxter responded would leave a lasting imprint on the company's relationships with patients and doctors, with employees, and, of course, with investors. The episode would, for better or worse, open a window onto Baxter's corporate soul.[25]

Despite not knowing what went wrong, Harry Kraemer quickly decided that the best course of action was to stop filter production at critical European plants. This was not an inconsequential decision: Baxter stock dropped and cost the company $189 million in earnings. But Harry Kraemer took the high road. Later it was determined that the problem went beyond Baxter's manufacturing department and involved other organizations in the supply chain. Yet Kraemer did not blame others, nor did he allow Baxter to postpone making the decision, and Baxter settled promptly with all affected families.

The values behind Baxter's actions led to a long-term, very positive esteem of the organization in its market. It supported pride in the employees and sustained trust in the health-care field, where trust is essential not only for the marketplace but also for healing. Al Heller, the president of Baxter's renal division, ultimately supported the effort to do what was right for the customers, the patients. This is a sharp contrast to the leadership of organizations in which there is fraud.

> Respect, responsiveness, results—people at Baxter actually believe that stuff. "Do the right thing"—Kraemer repeats it ad nauseum. So does everyone else. People know what it means. And it sticks. That's why Kraemer could drive off that Saturday confident that Heller would act responsibly. "If I didn't think Al would do the right thing on this one, I had a much bigger issue," he says.[26]

These values were product of the CEO and the leadership team (not quite the leadership picture at Tyco or Enron). This story also sharply contrasts with the way Richard Scrushy related to his leadership team. Larger lessons beyond those at HealthSouth help us to understand what happens when organizations drift away from a solid course like Baxter's to one that jeopardizes clients, employees, and even the credibility of entire markets.

The Science of Persuasion

As the case of HealthSouth illustrates, senior leadership (15 executives in all) wreaked havoc on an entire industry and in the end there was a $2.7 billion fraud. This example shows how the C-suite is the gateway for frauds escalating from the bushel to the crop. To understand the transitions, we must move out of the study of individuals and into the study of large groups. This requires an analysis of what happens when groups of people are persuaded to be deceived. As we examine this, we will see that the corrosive effects of the bad apple (and the mechanism used by the bad apple) drive the forces in the bushel and the crop.

Robert B. Cialdini, a professor emeritus of psychology and marketing at Arizona State University, is best known for his popular book on persuasion and marketing, *Influence: The Psychology of Persuasion*. It has sold more than 2 million copies and has been translated into 26 languages.[27]

In writing the book, Cialdini spent three years undercover, applying for jobs and training at used-car dealerships, fund-raising organizations, and telemarketing firms to observe real-life situations of persuasion. His book reviews many of the most important theories and experiments in social psychology and suggests six techniques that may be employed to influence others. The six techniques are listed next, with a short description of each and an integration of it with what has been presented thus far:

1. **Reciprocation.** This deeply embedded social rule is what makes us feel obligated to repay someone who has provided us with a gift, favor, or concession. People tend to return a favor—thus the pervasiveness of free samples in marketing. The good cop–bad cop strategy is also based on this principle.

   Reciprocations are highly emotionally weighted events and are connected to the mechanisms highlighted in the cases of the phisherman and HealthSouth as well as those on Wall Street.

2. **Commitment and consistency.** Most people act in consistent ways because this is valued by society, provides a beneficial approach to daily life, and simplifies adjusting to a new process by relying on past decisions. Harvard psychologist and philosopher William James observed that "habit is the enormous flywheel of society."[28]

   If people commit, orally or in writing, to an idea or a goal, they are more likely to honor that commitment because it is congruent with their self-image. Even if the original incentive or motivation is removed after they have already agreed to the idea, they will continue to honor the agreement. For example, in car sales, this is seen when the price is suddenly raised at the last moment because the buyer has already decided to buy.

When the written consent of the car buyer is thus exploited, we have a case of the social glue of shame and embarrassment being used maladaptively to take advantage of someone through intimidation rather than reinforcing social rules as noted in Part II.

3. **Social proof.** One important way people make decisions is by looking to see what others are doing or believing in that arena. This happens even more so in situations of uncertainty or when people believe that the others being observed are similar to themselves.

   People will do things that they see other people doing. For example, in one experiment, one or more confederates would look up at the sky, and the bystanders would then look up to see what they were seeing. At one point this experiment had to be aborted because so many people were looking up that they stopped traffic.

   Social proof highlights the power of relationships and how the core emotions we feel betray us when we are threatened by the loss of belonging. Again, it relies on the power of shame.

4. **Liking.** People are easily persuaded by, and want to buy from, people they know and like. Physical attractiveness, similarity, and familiarity are three qualities that increase this tendency. Cialdini cites the marketing of Tupperware in what would now be called viral marketing. People were more likely to buy the product if they liked the person who was selling it. Some of the many biases toward attractive people are discussed by Cialdini.

   In sales, there is the well-established know-like-trust-buy cycle, something that Bernie Madoff figured out only too well. Based on her interviews with Madoff, journalist Diana Henriques claimed that Madoff was quite the charmer, and "whatever their niggling doubts, [Madoff's clients are] reassuring themselves . . . about how trustworthy he is, as he spins out his vibrant, beautiful web of fantasy."[29]

   The effects of interest and excitement as well as the enjoyment of being with those we trust allow us to be fooled.

5. **Authority.** People tend to obey authority figures even when asked by them to perform objectionable acts. Cialdini cited incidents such as the Milgram experiments in the early 1960s and the My Lai massacre in the Vietnam War. There is a very

strong pressure in our society to comply with authority. Three triggers that Cialdini considered especially effective are the figure's title, clothing, and automobile.

Here the power of shame, again, reigns supreme: "Do this or you lose me!"

6. **Scarcity.** More value is assigned to messages or items that are scarce, censored, or hard to obtain. Messages that are restricted or hard to get make people want to receive them more, and the information comes across as more persuasive. This principle of influence works best when something is newly scarce and the individual is competing with others for it. Perceived scarcity will generate demand. For example, saying that an offer is available for a "limited time only" encourages sales.

Here we see the power of the effect of fear. We see this in the affects provoked in the phisherman e-mail as well as between the CFO and CEO at HealthSouth.

Conclusion

This chapter has provided the transition from the often small and insignificant bad apple fraud to the larger bad bushel or bad crop fraud. As power increases in the higher levels of management, it has the capacity to do good or bad (note that this is part of the construct of *capability* in Wolfe and Hermanson's "fraud diamond" representation). When power goes to the head of a leader who then becomes vain and insular, there is significant risk for harm. Along with missed financial targets and disrupted operations, the threat of fraud is significant.

Here is where the behavioral sciences can offer a great deal, yet the reversals of executives in terms of narcissism and psychopathy are not yet very well understood. This is the beginning of many explorations into what might be going on, based mostly on actual evaluations of senior leaders as well as relevant research into what allows large groups to be manipulated or deceived.

As Harry Kraemer has noted, when a business opportunity arises, instead of asking "Is this legal?," ask "Is this the right thing to do?" To end this chapter, we leave you with an excerpt from Kraemer's best-selling book:

> Values not only create competitive advantages when it comes to developing the workforce or customer relationships but also can guard against damage. Consider the CEO lament: "I

always thought that if what we were doing was legal, everything would be okay. As long as we adhered to the letter of the law, I never thought there would be a problem." There wouldn't be a problem if the line between legal and illegal were a solid black, immovable boundary. The truth is that the boundary between legal and illegal is a fuzzy gray, ill-defined line—and it moves. When organizations allow their actions to hug the line, there is a great danger that one of these days, they'll find themselves on the wrong side, even if their practices didn't change. What used to be legal became questionable, and then was determined to be illegal.

When this happens, most companies try to get back on the right side of the line as quickly as possible before anyone (especially the regulators) finds out about it. But once you're on the wrong side, it's very hard to cross back because often the line may have moved substantially. Then, in spite of all the good intentions to be compliant with the letter of the law, a company ends up violating it.

Rather than focusing solely on what's legal, a company would be far better off to consider what's right.[30]

Notes

1. For instance, according to the recently issued 2013 Internal Control Integrated Framework of the Committee of Sponsoring Organizations of the Treadway Commission, tone at the top refers to the consistent development and communication of expectations regarding internal control, including monitoring and is one of the most important features of an effective control environment. See www.coso.org. Ultimately we must ask the question so beautifully expressed by the second-century Roman poet Juvenal, "But who will guard the guards themselves?"
2. See "Executive Assessment" at Morrison Associates, Ltd., in Appendix B.
3. We wish to thank Harry Kraemer for this characterization, which he uses in his MBA class at Northwestern University in Evanston, Illinois.
4. Rick Anicetti, former president and CEO, Food Lion LLC, a U.S. organization of roughly 1,500 grocery stores and 72,000 employees, in personal communication with coauthor Daven Morrison, March 15, 2008.
5. Michael C. Jensen, "The Modern Industrial Revolution, Exit, and the Failure of Internal Control Systems." *Journal of Finance* 48 (1993): 831–880 esp. 863.
6. Michael Maccoby, *The Productive Narcissist: The Promise and Peril of Visionary Leadership* (New York: Broadway, 2003).
7. Ibid., 132.
8. Ibid., 244.

9. In the face of material fraud, the one thing that CEOs cannot do is use the "chutzpah defense," or what came to be called the "Aw, shucks" defense when WorldCom CEO Bernard J. Ebbers claimed that he had "no expert knowledge of accounting and no idea that any fraud was going on at WorldCom." See M. T. Biegelman and J. T. Bartow, *Executive Roadmap to Fraud Prevention and Internal Control: Creating a Culture of Compliance* (Hoboken, NJ: John Wiley & Sons, 2006), for a fuller description of such hollow defense strategies in the courtroom.

10. Maccoby, *The Productive Narcissist*, 134.

11. Personal communication with Daven Morrison.

12. Robert Hare and Paul Babiak, *Snakes in Suits: When Psychopaths Go to Work* (New York: HarperCollins, 2006).

13. Aaron Beam and Chris Warner, *HealthSouth: The Wagon to Disaster* (Fairhope, AL: Wagon, 2009), 12.

14. This is possibly true of Scrushy, but for ethical reasons we cannot make a diagnosis of psychopathy here. Narcissism, too, can be diagnosed only in person and by a trained mental health professional. This creates a dilemma in risk management. A leader who has enough power will never consent to be evaluated by a psychiatrist—especially if the leader is a narcissist, a psychopath, or both.

15. Jerrold Post, *Dreams of Glory: Narcissism and Politics* (Cambridge, UK: Cambridge University Press, in press).

16. Ibid.

17. Ibid.

18. Jerrold Post, *Personality and the Foundations of Political Behavior* (Cambridge, UK: Cambridge University Press, in press).

19. Jerrold Post, *Leaders and Their Followers in a Dangerous World: The Psychology of Political Behavior* (New York: Cornell University Press, 2004), 198–199.

20. Recent research appears to confirm such a possibility, viz., V. S. Khanna, E. H. Kim, and Y. Lu, *CEO Connectedness and Corporate Frauds.* Michigan Law Review: Public Law and Legal Theory Research Paper Series. Paper #283. June 2012.

21. Ibid.

22. Ibid., 109

23. Rudyard Kipling, "The Man Who Would Be King," in *The Phantom Rickshaw and Other Eerie Tales* (Allahabad, India: A. H. Wheeler, 1888).

24. Steven Law, "What Enron and the IRS Have in Common, *Wall Street Journal,* June 5, 2013.

25. Keith H. Hammonds, "Harry Kraemer's Moment of Truth," *Fast Company* 64 (October 2002).

26. Ibid.

27. Robert B. Cialdini, *Influence: The Psychology of Persuasion* (New York: HarperCollins, 2007).

28. William H. James, *Habit* (New York: H. Holt & Co, 1914). This work is now in the public domain at www.archive.org/details/habitjam00jameuoft.

29. Diana B. Henriques, *The Wizard of Lies: Bernie Madoff and the Death of Trust* (New York: Times Books/Henry Holt & Company, 2012), 363.

30. Harry Kraemer, *From Values to Action: The Four Principles of Values-Based Leadership* (San Francisco: Jossey-Bass, 2011).

Robert Weber, *The New Yorker*, August 26, 1991

"It's up to you now, Miller. The only thing that can save us is an accounting breakthrough."

PART

III

A CALL TO ACTION

Given that fraud, folly, and foibles are all part of human nature, what are the implications for fraud prevention, deterrence, and detection?

This issue raises an interesting question. All of the information, theories, and citations are nice, but do they affect your performance as a (risk) manager, an auditor, a regulator, an investor, a financial analyst, or a business leader? Can you improve in how you perform in your position? Depending on how you want to utilize what you have learned thus far, this can be a complex issue because it has many component parts.

We are dealing with one of the most productive and yet potent forces on the face of the earth: the human mind. We ask a simple but profound question: What causes people to do some of the things they do?

In answering this question we need to be concerned about two well-known biases in psychology: the fundamental attribution error, and the confirmation bias. The *fundamental attribution error* is a bedrock concept in social psychology. When we are trying to understand and explain another's behavior, we tend to do so in terms of that person's internal disposition, such as personality traits, abilities, and motives, as opposed to external situational factors (which may be highly relevant). This can be a result of the so-called actor-observer bias, because our focus is on the person more than the situation, about which we may know very little or nothing at all. We also could be quite uninformed, and even wrong, about how the person is interpreting the situation. Western culture exacerbates this error, since it emphasizes individual freedom and autonomy and people are socialized to prefer dispositional factors to situational ones. When we are playing the role of observer, typically when we look at others, we make this fundamental attribution error. When we are thinking about ourselves, however, we will tend to (properly) make situational attributions, perhaps because we understand our own situational context so much better.

Confirmation bias, in contrast, is our human tendency to engage in selective perception, to see what we want to see.[1] We judge the facts in light of the position we already hold or in a way that makes us look better than we really are. We simultaneously undermine and discount the facts that tend to contradict our position as being flawed. At least part of this tendency is unconscious.[2]

Yet given the analysis of those who commit fraud and the fundamentals of the human mind, as a reader of this book, you will now be much more fully aware, armed, and resourceful. Salespeople are aware that "a tactic known is a tactic blown." In the world of fraud, now that you know more about the fraudster's mind-set, the role of emotions and relationships and how they can be manipulated, and the power and capability of the C-suite, you are well prepared to perceive the warning signs of fraud and recommend deterrence measures.

What remains is to clarify as far as possible what has been shared in this book. As you will read in the appendices, fraudsters out there recognize the power of the lessons in these pages and would rather you not know them. See "The Art of Spinning" by convicted felon Samuel Antar that is reproduced in Appendix B.

So what does one do differently as a result of understanding what this book has presented in terms of behavioral forensics concepts, ideas, and insights? What ought one do differently on Monday morning?

Understanding fraudster motivation with primary reference to financial fraud—what makes white-collar con men and women tick—remains our principal concern. In this regard, we need to absorb and assimilate the following four things:

1. **Numbers and reality.** We live in a quantitative world—a cold, hard, and precise world of numbers. They just stare at us from a computer screen or a spreadsheet. They are "reality." Then again, they are not. A computer, a spreadsheet, or a general ledger, by itself, never produced a number in the history of human civilization. People produce the numbers and sometimes fabricate them. It can be useful to delve a little deeper and try to understand the motivations behind the numbers. Numbers are easily manipulated. Witness the implosion of major Wall Street firms in the last decade. The numbers appeared to tell the story, but the numbers did not create themselves. People did, for their own reasons. Much of the deception, it has been suggested, was to benefit the compensation packages of Wall Street executives. They got financial rewards for immediate results and thus tended to minimize long-term consequences. The numbers were there, but there was little consideration of why they were there. Known factors leading to previous stock bubbles and corporate malfeasance were simply ignored, and the so-called system of checks and balances effectively compromised.[3]

   Begin to realize the human and psychological aspects of what you see and deal with every day. Study the theories and the research about motivations for fraud. Attend seminars, listen to lectures, and read widely.[4] Try to learn more about the human side of your world. This will be a lifelong process, but you will get better at understanding what anthropologists call patterns *of* behavior as well as patterns *for* behavior.

2. **People's ability to change.** We have discussed this with reference to psychologist Michael J. Apter's reversal theory.

   An otherwise nice person may commit a cruel act at some point. A usually cruel person may exhibit some acts of kindness. The actions may change dramatically in a matter of minutes. A great case in point is illustrated in Truman Capote's murder mystery *In Cold Blood*. This was the true story of two small-time criminals in Kansas who, while in prison, heard of a rural farmer who was supposed to have a safe full of cash in his house.

Once released, they got a shotgun and drove to the farm-house in the middle of the night. They gained access easily because the doors were not locked. But there was no safe and thus no money.

The lead character was Perry, a small-time criminal. When his partner, also a small-time criminal, wanted to rape the farmer's 12-year-old daughter, Perry deterred him at gunpoint. While the farmer's son was tied up on a sofa in the basement recreation room, Perry put a pillow under his head so he would be more comfortable.

After their fruitless search was done, Perry went from room to room and killed each person with the shotgun. The criminals stole a transistor radio and six dollars in change. They were later arrested, tried, and executed.

Perry went from being a criminal with moments of compassion toward his victims to being their executioner in about 15 minutes.

This is an extreme example, but it is meant to show how quickly and how much people can change. The trusted employee or partner may change quite suddenly. Awareness of this psychological possibility can be useful. There is often no apparent logic to human behavior—at least none that we can readily see, much less comprehend.

3. **Fraud's tendency to evolve.** Because acts of fraud are very much inspired by calculated thoughts from one or more human minds, and because of the spectacular advances in technology and communication, the sophistication of fraud is increasing every day. Clearly, to keep abreast of all such evolution, public policy, legislation, and law enforcement need to evolve commensurately. A Nigerian proverb comes to mind: "When the mouse laughs at the cat, there must be a hole nearby." Trends in cybercrime indicate that some of the frauds being perpetrated in the twenty-first century (e.g., phishing and scamming, use of stolen credit cards, and other forms of identity theft) simply could not even be conceived of in the twentieth century because the Internet did not exist in its full-fledged form then. So one of the most fruitful collaborations in the fight against fraud is the combination of behavioral and digital forensics in conjunction with the impressive collection of financial/accounting analytical

approaches that now constitute the financial forensics body of knowledge.[5]

4. **The A.B.C. taxonomy.** Fraud can be perpetrated by a rogue executive (a bad apple, acting alone) or a colluding group of individuals (whether Enron traders or an insider trading ring), or it can occur in the context of a toxic culture—an entire industry, such as a pharmaceutical industry paying kickbacks or a corrupt political regime in a country. Thinking about fraud incidence in such broad terms can greatly assist with targeted fraud deterrence efforts and in developing appropriate response plans when fraud is discovered. It can also prompt reflection on how to avoid a repeat of such catastrophic risks materializing again.

In the closing chapters of this book, the point we wish to make is both simple and frustrating: People tend to focus on numbers rather than on the mind. The human mind is an elusive target, but it is there and it is important; we ignore it at our own peril. But we do not have a panacea or a silver bullet to present to you. Study, preparation, and awareness of the human factors can be very useful.

Notes

1. Perhaps we even want to hear what we wish to hear and already know. Consider Nobel laureate in physics Enrico Fermi's charming observation, "One should never underestimate the pleasure we feel from hearing something we already know."

2. Confirmation bias is related to cognitive dissonance that Stanford psychologist Leon Festinger described as a "state of tension that occurs whenever a person holds two cognitions that are psychologically inconsistent." Motivated reasoning, simply put, is biased reasoning. See blogpost by Sam McNerney, "Psychology's Treacherous Trio: Confirmation Bias, Cognitive Dissonance, and Motivated Reasoning," September 7, 2011, http://whywereason.com/2011/09/07/psychologys-treacherous-trio-confirmation-bias-cognitive-dissonance-and-motivated-reasoning/#.

3. A compelling narrative is provided in Bethany McLean and Joe Nocera, *All the Devils Are Here: The Hidden History of the Financial Crisis* (New York: Penguin, 2010).

4. Some excellent books on the subject of behavioral economics include: R. H. Thaler and C. R. Sunstein, *Nudge: Improving Decisions About Health, Wealth, and Happiness* (New York: Penguin, 2009); Daniel Ariely, *Predictably Irrational: The Hidden Forces That Shape Our Decisions* (New York: HarperCollins, 2008); Daniel Ariely, *The Upside of Irrationality: The Unexpected Benefits of Defying Logic at Work and at Home* (New York: HarperCollins, 2010); Daniel Ariely, *The (Honest)*

Truth about Dishonesty: How We Lie to Everyone—Especially Ourselves (New York: HarperCollins, 2012); and Daniel Kahneman, *Thinking Fast and Slow* (New York: Farrar, Straus and Giroux, 2011).

5. Darrell D. Dorrell and Gregory A. Gadawski, *Financial Forensics Body of Knowledge* (Hoboken, NJ: John Wiley & Sons, 2012).

8

Managing the Ecology of Fraud

WHAT YOU CAN DO ON MONDAY MORNING

This chapter begins with a discussion of the markets in order that we may more closely examine the moral foundations of capitalism. Specifically, we demonstrate that illegal and unethical behaviors, if condoned, soon snowball and have compound, ripple effects because, in the final analysis, markets are based on trust and confidence in the interactions of the market participants. In fact, it is to maintain market confidence that the whole auditing profession was devised in the first place. In the 1920s, University of Amsterdam professor Theodore Limperg propounded his "theory of inspired confidence." Limperg set forth a dynamic theory that connects society's need for reliable financial information to the ability of auditing methods to meet that need. He asserted that the confidence inspired by the independent auditor was the essence of the function, its very reason for existing.[1] We also explore the role of ethical behavior in sustaining organizations for the long run.

We then discuss what can be done to help executives stay on the right side of the line. After all, in the final analysis, leadership, especially stewardship, is about caring about one's employees, one's clients, and one's career, and that requires a great degree of competence and professionalism. "Good ethics is good business" and makes for healthy, sustainable organizations.[2]

Whenever questionable ethical behavior surfaces, emotions are likely involved. To understand emotional manipulation, there is no better place to go to than psychologist Robert Cialdini's work on the "science of persuasion," introduced in Chapter 7. When fraudsters put on the charm offensive, they pull it off in style, almost in the manner of applied psychologists. So it is helpful to understand exactly how they go about doing this. Appendix B provides more on the fraudster's specific modus operandi in this regard.

This chapter also looks at the role of lies and misrepresentation in trust violation and the perpetration of fraud. Research on detecting misrepresentation in the context of financial statements can help us to understand the two different kinds of lies: suggestion of falsehood *(suggestio falsi)* and suppression of truth *(suppressio veri)*.

As a companion to the conceptual fraud triangle (opportunity, pressure or incentive, and rationalization), which offers a framework to recognize the elements of fraud, we consider the operational fraud triangle. The elements of the operational fraud triangle are the act, the cover-up, and the conversion, and this triangle can be extremely useful in tracking the audit trail and in following the money. We will look at the psychological factors involved in each of these operational variables.

Finally, we present our thoughts on what you can learn from this book to do things differently on Monday morning.

The Financial Markets: The Moral Foundations of Capitalism

Economist Geoff Hodgson began his discussion of exchange value and costs by quoting Anacharsis of Scythia (ca. 600 BCE): "The market is a place set apart where men may deceive one another."[3] It is important, therefore, to understand what ethics and morals, if any, apply in the marketplace. The father of modern economics, Adam Smith, was actually a professor of moral philosophy in Glasgow, Scotland. He wrote *A Theory of Moral Sentiments* in 1759, a good 17 years before his magnum opus, *The Wealth of Nations*, was published. Jonathan Wight, an economics professor at the University of Richmond (Virginia), does an admirable job of describing Smith's stance on virtue and ethics in his own book, *Saving Adam Smith: A Tale of Wealth, Transformation, and Virtue.*

It is clear that we have come a long way from Smith's conceptions of the moral foundations of capitalism. Economics as a discipline today, dubbed an "amoral science," is quite distinct from moral and ethical considerations and concerns itself more with efficiency than with equity. *Economic incentives* has pretty much come to mean "more money," yet the behavioral sciences are pretty clear in showing that people are motivated by much more than money. Where pathology and deviance are involved, people may be driven by urges or frenzies they scarcely understand, and money is at best a symptom, not the cause, of their behavior.

The emergence of behavioral economics as a credible field of study is greatly adding to our knowledge of human behavior and helping to make economics real. Starting with the observation that human beings exhibit only "bounded rationality," Nobel laureate Herbert Simon emphasized that such realistic assumptions are critical in economic modeling. Only then would it be possible to adequately explain the causes of human behavior while taking into account the institutional framework in which people make decisions in the real world.

Behavioral economics incorporates much more than psychology, however. Morris Altman noted, "Models also need to make assumptions that take into account norms, peer pressure, culture, religion, differences in tastes and preferences, power relationships, gender, and past behaviors. Plus, assumptions need to capture the reality of the legal and overall incentive environment, which can differ across communities and societies."[4]

In particular, as a challenge to the conventional economics view that treats markets as perfectly rational and efficient, behavioral economics and an allied discipline, behavioral finance, have started taking a close look at the notions of economic efficiency (and inefficiency) and economic bubbles. Specifically, behavioral economists have introduced the idea of animal spirits.[5] Using this construct, it is possible to factor emotions, intuition, and social context into the modeling of business cycles and make the models more robust for both explanation and prediction.

Another important angle to consider is business ethics and integrity. It is more than curious that the notion of stewardship is hardly mentioned in the economics literature. The theory of stewardship draws from the disciplines of sociology and psychology. Stewardship asserts a model in which individuals act to serve the collective interests, in contrast to economics-based agency concepts of people as individualistic, opportunistic, and self-serving. Stewardship presumes that the board and management take their fiduciary obligations seriously and will act in the best interest of the firm's stakeholders, even when their interests are not aligned, because they place greater value on cooperation than on self-serving behavior.[6]

In her award-winning essay for the 2012 Ethics for a Connected World contest, Laura J. Rediehs, an associate professor of philosophy at St. Lawrence University, Canton, New York, persuasively wrote, "The biggest ethical challenge facing us today is that we have let economics replace ethics as a guide to life, and in doing so, we have devalued people and the associated virtues of respect, cooperation, empathy, and compassion."[7]

Lamenting how business schools may have failed in educating students, University of North Carolina at Chapel Hill professor Michael Jacobs wrote the following in the *Wall Street Journal*:

> Could we have avoided most of the economic problems we now face if we had a generation of business leaders who were trained in designing compensation systems that promote long-term value? And who were educated in the proper make-up and responsibilities of boards? And who were enlightened as to how shareholders can use their proxies to affect accountability? I think we could have. America's business schools need to rethink what we are teaching—and not teaching—the next generation of leaders.[8]

In 2006, Arizona State University professor Marianne Jennings wrote the very insightful book *Seven Signs of Ethical Collapse: How to Spot Moral Meltdowns Before It's Too Late*. An article summarizing the book stated the following:

> Since 2001, Marianne Jennings, professor of management at the W. P. Carey School of Business at Arizona State University, has kept a list of companies that have succumbed to ethical collapse, some for the second time. These are companies like General Electric, Merrill Lynch, AT&T, Arthur Andersen, [and] United Health Group. There are so many, in fact, that she's running out of room on the PowerPoint slide she uses for presentations and had to squeeze in the final entry "the stock options (160 companies)."[9]

Jennings believed that these were great companies that employed good people. But they made her list for one reason: They crossed a very bright and distinct ethical line; they were not close calls. The list grows almost daily. But it doesn't have to, she insisted.

In a presentation at the April 5, 2007, meeting of the Business and Organizational Ethics Partnership, Jennings noted the common characteristics of the misguided companies. Had they heeded the warning signs, she said, they could have employed potent antidotes (which she also presented) to prevent the moral meltdowns.

The seven common threads that Jennings found that make good people at great companies do really dumb, unethical things are the following:

Unethical Decisions Made by Employees
- Pressure to maintain numbers
- Fear and silence
- Young employees and a bigger-than-life CEO
- A weak board of directors
- Conflicts of interest that are overlooked or unaddressed
- Innovation like no other company
- Goodness in some areas atoning for evil in others

Lynn Brewer, a former Enron employee and now at the Integrity Institute in Seattle, argued that fraud has become a large part of the history of capitalism, and yet, unfortunately, it may actually be part of the glue that is holding the global economy together. In fact, she asserted, the global economy *depends* on fraud—so much so that if you asked Enron employees whether Enron was a highly ethical or highly unethical company, 90 percent would have said highly unethical. But if the same employees were asked if they themselves were highly unethical individuals, they would deny the claim, indicating an unconscious gap between the individuals and the corporation, which proved to be the greatest threat to the company's sustainability.

This illustrates the concept of *cognitive dissonance*, the driving force that compels humans to acquire or invent new thoughts or beliefs, or to modify existing ones, to minimize the amount of conflict between their actions and their values. It is a fundamental disconnect though, with serious ramifications for the individual, his or her organizations, and society at large.

We need a rethinking of the moral foundations of capitalism with reference to corporate governance models that are based on stewardship and stakeholder theory. This line of reasoning allows us to incorporate the perspective of a triple bottom line: economic returns (profit), social and community development (people), and environmental sustainability and conservation (planet).

Financial and stock market scandals in the last four centuries reveal that there are slick operators who are well motivated to swindle the unsuspecting investing public. They are able to do this because of the human desire to acquire "easy money" or "spectacular returns" (indeed, so spectacular that they are completely fabricated).

Helping Senior Executives to Stay on the Right Side of the Line

In the rush to make a deal, keep up with competitors, avoid a downturn in the market, and reward a "rainmaker"—a person who is capable of generating a tremendous volume of sales or recruiting a top talent—senior executive teams may turn to their legal counsel with the question of whether something they want to do is legal. A team typically asks for legal advice because it wants to exploit a competitive advantage in the hope of making something happen, but it knows that there is a risk as they look to see how close they can get to the line of legality.

Is It Legal?

"Is it legal?" is a seductive question. Smart people like to answer it, especially if they are in a playful mood of brainstorming or strategizing about what is possible. It is also easier when one is in the protective frame of a retreat or under the charms of a narcissistic leader. It is particularly challenging if the entire C-suite is excited about the opportunity that remains within the bounds of legality.

Senior executives are smart people. Legal advisors are also generally very smart and often want to satisfy their clients. They have bills to pay, too. Although intelligence is in many ways an advantage for problem solving, unfortunately, smart people are also better able to rationalize bad decisions. Their intellect gets in the way of the morally right answer.

This was evident on many levels at Enron. Writer Malcolm Gladwell noted that Enron had bought into the "all star effect": a model of intellect rewarding star performers above all else; a solution brought to the company by McKinsey, another organization known for having highly intelligent people.[10] Jeffrey Skilling, a McKinsey partner before he became Enron CEO, was infamous for responding to an interviewer at Harvard Business School (as portrayed in the documentary film *Enron: The Smartest Guys in the Room*), "Am I smart? I am f***ing smart!"

Is It the Right Thing to Do?

Because of this dilemma, the wrong question is asked or the whole issue is neglected. The right question is (as we noted in Chapter 7's example of Harry Kraemer's teachings) "Is it the right thing to do?" After asking the question, however, the other problem, as Kraemer effectively pointed out, is that the line between what's legal and what's right is not static—it moves. What is legal at one point in how business is done might not always be. He noted that many leadership teams get stuck because they find themselves on the wrong side and then dig in deeper trying to "lawyer" their way out. The essence of leadership and stewardship lies in being able to ask such difficult questions and arrive at the right answer every time.

Intelligent people are very capable at generating rationalizations. The more brilliant they are the better the reason given. This requires a senior leader to know his or her people well and to be able to tell when they are falling in love with their water-tight rationalizations.

Thus, what remains for organizations and individuals managing risk is to begin to master the skill of deconstructing rationalizations. Asking "Is it legal?" is the genesis of a rationalization. Rationalizations that lead to fraud must be pierced.

Piercing the Rationalizations

Given the complexity of the motivations, the capacity to reverse a course of honesty, and the power of shame to bully professionals and lower level staff, it is obvious that the ecology must not support rationalizations for fraud. We now present a framework for understanding how one might go about piercing the rationalizations offered up by convicted white-collar criminals. This framework has three levels:

1. **Background and context.** On the first level, we have information about the surface characteristics of the "crime scene" (i.e., the fraud scheme, the perpetrators and colluding parties, the amount of loss in assets or information, how the perpetrators reaped unlawful gains through their acts and

concealment, putative intent, and those harmed). We might call this the "tip of the iceberg."

2. **Stimulus factors or manifest variables.** On the second level, we start considering the proximate cause of the white-collar crime, including the rationalizations offered up by the perpetrators, either as a means of justifying their behavior (to themselves or to others) or of deflecting attention from the truth. We need to distinguish the apparent from the real reasons a white-collar criminal acted in a certain fashion. As we dig deeper through probing questions, we might discover motivations such as cognitive dissonance, revenge, crimes of passion, cultural norms such as honor killing, catch-me-if-you-can games, family pride, and noble cause corruption. This might be called "what meets the eye."

3. **Personality, psychological factors, and latent variables.** On the third level, explanations may occasionally correspond with level 2 rationalizations; however, it is also possible that we may never know. This might be called "more than what meets the eye." Careful study and analysis of convicted felons' biographies may yield more psychological insights.

As we construct this framework of analysis, other theories, such as counterfactual thinking and reasoning, become relevant. This "woulda, coulda shoulda" reasoning is very common among fraud perpetrators and typically precedes the commission of a crime.[11] It involves the interjection of the conscience. The conscience is what guides us and informs us if something is the right thing to know or do. It is the last and final possibility that the fraud perpetrator will decide not to engage in behavior—the point after which there may be no turning back.

Here are some telling level 2 examples:

- To the question "Why do you rob banks?," famous bank robber Willie Sutton allegedly replied, "Because that's where the money is."
- Former Satyam Computer Systems CEO B. R. Raju described his cooking-the-books compulsion thus: "[It was] like riding a tiger without knowing how to get off without being eaten."
- Bernie Madoff: "I was surprised that I wasn't caught earlier by the SEC."

These examples demonstrate that the conscience did exist in these criminals, and that the approach of delving into the mind of the fraudster has merit and potential. However, we are at a fairly nascent stage of research on this topic of piercing rationalizations.

Emotional Manipulation

Beyond the interpersonal emotional manipulation of an actual fraud, there are broader dynamics known that can be watched for in order to be able to pierce rationalizations before they take root. Understanding what is healthy and what is more maladaptive is important to clarify. Arizona State University psychologist Robert Cialdini's work is instrumental for recognizing the difference between persuasion and manipulation.

Popular uses of emotion to influence decisions are well-known, especially in the emerging science of persuasion. Not all of these uses are criminal. People in marketing routinely use emotions to excite us about a product or service—this can only be called an attempt at persuasion. As seen in Part II, others are clearly criminal in their exploitation of emotions, making such efforts clear cases of psychological manipulation.

Social engineering in the world of computer technology, to access personal information or protected passwords, is currently a popular subject for information technology security, but the tactics used are as old as crime itself. They include a sense of distress ("I'm lost—I could use your help") or anger ("I'm a powerful person and you will be in trouble if you don't comply") and are just a step away from the Nigerian e-mail scams—the "phisherman" model that was described in some detail in Part II. Serial killers are infamous for playing helpless to seduce their victims.[12]

Fraudsters use fear to frighten us about losing our money. For example, there have been frequent e-mail scams and phishing incidents in which a threat is quickly amplified, but the victims are told that by giving out their personal information, their fear will be taken away.

Fraud is a particularly pernicious and diabolical manipulation of emotions. It is a human act that is not hidden; it happens openly in the books and records—it is there for all to see (although complexity can mask fraud). We believe that part of the distraction, similar to the bump of the pickpocket, is the manipulation of emotions in key gatekeepers, from the supervisor who assumes the salesman is being honest with his expense report to the audit engagement partner who assumes the CEO and CFO are sharing all the relevant information. In most cases, when an auditor's independence has been impaired or a conflict of interest manifests itself, the gatekeeper has had his or her silence or acquiescence purchased through personal gain.

As in e-mail frauds, senior officers may use the same negative emotions of fear and distress. They may also use the positive emotion of excitement about large bonuses or raises to distract and cajole. In addition, given their experience with power, it is likely that they are also using shame and the related emotions of contempt and disgust.

The C-suite fraudster manages to distract those who would discover the crime by essentially dismissing the questions as small-minded or the auditing profession as "bean counters." The specific tactic used on the governance or audit committee is to bypass the processes or force them to go too fast to do a proper job. Their tactic is to shame the function and the people within it. To make the leadership team, function, business unit, or even whole organization turn against the audit committee, they use their power to attack.

This works because of the power of embarrassment, or the affect of shame. In our experience, shame is a critical emotion, if not *the* critical emotion, that disrupts all workplaces. When the threat of shame is greatest, that is when the most aggressive attacks will come. All of the authors of this book are familiar with this in confronting someone who has committed a crime and is avoiding capture.

Blogger Bob Burg offered the following insight:

> Persuasion and manipulation are certainly "cousins," and to deny that is to deny reality. After all, both are based on certain principles of human action and interaction. Good persuaders . . . and good manipulators understand those principles and know how to effectively utilize them. That's why there is perhaps nothing more dangerous than a bad person with good people skills. Yes, the principles are similar; often even the same. In actuality, however, the results are as different as night and day. The big difference—in my opinion—is the intent.[13]

In his magnificent book, *The Art of Talking So That People Will Listen*, Paul Swets provided an outstanding explanation of both intent and outcome:

> Manipulation aims at control, not cooperation. It results in a win/lose situation. It does not consider the good of the other party. Persuasion is just the opposite. In contrast to the manipulator, the persuader seeks to enhance the self-esteem of the other party. The result is that people respond better because they are treated as responsible, self-directing individuals.[14]

Persuasion aims to serve; manipulation, to hurt. Even if manipulators don't intend to hurt, they are indifferent about doing so because they are simply so focused on themselves and their own self-interest that—like any other totally self-serving organism—they do only what they think is for their own benefit; if someone must suffer as a result, then so be it.

What they don't realize is that not only is this not good life practice, it's also not good business practice. Manipulators can have employees, but never a team. They can have customers, but rarely ones who will be long-lasting and a source of referrals. Once manipulators are discovered, their customer base tends to crumble like a stale cookie. They can have friends and family, but rarely are these relationships fulfilling and happy.

Both persuaders and manipulators know the how and why of human motivation, and both utilize their knowledge to cause the action they desire a person to take. However, the crucial difference between the two is that while manipulators use that knowledge to their own advantage, persuaders use it to the other person's advantage or to mutual advantage. This ties perfectly into the notion that your influence is determined by how abundantly you place other people's interests first. That's persuasion and leadership at its best.

On Lies and Misrepresentation

Rationalizations that become fraud need to be covered up. How a cover-up works is actually well studied. In fact, excellent research, albeit in a laboratory setting, has been done on detecting deception in the context of financial reporting fraud. Since there are two different types of misrepresentation—suggestion of falsehood and suppression of truth—different tactics are utilized by those who are attempting to deceive others.

The following are some deception tactics used for creating a financial deception:[15]

- **Masking.** Failing to record or disclose an expense or a liability.
- **Dazzling.** Disclosing information in the footnotes to the statements rather than in showing it in the body of the text.
- **Decoying.** Emphasizing legal issues (blind alleys) that after a close examination turn out to be immaterial or handled appropriately.
- **Repackaging.** Changing the descriptions or labels that characterize economic entities or reframing issues to maliciously justify the use of favorable accounting procedures.
- **Mimicking.** Creating fictitious transactions or transactions without substance.
- **Double play.** Improperly applying general accepted accounting principles to an item that is not individually material.

It is instructive to reflect on the ways in which lies may be used to mask the truth, so that one is able to pierce the veil of deception. Although the focus here is on the cognitive orientation that appeals to rationality and logic, it is not difficult to imagine that whenever lies are spread, the deceiver may also exploit human emotions (knowing the vulnerability of the victim).

New York Times reporter Floyd Norris cited the example of Nick Leeson, the rogue trader who brought down Barings Bank nearly two decades ago:

> When auditors and bosses asked how he was making all that money, Mr. Leeson later explained, he responded with meaningless but impressive sounding jargon.
>
> "Luckily for my fraud, there were too many chiefs who would chat about it at arm's length but never go further," Mr. Leeson wrote in his memoir. "And they never dared ask me any basic questions, since they were afraid of looking stupid about not understanding futures and options." Not much has changed.[16]

Note that the fear of looking stupid is very much an aspect of shame, the emotion that fraudsters exploit to their advantage, and thus it allows their risky behavior to remain unchallenged and unhindered. Knowing what you do now, how do you or your team avoid getting caught up in predator-prey dynamics? It is also worthwhile thinking about how to lead an organization that minimizes the risk of accidental fraudsters. Which code-of-conduct policies and ethics training programs will deter and dissuade accidental fraudsters from exploiting opportunities that present themselves?

Organizational culture can be conceived of as an antidote; beyond economic incentives, how do you go about building authentic relationships and underscoring stewardship in preference to leadership?

It is critical to imagine the ways you can be deceived, bringing the modus operandi of the fraudster sharply into focus. The more fruitful approach is less about the profile of the fraudster and more about how he or she goes about the act, the concealment, and the conversion.

In this regard, the thoughts of convicted felon Sam Antar of Crazy Eddie on what he called the art of spinning are noteworthy. An excerpt from his web site can be found in Appendix B.

The Operational Fraud Triangle

In exploring how fraudsters prey on their victims, we will look at the operational fraud triangle, methods of lying and lie detection, and commonsense approaches to guarding against deception. We have already discussed the conceptual fraud triangle, which consists of the three vertices of opportunity, incentive or pressure, and rationalization. In contrast, the operational fraud triangle consists of the three vertices of the act, the concealment or cover-up, and the conversion. See Exhibit 8.1.

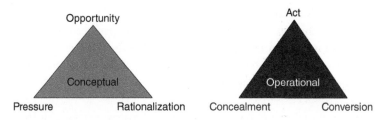

Exhibit 8.1   The Two Fraud Triangles

There is a psychology associated with each of the vertices, and we can divide the fraud life cycle into the following phases: before the fraud occurs, during the allegations and investigation, and the postfraud remediation process. Thus, whether the perpetrator operates alone or in concert with others in a toxic culture, there is a certain process that exploits the prevailing circumstances and that affords both the opportunity and the victims (who either are trusting or are thoroughly taken into confidence by the fraudster and then betrayed). The operational fraud triangle can be an extraordinarily useful aid to an investigator's or auditor's thinking. Specifically, it can lay bare the "too good to be true" syndrome and better track a follow-the-money strategy to detect fraud.

The act itself may be unethical or illegal, and it usually starts small. But once the fraudster gets away with it, he or she is emboldened to try a larger heist. In many cases, this is not the first time the white-collar criminal has engaged in deceptive behavior. Hence, these people are in a position to offer quick and convincing explanations should suspicions arise. They are frequently operating in collusion, so their confederates play a role in deflecting any doubts expressed by overly inquisitive people, including auditors or regulators. Of course, in the worst circumstances, the whole culture of the organization has become criminogenic, and crime is just the routine behavior of everyone involved. Organized crime is a good example of this.

Let's consider the triangle's second vertex, concealment, especially in the context of collusion. In the Sicilian Mafia, the code of silence and refusal to cooperate with the police and other regulatory authorities is called *omerta*. We saw this happening in Lance Amstrong's cycling team to keep the deception going for a long time. Several decades ago, Everett Hughes described it as follows:

> That people can and do keep a silence about things whose open discussion would threaten the group's conception of itself, and hence its solidarity, is common knowledge. It is a mechanism that operates in every family and in every group which has a sense of group reputation. To break such a silence is considered an attack against the group; a sort of treason, if it be a member of the group who breaks the silence.[17]

White-collar crime has long suffered interminable definitional controversies, so E. W. Burgess has suggested a subjective definition:

"White-collar crime should include only those who consider themselves to be criminals."[18] J. Katz pointed out that such a definition suddenly makes a lot of sense if we focus on behavior that is "felt by actors to require cover-up." Thus, he argued, "One might try to cover up an act or activity because one knows it is criminal, because unprincipled adversaries might try to get enforcement officials to treat it as criminal, because revelation might lead to legislation making it criminal, or merely because it might appear improper to a public audience."[19] In addition to resolving the definitional controversy, this sort of emphasis by the investigator allows for a laserlike focus on the act of fraud itself, by the very fact that an attempt was made to conceal its commission.

In this context, the fallout from the U.S. government's prosecution of Raj Rajaratnam of Galleon Funds, followed by the successful conviction of former Goldman Sachs director and former McKinsey managing director Rajat Gupta, is truly remarkable. This is considered the largest insider trading ring in the history of Wall Street.[20] The government is currently pursuing Stephen A. Cohen of SAC Capital Advisors and has successfully levied a record $616 million penalty, as of this writing.

As in the previous cases, many cooperating witnesses are being sought out. And there is a whole psychology associated with the unindicted co-conspirators in such cases, who are being pressured to assume the role of cooperating witnesses. Blogger Walt Pavlo has written about the fairly recent case of Matthew Martoma, affiliated with SAC Capital Advisors (this can be found in Appendix B). As of this writing, Rengan Rajaratnam, the brother of the jailed Raj Rajaratnam, has also been brought in for questioning, because he too was previously affiliated with SAC Capital Advisors.

The last vertex of the operational fraud triangle, conversion, is critically important because it helps us to follow the money. After all, the person who is reaping the benefits of illicit money can safely be assumed to have some involvement in the fraud. The money trail is a key indicator of not only the scheme but also the person or people who hatched the plot and executed it. Even "accidental" or "unlikely" beneficiaries are potential persons of interest.

What You Can Do Monday Morning

Here are some pointers you can put into action. They are offered around a new triangle of how fraud comes to life or is operationalized.

Through that model, ideas on how to pierce the rationalizations, to halt the start, or catch the cover-up of a fraud are given. And, of course, to think about how fraud might take root requires one to consider the psychology of fraud itself.

The Psychology of Fraud

Allow for the psychological element. It may be elusive, but it is there. Are the numbers you see just cold, hard facts, or were they produced for a reason? If so, what was the reason, and who produced them? This is a challenge, for those of us in the accounting and finance functions are most comfortable in the realm of numbers. Human behavior is a much more difficult issue to deal with. Many are untrained in such issues, but we must make it a habit to look beyond the numbers. Human nature, as we have noted, can change. We often feel uncomfortable in asking the simple but important questions: Why did you do this? What were you trying to achieve? What forces or impulses drove your behavior?

Such questions are difficult because we often know, or at least think we know, the people involved. They are Susan or Bob down the hall. They are the soccer moms and dads. They are like us in many ways.

We have also commented on the findings from the ACFE's *Report to the Nations*. This biannual compilation and analysis of fraud data provided by certified fraud examiners on their largest and most recent cases will and should scare you. The most common offenders in occupational fraud have the following profile:

- Either male or female
- 45–55 years of age
- 10–15 years with the organization
- College degree
- No criminal record
- Never seen as a problem employee
- Known and trusted

The point here is not to profile people, but to recognize the futility of profiling. The returns on profiles will be minimal compared to the harm from unnecessarily shaming and harassing innocent people due to "false positive" identification. It is important to remember who the typical fraudsters are. These are not the clever con artists who come in for two or three months, steal money, then disappear. They are the people we thought we knew and thus trusted. They are in an excellent position to become trust violators after the fact.

Certainly there are outside frauds, carried out by career criminals who are clever in what they do, but they are not the most common problem. According to the ACFE research, the average organization loses 5 to 7 percent of its potential profits to internal fraud each year. And this range of loss has remained quite stable over the years the *Report to the Nations* has been published, from 1996 to 2012.

As the guardians of the financial books and records begin to better appreciate the psychology of fraud, they must consider two further ideas previously outlined in Part II: profiling the fraudster and the organizational culture.

Don't Build a Profile, But Do Watch the Culture (and "Let Them Know Someone's Watching")[21]

You may be thinking, "Does this mean I have to be paranoid about every person I work with or know?" To a large degree the answer is no, but to some degree it's yes. The data on fraud as well as lying and deception point less to a kind of person and more to the environment a person works in. If it is possible that anyone can commit fraud then the implication is that there is a need to protect those who work in your organization from factors that will tempt them. Building this safer environment requires vigilance.

In accounting and auditing, there are professional standards that call for skepticism. Depending on your position, you are required by the professional standards to be alert to things that may be going on, to notice numbers that do not seem to add up, to ask questions that need to be asked, and to evaluate the answers. Then there is more digging to be done. This can be an uncomfortable position, especially if you are an in-house auditor. You have to live with these people. It is not much easier if you are an external auditor, because the people you are asking the questions of are the same people who hired you and are paying your fees.[22]

There has been much discussion in the professional literature of the inherent conflict that seems to come with the position of auditor. The story of the demise of Arthur Andersen, the once venerable and great accounting firm, is replete with theories of why the firm got into trouble with its client Enron. One of the more common conjectures is that its senior people just got too close to the client and did not ask enough tough questions. Others have noted how could they not go along when analysts in the stock market adored them and investment banks constantly were courting them. In the end, the case against Andersen was overturned and they were found not guilty. It was largely a symbolic victory, and it came too late, though, because the Supreme Court's verdict vacating the case against Andersen came in 2005, long after the firm had pretty much become defunct by the end of 2002.[23]

Affinity Risk

Because those who commit fraud look much like the rest of us, there is a tendency to trust them. In the investigation of fraud, this is called an *affinity scam*. Bernie Madoff created a Ponzi scheme (using new money to repay old money), but it was also an affinity scam. He relied on the fact that people much like himself would tend to trust him. Madoff was wealthy, was Jewish, had a career on Wall Street, lived in the "right" neighborhood, belonged to the "right" clubs, and made all the right moves to ingratiate himself with his clients and prospects. So did his victims, who did not believe he would deceive them because he was so much like them. That is what makes an affinity scam work.

In the case of the affinity scam, the importance of practicing a healthy skepticism is protective. Avoiding the "fair-haired golden one" who turns sour is easy in retrospect, and in the case of Enron required Bethany McLean and others to see the façade. To make the right call and exercise skepticism before the fact is key, for we can be easily deceived into thinking that "we knew or suspected it all along" (called *hindsight bias*, an exact science!).

Recognizing Tipping Points (of the Mind)

A house is a heap of stones, but a heap of stones is not a house. Which stone is it—the 27,866th one—that with certainty allows us to claim that a house has been built? The phenomenon of vagueness makes it difficult for us to arrive at a definite answer in these little-by-little arguments.

Similarly, the first cigarette you smoke does not give you lung cancer, but neither does the last. The first drink you take does not make you an alcoholic, but neither does the last. At some point you crossed the line or, as Malcolm Gladwell noted in his book *The Tipping Point*, reached the point where turning back seemed impossible. Once you hit that point, in the logic of some, you might as well continue and hope for the best. To some degree, you are playing the odds.

A bank robber in New York City in the 1970s had robbed 11 banks before the FBI arrested him. When asked why he had continued to rob banks, thus increasing his chances of getting caught, he allegedly replied, "My man, you don't get no more time for eleven than you do for one." He understood the system very well. He knew the government was not going to spend the time and resources to try him eleven times. Thus, his tipping point was the first robbery.

Such logic also applies to the white-collar offender. The climate in the court system has begun to change in recent years, but for many years the white-collar offender was treated much differently from the street criminal. The person who stole $10,000 using a pen usually received a much lighter sentence than the person who stole $10,000 using a gun to rob a bank. Investigators followed much the same logic. Nobody got hurt with a pen, but the bank robber's gun could have hurt or killed someone. The bank is a big institution; it has lots of money and insurance. The elderly person who is robbed at home may have lost his or her life savings. Thus, armed robberies have usually gotten more attention than white-collar crimes.[24]

There is an axiom among experienced fraud investors: Did you ever hear of anybody stealing a million dollars and working their way down? Indeed, experience tells us that fraudsters shoot big, then bigger. "Free" (stolen) money becomes addictive to many. Perpetrators often start small and, if successful, tend to incrementally increase the amount of each theft. They do not usually go from a theft of $100 to a theft of $100,000; they more likely go from $100 to $500 to $1,000, and so on. To a degree they are testing the ability of the system to detect them and are also refining their techniques.

As they progress—the average occupational theft lasts for 18 months—the lifestyle of most tends to change to include expensive cars, lavish vacations, expensive jewelry, and the like. They often brag about their new wealth, attributing it to success in the lottery or at the casino, a gift from a relative, or some other unexpected source. Indeed, lifestyle changes are one of the more common methods by which fraudsters are detected. Their addiction finally betrays them, because just as with a chemical addiction, there is always a need for more.

The Appetite for Risk and Danger

Michael Apter, whom we cited earlier in our discussion of the reversal theory of motivation, has also written a book titled *Danger: Our Quest for Excitement* about the human appetite for risk. This may seem odd at first. We carry automobile, homeowner's, health, and life insurance. We are wary of risk and want to protect ourselves from it. We wear seat belts and have smoke detectors. We do not seem to like risk.

Yet in other ways we do enjoy risk. Any game, from checkers to high-stakes poker, is interesting because it involves an element of risk. Imagine a football game with only one team on the field. It would score a touchdown on every play. How many games would you go to? Without the element of risk, no game is any fun. There is no challenge, no drama, no excitement when you win, and no test of strength or skill.

Apter asserted in *Danger* that while all humans have an appetite for risk, some have a larger appetite than others. Think of the extreme-sports shows you see on television. Those sports' athletes are people with a high need for risk. Could this be an explanation for financial misbehavior? Do some simply want to see if they can beat the system, much as with a game in a casino, even though they know the odds are against them? This kind of reasoning certainly seems to have appealed to Frank Abagnale, the man who inspired the book and the movie *Catch Me If You Can*.

The Path to Fraud, Then Misery

The intelligence community in the United States—the collection of agencies that includes the Central Intelligence Agency, the Federal Bureau of Investigation, and about a dozen others—uses the term MISR (pronounced "miser"), which stands for *money, ideology, sex,* and *revenge,* to identify what are believed to be the most common reasons people in sensitive positions choose to betray their countries. This betrayal of loyalties by a spy must be a reversal of motivation at some level and, as noted here, is very much tied to that person's values. The catastrophic reversal of a spy's honesty is, thus, exactly like the one highlighted in Chapter 5 when the accidental fraud was discussed. It may also fit the issues around narcissism and shame that we discussed in Part II.

Sometimes the motivations are combined. For example, Robert Hanssen was a career FBI agent who also spied for the Soviet Union for more than 20 years (his story was presented in the movie *Breach*). As best we know, Hanssen was motivated by money (he received more than $1 million), sex (he supported a young woman who worked in a strip club), and revenge (he was bitter because he believed his talents had not been properly recognized by his FBI superiors).

More than 50 years ago, American psychologist Frederick Hertzberg developed a theory about money. He acknowledged that money has an absolute value (e.g., $10 can buy more than $5), but he introduced the new perspective that money also has a relative or symbolic value, which can have a powerful influence on the actions of humans.

Herzberg explained the value of money to companies to motivate employees. An employee's salary fits into a motivational category he called "hygienic," in which things are noticed only when missing.[25]

Suppose you apply for a job and get it, with a salary you find acceptable and adequate. Then two weeks later you discover that the person you replaced made twice as much. The salary you once thought satisfactory is now unsatisfactory, because you feel foolish and devalued. This is the experience of shame. What comes next you now know depends on the person's competence with shame. The risk exists that if they experience shame at too high a level, and it becomes intolerable, they may choose to attack. This may take the form of taking advantage of their organization through fraud.

Already vigilant to this dynamic, thoughtful HR departments manage this information very closely. Despite the best intentions, this information can be revealed. The tone at the top, the capacity to manage emotions competently and the overall distractability of the organization (or organizational inertia) are just a few of the risk factors related to fraud discussed thus far. Having protected time to discuss issues of compensation and other incentives is something a leadership team can do on Monday morning.

Conclusion

The capacity to understand others, especially as it relates to psychology and the human mind, at the workplace is a powerful tool for protecting an environment at risk for fraud. A portion of Part II of this book was intended for leaders and other professionals concerned with fraud risk to be more aware of the dynamics that underlie fraud. How the organization relates to the taking of profits and distributing that profit to those who work there is very important on an affective (emotional) level.

At times, leadership may miss when individuals that work in an organization are hurting or take offense and do not have the capacity to express their upset or even become aware of it. Thus, for Monday morning, leaders must avoid their biases, especially professional jealousies and feelings aroused by making social comparisons. Specifically we recommend leaders ask questions around "Is it the right thing to do?" relative to the people in an organization. Leaders may dismiss raised concerns about employees with "don't worry, they are okay with that." Thus, those of us in fraud prevention may miss the inherent biases that leadership has toward thinking employees are "okay with that" when they have been harmed and are at risk of considering sabotage like fraud.

Specifically, in a materialistic culture, with the attitude that "whoever has the most toys, wins," CEOs can become narcissistic and covet wealth, fame, and power. It is critically important to maintain a sense of balance; otherwise, it is possible for a CEO to do untold damage to an organization because of his or her own insecurities and associated behaviors. For instance, does a high-flying CEO compare himself to others and feel taken advantage of in terms of salary, stock options, and benefits? Does this prompt him to get even when he thinks he deserves more?

Needless to say, it is critically important that auditors and investigators put on their thinking caps and exercise a high degree of professional skepticism when they suspect they are dealing with high-risk environments susceptible to fraud. They should ask commonsense questions: Does this sound too good to be true? This story doesn't make sense, so what follow-up action is demanded of me to get at the facts?

Being curious is indispensable, and asking the right questions is the only way to get to the bottom of things. Once fraudsters realize that they are not dealing with fools, they are usually smart enough to back off. The potential fraud is then nipped in the bud or successfully foiled. The power of asking the right question increases logarithmically as one moves up the organization; indeed, the most important omission is the unasked question. At the most senior levels there are two questions that frame critical discussions. One takes the leadership down a path of long term sustainability; the other can be a path of ruin.

Notes

1. D. R. Carmichael, "The PCAOB and the Social Responsibility of the Independent Auditor," *Accounting Horizons* 18, no. 2(2004): 127–133.
2. See for instance, R. C. Solomon, *It's Good Business: Ethics and Free Enterprise for the New Millennium* (Lanham, MD: Rowman & Littlefield Publishers, 1997).

3. Geoff Hodgson, *Capitalism, Value, and Exploitation: A Radical Theory* (Oxford, UK: Martin Robertson, 1982).
4. M. Altman, *Behavioral Economics for Dummies* (Hoboken, NJ: John Wiley & Sons, 2012), 10.
5. G. A. Akerlof and R. J. Shiller, *Animal Spirits: How Human Psychology Drives the Economy, and Why It Matters for Global Capitalism* (Princeton, NJ: Princeton University Press, 2010).
6. J. H. Davis, F. D. Schoorman, and L. Donaldson, "Toward a Stewardship Theory of Management," *Academy of Management Review* 22, no. 1 (1997): 20–47.
7. Laura J. Rediehs, "Economics Has Replaced Ethics," Carnegie Council for Ethics in International Affairs, 2012, www.carnegiecouncil.org/publications/articles_papers_reports/0139.
8. Michael Jacobs, "How Business Schools Have Failed Business," *Wall Street Journal*, April 24, 2009. http://online.wsj.com/article/SB124052874488350333.html.
9. Marianne Jennings, "Seven Signs of Ethical Collapse: How to Spot Moral Meltdowns Before it's Too Late," Markkula Center for Applied Ethics, Santa Clara University, April 2007, www.scu.edu/ethics/practicing/focusareas/business/bcep/meltdown-signs.html.
10. Specifically, Gladwell observed, "The one Enron partner that has escaped largely unscathed [from the Enron fallout] is McKinsey, which is odd, given that it essentially created the blueprint for the Enron culture. Enron was the ultimate 'talent' company." Malcolm Gladwell, "The Talent Myth: Are Smart People Overrated?" *New Yorker*, July 23, 2002, 28–33.
11. Called *counterfactual thinking or reasoning* in psychology research, this tendency of human beings has been extensively studied. See N. J. Roese and J. M. Olson (eds.), *What Might Have Been: The Social Psychology of Counterfactual Thinking* (Hillsdale, NJ: Lawrence Erlbaum Associates, 1995).
12. In this connection, consider the applications of *paedomorphism*—the retention of infantile and juvenile characteristics in the adult—in the context of the predator-prey dance. Among animals, the domesticated dog or cat is actually a transformed creature—the real thing is the wolf or the tiger in the wild. How fraudsters might use their childlike characteristics to make victims let down their guard would be a worthwhile area of behavioral forensics research.
13. Bob Burg, "Persuasian vs. Manipulation," August 3, 2010, www.burg.com/2010/08/persuasion-vs-manipulation.
14. Paul Swets, *The Art of Talking So That People Will Listen: Getting through to Family, Friends, and Business Associates* (New York: Prentice-Hall, 1986).
15. See S. Grazioli, K. Jamal, and P. E. Johnson, "A Cognitive Approach to Fraud Detection," *Journal of Forensic Accounting*, 7 (2006): 65–88.
16. Floyd Norris, "Masked by Gibberish, the Risks Run Amok," *New York Times*, March 22, 2013.
17. Everett C. Hughes, "Good People and Dirty Work," in *The Other Side*, ed. H. S. Becker (New York: Free Press, 1964), 28.
18. E. W. Burgess, "Comment," in *White-Collar Crime*, ed. G. Geis (New York: Free Press, 1977).

19. J. Katz, "Cover-Up and Collective Integrity," *Social Problem* 25 (1977).
20. See Anita Raghavan, *The Billionaire's Apprentice: The Rise of the Indian-American Elite and the Fall of the Galleon Hedge Fund* (New York: Hatchette Book Group, 2013).
21. A classic piece of advice from the ACFE Founder and Chairman, Dr. Joseph T. Wells, in his May 2002 *Journal of Accountancy* article. "Let Them Know Someone's Watching."
22. Consider the following well-known quip from internal auditing: What are the two greatest lies of internal auditing? First lie: When the auditor says to the client, "We are here to help you!" Second lie: When the client responds: "We're so glad you are here!"
23. See http://www.cnn.com/2005/LAW/05/31/scotus.arthur.andersen.
24. In this connection, the title of Walter Pavlo and Neil Weinberg's book is revealing: *Stolen without a Gun: Confessions from Inside History's Biggest Accounting Fraud—the Collapse of MCI WorldCom* (Tampa: Etika Books, 2007).
25. Frederick Herzberg, *The Motivation to Work* (New York: John Wiley & Sons, 1959).

The Future of Behavioral Forensics

DEVELOPING PSYCHOLOGICAL AWARENESS TO COMPLEMENT FINANCIAL FRAUD SUSPICIONS

The accounting profession has developed methods to uncover fraud. The fields of criminology and forensic accounting have improved and refined them. Our book proposes that psychology must be added in order to round out these professions and add to deterrence and detection. Thus far, we have intentionally added to the understanding of *how* people are motivated to commit fraud, and we have also added to the potential reasons for the *why* of fraud. We have been less direct on the ties to deterrence, detection, and prevention. But the answers are there and become clearer as the understanding of the ecology of fraud—the players, the game, the context, and the outcomes, indeed the whole terrain—deepens.

A known tactic—for example, the role of emotions in the simple but intentionally deceptive steps of the phisherman—provides a great deal of understanding of any fraud. The con men and women may change, but the "play" remains the same.[1]

For many, this will be enough. This is not new as it relates to understanding and changing behavior to be more adaptive. For example, merely knowing that smoking is associated with cancer, or obesity with heart attacks, is enough for many to choose to live a healthier life. Others take much longer to be convinced, allowing deceptive or even fraudulent science to harm many people, and simply continue to deny or diminish the relevance of behavioral forensics.

Understanding provides the path to action steps in this frame of mind. For those who are skeptical about emotions or about the reversals of motivation, who are confused by the relevance of narcissism in leaders, or who cannot see the dangers of the charismatic leader-follower dynamics, their concerns must be heard. Clarifications will come out of this dialogue, and we will all be better off for it. After all, the losses from fraud are an avoidable leakage in the economic system and a deadweight loss to society (i.e., it is only the fraudster who benefits; everyone else loses).

Fraud: A Global Scourge

The scale and cycle of frauds have been increasing since the massive savings and loan scandal of the 1980s, costing more than $300 billion and culminating in the Wall Street financial crisis of 2007–2009 with an estimated loss of 8.8 million jobs and $19.2 trillion in lost household wealth.[2] We are not necessarily suggesting that the Wall Street financial crisis involved widespread fraud, but it did feature scandalously dishonest programs designed to trick homeowners into bad loans. Since this infection spread to the world of collateralized debt obligations, or CDOs,[3] and into the larger financial marketplace, it is clear that the so-called system of checks and balances failed and weak regulation was exposed. It also revealed that highly touted risk management systems and corporate governance mechanisms were, in reality, grossly inadequate. In sum, the ubiquity of fraud incidence remains a serious concern not only in America, but all over the world.

Many of these systemic deficiencies had at least one root cause that could be traced back to human behavior. One pair of researchers offers the following psychological factors ("animal spirits"): confidence, fairness, corruption, bad faith, money, illusion, and stories.[4] Indeed, we can confidently assert that the human side of governance has been given short shrift, and it is high time that we devote more attention to the people and behaviors that led to these scandals. After all, that is precisely the proper domain of the emerging field of behavioral forensics, isn't it?

Fraud Is Not a Problem with an Easy Answer

Fraud is not going to be solved with quick tips on the detection of lying, by unfairly characterizing every senior executive as a criminal, or by regulatory overload—adding to the plethora of existing laws and regulations. As in military tactics, every advance has the potential to be countered. Understanding and self-awareness is at the heart of the work required of all employees, but in particular senior leaders, to not allow fraud to harm an organization. That brings us full circle to the mission of this book.

This book has discussed behavioral forensics in terms of the perpetrator, the victim, the overseers, and a new taxonomy for the larger impact of fraud. Along the way, we have endeavored to furnish not only new understandings but also suggest feasible solution approaches in prevention, deterrence, and investigation. The A.B.C. theory contains the core premise that there is always at least one individual involved in the perpetration of every fraud. If the human factor is so fundamental to fraud, then, given our extreme displeasure at the massive and devastating financial losses that result, it behooves us to study what it is that causes people to behave in such a fashion. But how can we use our enhanced understanding to possibly preempt or deter their egregious unethical or illegal behavior?

A Multidimensional Problem Requires a Multidisciplinary Team

Given the complexity of our financial systems and our increasingly more powerful technology, the need for a comprehensive method to inoculate against and investigate fraud will require more than one profession. We must have a multidisciplinary approach. Fraud requires not only expertise in accounting, law, criminology, computer science and information technology, economics and statistics, but also the hybrid profession of forensic accounting. And given the complexity of human behavior, it requires psychiatry and psychology, even anthropology.

Consider the inverse. If this were a textbook on governance failures arising out of fraudulent financial reporting meant to educate psychologists, it would be logical to include coverage and discussion of accounting principles and concepts ("debits and credits"). Thus it is fundamental that the crisis of fraud includes the worlds of psychiatry and psychology. The middle section of this book builds this

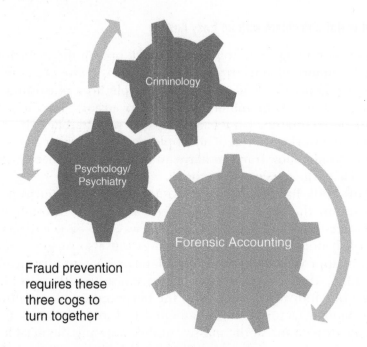

Fraud prevention
requires these
three cogs to
turn together

Exhibit 9.1   The Multi-disciplinary Team for Managing Fraud

case. Exhibit 9.1 models how the three professions can integrate in minimizing the risk of fraud.

From the Wall Street subprime mortgage crisis to alleged money laundering to benchmark interest-rate rigging, the global financial services industry has experienced more than a black eye in terms of shattered reputation. The resulting fines, litigation, and reputational damage have even made insurers such as AIG shy away and scale back their financial services industry insurance coverage and protection.[5] Yes, "uninsurable risks" are those that even insurance companies shy away from!

Consider the still unfolding rigging case of the London interbank offered rate (LIBOR) through the British Bankers' Association. LIBOR is a benchmark rate based on daily estimates from a group of banks of how much it would cost them to borrow from one another. Since mortgages, student loans, financial derivatives, and other financial products often rely on LIBOR as a reference rate, the manipulation of submissions used to calculate those rates can have significant negative effects on consumers and financial markets worldwide. LIBOR is a collection of rates generated for various currencies across 15 different time periods. The quotes are used as benchmarks for roughly $10 trillion in loans and some $350 trillion in derivatives.[6]

Over the last few months, Barclays, Royal Bank of Scotland, and UBS have all been fined almost $3 billion combined after regulators alleged rate manipulation, and all three banks admitted wrongdoing as part of their settlements. On March 19, 2013, the *Financial Times* reported that Freddie Mac has sued more than a dozen banks, as well as the British Bankers' Association, alleging that it has suffered "substantial losses" as a result of the LIBOR manipulation.[7]

Market confidence has been shaken, and internal audit departments at Barclays and UBS have confessed that their compliance reviews failed to detect persistent rate manipulation efforts. Even more troubling is that RBS "has acknowledged that it did not even realize there was a potential problem with having the same people help set the rates that they then traded on."[8] There could not have been more conflicted traders than those who got to set the price at which they would then trade.

This is clearly a prime example of a bad-crop situation, with more large banks likely to get ensnared in the LIBOR manipulation saga in the coming months. And the real difficulty is that member institutions of the financial services industry cannot help but participate. Charles Prince, the former CEO of Citigroup, noted in the summer of 2007, "When the music stops, in terms of liquidity, things will be complicated. But as long as the music is playing, you've got to get up and dance. We're still dancing."[9]

As for solutions and responses, on March 25, 2013, Britain's Financial Services Authority promulgated rules on regulating benchmark rates, kicking off a string of reforms aimed at preventing a repeat of the alleged widespread rate-rigging attempts. Kevin Milne, the chief executive of Rate Validation Services, a benchmark provider, commented, "A reliable benchmark is one that is based on transaction evidence, is automated, and is supported by an independent governance process which guarantees the accuracy and the neutrality of the output." To that the reporter added, "Cabals are less likely to form when rate-setters include institutions with fundamentally different interests."[10]

This chapter addresses the following topics through Stanford University professor James March's high-level characterization of a "culture of cleverness" in a competitive setting:

- The ecology of fraud: environment and context.
- The players: predatory or accidental fraudster (whether or not in the C-suite), prey or victim, auditors, and investigators.
- The behaviors: lying and misrepresentation, purposeful acts designed to deceive others, cover-up and concealment activities, and conversion (or benefiting from ill-gotten gains).
- The outcomes: losses to society as a whole, bankruptcy of companies, loss of investor confidence, and erosion of trust overall.

This chapter discusses the overarching idea of the multidisciplinary team as a conceptual framework for analyzing corporate governance failures. Infusing it with behavioral insights allows us to come up with an anatomy of present and future scandals, with the prospect of arriving at responsible and effective solutions. We have issued a clarion call for carrying out "a psychological autopsy" of every future governance failure whether or not they involve fraud. The lessons learned from a behavioral forensics perspective may be the most valuable lessons after all.

The environment that will support fraud behavior is one that supports intellect over meaning. It is suitably characterized and identified as a culture of cleverness.

A Culture of Cleverness

To effectively execute a fraud, several steps must be taken by the perpetrator. Each of these steps must somehow distract or deceive the formal checks and balances designed to catch them.

Predator (the headline grabbers)
1. Recognizes the potential exists to exploit the system.
2. Intimidates those who are inside the organization to override regulatory functions (often using coercion through reward and threat).
3. Intimidates the internal and external auditors, regulators, and governing board.

Accidental Fraudster (the-run-of-the-mill fraud)
1. Discovers by accident a hole in the accounting processes.
2. Rationalizes the rule breaking using Apter's reversal theory.
3. Sustains the fraud over time using the eight areas of motivation from reversal theory.

Either of these types of fraud can bypass the best formal accounting or enterprise resource planning systems if the person has the power or the intellect. Even with best practices, the human element can outmaneuver fraud detection systems and processes. In addition, these can be costly frauds, because either can ultimately involve large groups of people in the bad bushel or bad crop taxonomy. The culture of cleverness demonstrates how psychological dynamics generate fertile ground for fraud. How does this work?

At the 1986 annual meeting of the American Accounting Association, the theme of which was "Accounting and Culture," Stanford University professor James March delivered a stirring and thoughtful address in which he described the environment of decision making in this simple and direct way: "Modern theories of interactive decision making and competition are theories of calculated cleverness in the interest of the self." Obviously, when one such decision maker, acting purely in his or her self-interest, crosses the line, we see the perpetration of fraud. March then described the culture of cleverness as a key aspect of the *ecology of fraud*:

> We imagine a world of self-interested decision makers nested within organizations that are in turn nested within markets, communities, and political institutions. Each of the actors within this world attempts to make and influence decisions in a way that advances his or her self-interest as he or she calculates it by considering alternatives in terms of their expected consequences. These considerations pervade the decision process and the production of information involved in decisions. . . .
>
> Consider, for example, the production of income statements. There are ample signs that managers, investors, and workers attend to income statements. Because income statements matter, many clever people try to make the statements say what they would like them to say. Clever managers try to outwit clever accountants and clever analysts, who are at the same time trying to outwit them. Clever investors and clever public officials try to

interpret the information provided through this culture of cleverness. And clever economists try to develop theories specifying the equilibria of clever processes, that is, processes involving multiple interacting clever people and the pervasive cleverness of calculation.[11]

March also wrote a book in which he said the following:

In the beginning:

God created innocents and sophisticates. Sophisticates are clever; innocents are not. Cleverness pursues self-interest with as much guile and imagination as possible. Information is an instrument in the service of the clever, and competition rewards people in proportion to their relative cleverness with information instruments. . . .

Before long:

Competition destroys innocence. Less clever people are eliminated from the competition, either by losing their innocence or by losing their livelihood. Once the innocent are gone, variations in cleverness are small and the effect of cleverness on the distribution of winnings is nil. Everyone in the game is clever (or can hire someone who is). . . . The key conclusion is that the cleverness of competitors makes cleverness necessary but insignificant in affecting distributional outcomes. Since only very clever people survive, no one outwits anyone else—though everyone tries.

But ultimately:

Sophistication loses both victims and competitive advantage. The elimination of innocents reduces the competitive value of the kinds of cleverness that eliminated them. However, it is in the interest of each surviving participant to continue being clever as long as the others do, even though the effect of clever behavior on the relative competitive strength of survivors is nil when all engage in it. The energy devoted to cleverness is not devoted to other things, thereby making all of the clever participants vulnerable to new kinds of predation from outside. Thus, a clever system of account management is likely to be destroyed by the depletion of innocents to exploit and the specialization of managerial competence to skills that are irrelevant to new threats.

The story is an old one, hardly unique to information engineering. . . .
The ecological difficulty with calculated self-interest and cleverness is
not that they are immoral in the usual sense, but that they are forms of
incompetence.[12] (Emphasis added)

Yale mathematics graduate and big hedge fund manager Andrew
Redleaf and his colleague at Whitebox Advisors, Richard Vigilante,
give a twenty-first-century description:

> The ideology of modern finance replaces the capitalist's appre-
> ciation for free markets as a context for human creativity with
> the worship of efficient markets as substitutes for that creativ-
> ity. The capitalist understands free markets as an arena for the
> contending judgments of free men. The ideologues of modern
> finance dreamed of efficient markets as a replacement for that
> judgment and almost as a replacement for the men. The most
> gloriously efficient of all, supposedly, were modern public secu-
> rities markets in all their ethereal electronic glory. To these most
> perfect markets the priesthood of finance attributed powers of
> calculation and control for exceeding not only the abilities of
> any human participant in them but the fondest dreams of any
> Communist commissar pecking away at the next Five Year Plan.[13]

Our embrace of what is clever has a dark side. To be infatuated
with a superior intellect or fantastic innovation has its drawbacks; it
can be a sign of individual and group incompetence, as March suggests, or even a wounded or vulnerable organization.[14] Recall Duane
Kullberg's foreboding warning of partners' hubris at Arthur Andersen
as well as the echoes in the bubble around the leader that walls off
warnings about being too clever or too full of oneself. Ultimately, this
is a step toward the suicidal charismatic leader-follower infatuation.
Wounded organizations may come in the form of what appears to be
a "perfectly adapted" species as the adaptation is incomplete.

All Aspects of Fraud Must Be Understood

If we are to make any progress in combatting fraud, bold confrontation is required to stem the tide of the escalation of bubbles and
bursts, phenomenal wealth creation, and catastrophic frauds.[15]
Financial forensics and its role in fraud has clear ties to market

expansions. The argument to question "cleverness" also demands, first, an acknowledgment that the status quo is unsustainable, and, second, the direct confrontation of a culture that adores the free market and lives in fear of any regulation. For a person of this frame of mind, regulation is poison. It actually makes more sense to cleanse and regulate the market on occasion.

How do we restore honesty and decency to the capital markets? How can we stem the moral decay evident in the business world? Our focus must be on the people involved, and we must have systems of ethics, values, and morals that all can strive to adhere to and eliminate the blight—the bad crop situation we are experiencing in contemporary business.

Let's start with a foundational comment on the capital markets ecology—the regulatory principle—as persuasively noted by Nobel Laureate in economics George Akerlof and his coauthor, Robert Shiller: "The public, and the regulators who were supposed to act on their behalf, had failed to understand a fact of life that is totally obvious to everyone who has played a serious team sport: there have to be rules and there has to be a referee who enforces them—and a good and conscientious referee at that. Otherwise there will be random cheating that destroys the sense of the game, and dangerous and aggressive play, so that many people will get hurt and the game will cease to reward good play."[16] Regulators seen as a threat will never be allowed to fully contribute to the process in an adaptive manner. If, however, they are seen as part of the larger community, like a solid police or fire department, they can be active in fraud deterrence and detection and be protective of the marketplace.[17]

Emotions lie at the heart of our values. When we compromise them as Patti Smith did in the anecdote told earlier in this book about her attempt to steal the encyclopedia, we are sickened when we have to confront the failure to live up to our ideals. Regulators help remind us of these ideals and also catch us sooner in the process. Smith's regulators were her mother and grocery store manager. As we grow older, these regulators take a form in our shared ethics and those of our superiors.

Lynn McGregor noted, "The organizations that survive and flourish in the longer term are the ones that get the human side of governance right."[18] Within organizations, internal auditors have a vital function. The internal audit function can take the ethical temperature of the organization, assess information integrity risk, and thus be a critical line of defense in alerting the C-suite and the board of the most serious staff risks who warrant attention. Swift responsive action can even prevent corporate collapse.[19]

When conducting an ethics audit, it is fundamental to ask, "Do you ever feel pressured by your organization to act contrary to your own moral judgment?" If the answer is yes, a corporate ethics audit of considerable depth is required, including the following:

- What sort of pressure?
- Where does it come from?
- Is it real or imagined?
- Is it personally worth the cost of staying with the company?
- Does it demand formal reporting to the board of directors or even outside agencies?

If the answer is no or very rarely, the corporate ethics audit is nevertheless revealing, for it raises the most important existential question: Is this the person I want to be?[20]

Profile a Criminal When There's a Crime, Not for Prevention

Many are tempted to say that numbers are "hard," and psychology is "soft," and therefore of little benefit. We disagree with this assessment and will explain our logic. The profiling unit of the FBI makes this case.

The FBI Profiling Unit has been around for thirty-plus years and has gained public recognition. It has been featured in news reports, articles, TV shows, and movies (an early member of the unit was the technical advisor on the movie *Silence of the Lambs*).

The perception of profiling as adding value counters the perception that psychology is soft, but before profiling is embraced as the ultimate solution, it is important to understand what profiling can and cannot do. By studying a crime scene or a series of crimes, the unit can begin to develop a psychological profile of the likely offender. It helps focus investigative resources by looking for perpetrators with certain characteristics:

- Did they have a relationship with the victim?
- Did they live close to the victim?
- Are they organized offenders, who tend to follow a pattern?

- Are they disorganized offenders, who strike at random and are sloppy with regard to physical evidence left behind?

Profiling has limits. The average person who commits fraud has no prior criminal record. To profile the typical fraudster in a program designed for prevention is to attempt to boil the ocean.

In addition, there are limits to the use of the profile. The hypothetical profile that the FBI generates is a problem-solving exercise intended to focus the minds of the crime solving team, yet no matter how well done, it has zero value in court. Besides helping focus the investigation, the profile is nevertheless useful in conducting an interview of a suspect. In short, you have a better idea of what makes the person "tick." To move such considerations to the realm of fraud, consider the following examples.

Case one: A young reporter for a financial magazine was assigned to get an interview with the star CEO of a high-flying company. She was not well-known, and it took her many attempts to gain half an hour of his time. When she did, the "interview" was one question and the scheduled half-hour interview was over in three minutes. Her question was "How does your company make money?"

The CEO came out of his chair screaming at her that she was inexperienced, unprofessional, and unprepared. She made the long journey back to her office. She had brave editors with a significant amount of integrity, and they told her to go with her story. The rest is history. The reporter was Bethany McLean, the CEO was Jeff Skilling, and the company was Enron. McLean's story was one of the first cracks in the façade that was Enron.

What role does psychology play here? Skilling was trying to intimidate McLean. He sought to bully her with shame. Her question, so direct, and so deserving of an answer, "deskilled" him, and he wanted her to go away, to dismiss her because he could not answer it.

As an investigation (or in the case of Skilling, just an interview) gets close to exposing a fraud, one sees other forms of such behavior fairly frequently; responses such as "Do you know who I am? I have been with this company for thirty-five years! Who are you to question me? I was an executive when you were in grade school." Investigators know that those who commit fraud have standard lines of response that have worked for them in the past, and they tend to stick to them.

Case two: Most of us who are interested in eliminating fraud will see and do more by tackling the everyday frauds. This type of fraudster is less dramatic, but more subtle and harder to capture. In this situation an even milder, but similar, line of defense is the model citizen: "You know I have six kids, and two of them are special-ed kids. Look at all these plaques—I work some long hours, but I am always active in the community." The effort is to avoid the question by, in essence, saying, "I am a good person and have a lot on my plate. I can't believe you think I did anything wrong." These are the deceptive and defense tactics of the accidental fraudster during investigations.

And what role does psychology play as the investigation unfolds in this case? The core affects are still relevant. It is a way of dismissing the shame in a different manner than the all-out direct assault. Like the phisherman, specialness or exceptionalism is emphasized as proof of innocence. In a manner similar to a pickpocket's use of distraction with a bump or spilling something on the victim, the attention is directed away from the line of questioning that will expose the fraud.

Our challenge is to integrate the concepts and cases into actionable concepts now. We have clarified the following:

- Rules and referees matter.
- Fraud is a complex phenomenon.
- The environment for supporting or deterring fraud matters.
- Profiles matter after fraud has occurred.
- Understanding interpersonal dynamics is the first step to delving into the antecedents of fraud. Answering the "how fraud was committed" question may not always help answer the "why she committed fraud" question.

To add to the resources and to deepen understanding we recommend a robust investigation into what is happening with fraud. This would include an "autopsy" of what went wrong psychologically and interpersonally.

A Psychological Autopsy of Fraud

In cases of fraud, there are many often-cited reasons: poor controls, an urgent need to take action caused rules to be bypassed with short-cuts, management override of controls, and so on. But what is not uncovered is the role the emotions played. What role did bullying and shame played. How did the reversals happen? We recommend that beyond the typical review and summary of lessons learned, there ought to be a psychogical autopsy. The immense losses to fraud during the Iraq War is a case to consider.

Stuart Bowen, the special inspector general of the Iraq reconstruction, was involved in evaluating the accounting of funds in Iraq. He was able to see the projects and knew of the plan for the disbursement of funds early on, after the end of hostilities with Saddam Hussein's army. When asked by journalist Judy Woodruff of the PBS NewsHour whether the frauds and their severity were to be expected as reasonable, he noted clearly that Iraq represented real problems.

> *Stuart Bowen:* There was something particular to Iraq, Judy. The lack of controls at the outset created what some—what one person called a free fraud zone in Iraq. And the Bloom-Stein conspiracy, we broke in Hillah, Babylon, in 2004, convicted a colonel, three lieutenant colonels. Philip Bloom, the contractor, who has had a previous felony conviction, and Robert Stein, the comptroller for the south-central region.
> *Judy Woodruff:* These were Americans.
> *Stuart Bowen:* Yes, essentially, the comptroller for the south-central region had a previous felony conviction. This is a man who had control over hundreds of millions of dollars. And he told me when we interviewed him a few years ago that, hey, if there had been a powerful, robust oversight presence on the ground, that the crimes that they engaged in wouldn't have happened.[21]

Felons were overseeing huge sums of money, the military was involved in the corruption, and oversight was weak to the point of being nonexistent.[22] A psychological autopsy would ask questions such as the following:

- How did the comptroller get hired despite being a felon? Were there any background checks done? Is this a case of a variation on the phisherman dynamic (like Enron traders and the HealthSouth Scrushy-Beam interactions)?

- What role did shame play in making the oversight function so weak?
- How did the leadership groups avoid asking questions about competence and motivations?
- Assuming the army officers were not always dishonest, when did they turn and why? (What was the story of their reversals?) Also, were they getting paid off and in on the act and had their silence purchased?
- How did the contractor intimidate or bully the U.S. government into not following through on any form of a powerful, robust oversight presence?
- What role did the protective frames of K Street, Congress, and the contractor's organization play in ignoring risk and seeing this life-threatening and life-sustaining work as "play"?
- What role did the charismatic leader-follower dynamic play in this fraud?
- Was pathological narcissism present?

Thoughtful debriefings of the critical people involved by a multi-disciplinary team can deepen our understanding, help with limiting the damage, and even suggest ways to preempt recurrences of such nightmarish scenarios.

The Future of Behavioral Forensics

You may come away from this table still hungry. The authors of this book have a combined total of almost 100 years of experience in dealing with the human motivations that produce fraudulent behavior. But yet it is difficult to totally understand human behavior. We wish you luck in your pursuit, and we hope that the information in this book helps you to frame questions when seeking evidence of fraud and dealing with its perpetrators.

We should reflect upon Oxford historian Arnold Toynbee's profound remarks in his masterpiece, *The Prospects of Western Civilization*: "Man is astonishingly good at dealing with the physical world, but he is just as astonishingly bad at dealing with human nature: therefore an inch gained in the understanding of and command over human nature is worth a mile gained in the understanding of and command over physical nature."[23]

Why people do what they do is a complex subject. We cannot give you an all-encompassing checklist, but we have given you guidelines to consider. Of these guidelines, some are areas for future research and some are general theories that seem to apply to instances of fraud. Use them as you see fit. We have tried to start you on the journey, and we think that if you give it some effort and consideration, you will be better off. We have learned from study and experience and hope you will, too.

In the future, the combination of behavioral and digital forensics will be powerful. As the sophistication of fraud evolves and it goes truly global, with a multi-country organized-crime presence, we will need commensurately sophisticated techniques to combat such an environment. Note that organized crime now has a dispersed geographical presence, but national standard-setting and regulatory and policing organizations may not be so well organized and coordinated internationally. And each case of poor coordination is a gap that invites the blow—it offers more encouragement to potential fraudsters (as the risk of being caught is perceived to be negligibly low).

Multidisciplinary teams are necessary to more fully understand fraud and cope with the ramifications for future fraud risk management. They will include industry experts, accounting and auditing practitioners, lawyers, computer scientists, psychologists, sociologists, and criminologists, anthropologists, statisticians, technology professionals, forensic and regulatory experts, and national agencies such as the FBI and the CIA. Clearly, bringing such a diverse group together and making meaningful progress will be a challenging task.

However, the Institute for Fraud Prevention, cofounded by the Association of Certified Fraud Examiners and the American Institute of Certified Public Accountants and housed at West Virginia University in Morgantown, is starting to get traction. There is also considerable interest on the part of professional organizations and regulatory bodies in curbing fraud, because fraud is an issue that cuts across all organizations and results in a deadweight loss to society.

Fraud prevention will entail developing a comprehensive conceptual framework, and must be inspired by the disciplines underlying behavioral, computer, and financial forensics as well as by ongoing research. Antifraud professionals will need to look into practical ways of translating behavioral/computer science insights and integrate them with the methods of financial forensics—operating in the context of finance, accounting, and economics, and the markets and delivering actionable intelligence and implementable solutions.

Implications for law and policy must also be carefully considered, evaluated, and addressed timely.

Businesses will benefit from instituting culture and ethics audits to help them go beyond the numbers and explore the behaviors and actions of the people behind the numbers at their companies. One of the most important risks for organizations is the behavioral and integrity risks from members of the C-suite.

The one certainty is that fraud will continue and propagate across cultures. It will have higher levels of complexity, and fraudsters will take advantage of, and perhaps "arbitrage," cultural and ethical differences. This is where the engagement of anthropologists and ethnographers will become crucial.[24]

Vive la behavioral forensics!

Notes

1. Interestingly, even with all the global communication and technology advances, the interaction between fraudster and victim, between predator and prey, still follows the French expression *plus ça change, plus c'est la même chose.* In English, it is the observation that "the more things change, the more they remain the same."
2. U.S. Department of the Treasury, *The Financial Crisis Response: In Charts* (Washington, DC: U.S. Government Printing Office, 2012).
3. CDOs, or collateralized debt obligations, are investment-grade securities that are backed by a pool of bonds, loans, and other assets. CDOs do not specialize in one type of debt but are often nonmortgage loans or bonds and represent different types of debt and credit risk. See http://www.investopedia.com/terms/c/cdo.asp for more information.
4. G. A. Akerlof and R. J. Shiller, *Animal Spirits: How Human Psychology Drives the Economy, and Why It Matters for Global Capitalism* (Princeton, NJ: Princeton University Press, 2010).
5. Alistair Gray, "Protection Becomes a Scarcer Resource," *Financial Times,* March 19, 2013. Ramesh Singh, an AIG financial institutions expert, is quoted as saying, "We've seen carriers [insurance providers] starting to tail back their capacity for large financial institutions."
6. See CNN Money article by Alanna Petroff, LIBOR Moving to NYSE EuroNext. July 10, 2013, http://money.cnn.com/2013/07/09/investing/libor-nyse-uk/index.html.
7. In a symbolic blow to the British financial industry that has been rocked by a series of scandals, the UK Treasury has handed over the administration of LIBOR to NYSE Euronext from 2014 onward.
8. Brooke Masters, "Objective Evidence Offers Better Guarantees in a Brave New World," *Financial Times,* March 19, 2013.
9. M. Nakamoto and D. Wighton, "Bullish Citigroup Is 'Still Dancing' to the Beat of the Buy-Out Boom," *Financial Times,* July 10, 2007.

10. Masters, "Objective Evidence." The choice of the word *cabal* in such a context is noteworthy. Typically, it refers to a group of people united in their (evil) designs by artifice, intrigue, and conspiracy. The term usually carries strong connotations of shadowy corners, backrooms, and insidious influence; it is also suggestive of gang behavior and *omerta*, the code of silence and refusal to cooperate with the authorities in investigations. In the context of the A.B.C. theory, we thus see an interaction effect between bad bushel and the bad crop, with cabal being the relevant unit of analysis.

11. James March, "Ambiguity and Accounting: The Elusive Link between Information and Decision Making," *Accounting, Organizations and Society* 12, no. 2 (1978): 153–168.

12. James March, *Morality Play in Three Acts* (City: Publisher, 1986).

13. Quoted in Bethany McLean and Joe Nocera, *All the Devils Are Here: The Hidden History of the Financial Crisis* (New York: Penguin, 2010), 261.

14. For instance, it has been suggested that Enron had taken its "penchant for innovation just a little too far." It had used highly complicated, yet suspect financial engineering ploys such as "convoluted partnerships, off-the-books debt, and exotic hedging techniques . . . to hide huge losses." It was a sign of the times that, "a Harvard Business School study was approvingly titled 'Enron's Transformation from Gas Pipelines to New Economy Powerhouse.'" John Micklethwait and Adrian Wooldridge, *The Company: A Short History of a Revolutionary Idea* (New York: Modern Library, 2003), 152.

15. Charles P. Kindleberger and Robert Aliber, *Manias, Panics, and Crashes: A History of Financial Crises*, 6th ed. (Hampshire, UK: Palgrave Macmillan, 2011).

16. Akerlof and Shiller, *Animal Spirits.*

17. In the early twentieth century, U.S. president Teddy Roosevelt proclaimed, "I believe in corporations. . . .They are indispensable instruments of our modern civilization; but I believe that they should be so supervised and so regulated that they shall act for the interests of the community as a whole." Quoted in Micklethwait and Wooldridge, *The Company*, 182.

18. Lynn McGregor, *The Human Face of Corporate Governance* (Hampshire, UK: Palgrave Macmillan, 2000).

19. M. M. Krupp and S. Ramamoorti, "Sleeping with the Enemy: The Internal Audit's Role in Extreme Governance Breakdowns," *Journal of Forensic Studies in Accounting and Business* 3(1)(2011): 47–65; and S. Ramamoorti and R. Evans, "The Corporate Ethics Audit," *Internal Auditor* 68(4)(2011): 25–27.

20. See S. Ramamoorti and R. Evans, "The Corporate Ethics Audit," *Internal Auditor* 68(4)(2011): 25–27.

21. "Report Finds U.S. Failed to Consult Iraq's Needs in Rebuilding," *PBS Newshour*, March 6; 2003.

22. This factual description begs the colorfully expressed "the fox guarding the chicken coop" problem!

23. Arnold Toynbee, *The Prospects of Western Civilization* (New York: Columbia University Press, 1949).

24. We have a start with a recent book by an anthropologist studying the culture of Wall Street. See Karen Ho, *Liquidated: An Ethnography of Wall Street* (Durham, NC: Duke University Press. 2009).

Afterword

For many years, the business community has assessed and managed the risk of financial fraud within, by, or against organizations using numbers, matrices, and charts. As this book illustrates, these matters also require an understanding of what influences behaviors that result in financial fraud—if you will, the human element of fraud. Knowing this, management can train its workforce to understand and recognize potentially fraudulent behavior when it happens. This training, combined with appropriate reporting processes and mechanisms, will allow for the recognition and reporting of fraudulent behavior on a real-time basis by rank-and-file employees and can substantially reduce losses caused by financial fraud.

Working as a professional in the corporate fraud prevention, detection, and response area, I have participated in sophisticated approaches to financial fraud risk identification and evaluation. In some cases, the work was dominated by stakeholder brainstorming, theoretical discussions, industry comparisons, and database analyses. They were highly technical exercises dominated by specialists. The results were documented using heat maps, massive spreadsheets, and professional jargon. Rarely were the triggering events, specifics of the deceptive acts, and prevention mechanisms effectively communicated to the entire workforce in an effort to reduce fraud risk.

Now consider the complexities added by recent federal oversight. Legislation like the Sarbanes-Oxley and Dodd-Frank acts, together with associated regulatory enforcement, has upped the ante for boards of directors and management to prevent, timely detect, and respond to financial fraud. However, the laws, rules, and regulations provide scarce guidance on how to do this. To assist with this challenge, I coauthored a white paper on accounting complaint handling called *Hear That Whistle Blowing*, published in the *Anti-Corruption Handbook* and written by a fellow member of the Forensic and Valuation Services National Leadership team, William P. Olsen. In this piece, I discuss the tough task of evaluating how to handle complaints that involve both financial and human resources issues. This book moves another step closer in helping directors, management, auditors, and regulators understand the interconnectivity between financial fraud and human behavior.

In my experience, people trump internal policies, processes, and controls and people respond to incentives. To the fraudster, comprehensive and well-documented policies, procedures, and controls provide the landscape to navigate in order to commit fraud. In other words, fraudsters know what is being watched and how to avoid these areas to go undetected in their transgressions. For many of these bad actors, the creative process used to find ways around systems is stimulating and rewarding. The fecundity of the mind provides great incentive.

This has potentially wide-ranging implications for directors and management as they use this approach to assess financial fraud risks in the future. Company culture, international behavioral norms, and cues and patterns will be identified and weighed as important attitudinal issues affecting fraud risk. There will be an acknowledgment that certain financial programs unintentionally encourage bad behavior and, therefore, must be eliminated, modified, or actively managed. As a result, internal and external auditors, as well as regulators and oversight authorities, will be required to pay more attention to the human side of fraud. Inquiries and investigations into financial fraud will include objectives to determine whether an organization has a bad "apple," "bushel," or "crop"—the A.B.C. approach to fraud.

In this book, we now have a resource to close the gap between traditional financial "fraud risk assessment by the numbers" and the human element of fraud. Directors, management, and other stakeholders can learn how to identify and evaluate the people part of financial fraud. Most important, rank-and-file employees can be taught to understand and recognize the daily behaviors of their coworkers. Armed with this knowledge, they will be in the best position to help reduce financial fraud—just like the well-known U.S. Department of Homeland Security campaign slogan "If You See Something, Say Something," especially if it relates to A.B.C.!

Bradley J. Preber, CPA/CFF, CFE
National Managing Partner of Forensic and Valuation Services,
Grant Thornton LLP

APPENDIX A

The Psychology and Sociology of Fraud: Integrating the Behavioral Sciences Component into Fraud and Forensic Accounting Curricula

Sridhar Ramamoorti

The most incomprehensible fact about the universe is that it is comprehensible.
—Albert Einstein, Physics Nobel Laureate

The most comprehensible fact about human behavior is that it is incomprehensible.
—David Fisher, Professor of Cosmochemistry, University of Miami

INTRODUCTION

The 2008 *Report to the Nation* issued by the Association of Certified Fraud Examiners indicated that U.S. organizations lose almost 7 percent of their revenue to fraud, and that the Gross Domestic Product (GDP)-based annual fraud estimate for the United States alone was $994 billion (ACFE, 2008). Of course, we all now recognize that the scourge of fraud is a global phenomenon that extends far beyond the borders of the U.S. However, the study of white collar crime has hitherto been relatively sparse because "few areas of criminological investigation are plagued [with such] intractable controversies [including] conceptual ambiguities, distinctions, and taxonomies" (Shover 1998). Nevertheless, future business professionals, and especially accounting majors, must have a keen understanding of the new 21st century era of governance and accountability spawned by the post-Enron/WorldCom environment. In this regard, colleges and universities must do their part by encouraging business, criminology, and law faculty to carry out much-needed research in this important area and teach courses in fraud and forensic accounting (FFA). Because any organization can be plagued by fraud, organizations should strive to understand the behavioral root causes of fraud—who commits fraud and why—and thus, proactively manage their fraud risk exposure. Indeed, these are the fundamental premises underlying the model FFA curriculum developed by and implemented at West Virginia University (2007).[1] In this paper, I will make the case for looking seriously to the behavioral sciences—

Sridhar Ramamoorti is a partner in the National Corporate Governance Group of Grant Thornton LLP.

I would like to thank Professors Dick Riley and Tim Pearson of West Virginia University, Andy Bailey and Denis Posten of Grant Thornton, and especially, Professor Bruce Johnson of The University of Iowa for their comments on previous versions of this article.

[1] The West Virginia University model FFA curriculum had its genesis in a $614,000 project grant from the National Institute of Justice led by Professors Richard Riley and Bonnie Morris from the WVU Accounting Department and co-investigator, Professor Max Houck. Broad-based counsel was provided by a Technical Working Group (TWG) of which, the author of this paper, Dr. Sridhar Ramamoorti, was a member. (See http://www.ncjrs.gov/pdffiles1/nij/grants/217589.pdf)

psychology, sociology, criminology, and anthropology—to support the interdisciplinary field of fraud examination and forensic accounting in theory development and in practice, and in fraud prevention, deterrence, and detection.

Fraud involves intentional acts and is perpetrated by human beings using deception, trickery, and cunning that can be broadly classified as comprising two types of misrepresentation: *suggestio falsi* (suggestion of falsehood) or *suppressio veri* (suppression of truth).[2] As Ramamoorti and Olsen (2007) have argued: "Fraud is a human endeavor, involving deception, purposeful intent, intensity of desire, risk of apprehension, violation of trust, rationalization, etc. So, it is important to understand the psychological factors that might influence the behavior of fraud perpetrators. The rationale for drawing on behavioral science insights is evident from the intuition that one needs to 'think like a crook to catch a crook.' Many business professionals, especially those in the financial arena, tend to discount behavioral explanations. But as the incidence of fraud continues to grow, placing the spotlight on behavioral factors may be an important approach not only to fraud detection but to deterrence as well." In other words, when discussing the topic of fraud, we must inevitably bring in the human factor.

Consider the scathing criticism from five decades ago of Carl Devine (1960), now widely acknowledged as a pioneer of the "behavioral accounting research" paradigm: "Let us now turn to that part of accounting which is related directly to the psychological reactions of those who consume accounting output or are caught in its threads of control. On balance it seems fair to conclude that accountants seem to have waded through their relationships to the intricate psychological network of human activity with a heavy-handed crudity that is beyond belief. Some degree of crudity may be excused in a new discipline, but failure to recognize that much of what passes as accounting theory is hopelessly entwined with unsupported behavior assumptions is unforgivable." It is now evident that too many in the marketplace have been consumers of "creative accounting output" and have certainly been "caught in its threads of control" leaving them financially poorer. We need to understand, from a behavioral science standpoint, the motivations of these "criminals with clean fingernails" who can easily "steal without a gun" (Pavlo and Weinberg 2007; De Angelis 2000).

More recently, other knowledgeable commentators from practice, including supposedly "reformed fraudsters," have called for integrating the behavioral sciences component into FFA curricula. For instance, convicted felon Samuel Antar, of "Crazy Eddie" notoriety, makes the following insidious remarks on his website (http://www.whitecollarfraud.com): "You are not getting courses in criminality or psychology. You are not getting courses in what motivates people like me to commit the crimes that I committed that are going to possibly destroy your careers. They are going to cause investors to lose hundreds of millions of dollars."[3] Similarly, Joseph Wells, the founder and chairman of the Association of Certified Fraud Examiners (ACFE), has wryly observed: "As a group ... the majority of CPAs

---

[2] See the research by Grazioli et al. (2006) for a very interesting development of a cognitive psychology approach to detecting financial statement fraud deception tactics such as masking, dazzling, decoying, re-packaging, mimicking, and double play.

[3] Students are not getting courses in critical thinking either. For instance, Ruggiero (1995) noted such a desperate need in his preface to the first edition of a book on critical thinking, "because we live in an age of manipulation. Armies of hucksters and demagogues stand ready with the rich resources of psychology to play upon our emotions and subconscious needs to persuade us that superficial is profound, harmful is beneficial, evil is virtuous. And feelings are especially vulnerable to such manipulation ... in virtually every important area of modern life—law, medicine, government, education, science, business, and community affairs—we are beset with serious problems and complex issues that demand careful gathering and weighing of facts and informed opinions, thoughtful consideration of various conclusions or actions, and judicious selection of the best conclusion or most appropriate action."

are still ignorant about fraud ... for the last 80 years, untrained accounting graduates have been drafted to wage war against sophisticated liars and thieves. And as multi-billion dollar accounting failures have shown, it hasn't been much of a fight" (Wells 2004).

This paper is organized as follows: I will first provide definitions of psychology, sociology, and criminology to form the basis for subsequent discussion of the relevance of these behavioral science disciplines to the study of white collar crime. Next, examples of constructs from these disciplines will be used to highlight theories and explanatory variables that may be useful in understanding the sociology and psychology of the fraudster (e.g., lying and misrepresentation, social engineering, the science of persuasion, industrial psychopaths, heuristics and biases in decision making). This is followed by a similar application of these constructs to auditors, boards of directors and oversight bodies, structures, and processes. Concluding remarks are then offered, along with the Appendix, which contains behaviorally inspired solutions to the fraud problem, its prevention, deterrence, and detection.[4] The behavioral sciences are also relevant to fraud investigation and remediation efforts, but I have treated these as being beyond the scope of this preliminary overview paper.

DEFINITIONS OF PSYCHOLOGY AND CRIMINOLOGY

Psychology is the study of the nature, functions, and phenomena of behavior and mental experience; simply put, it is the science of human behavior[5] (Colman 2003). In general, psychology seeks to understand, explain, predict, and control individual and group behavior. Specifically, personality psychology studies individuals; social psychology looks at group behavior; cross-cultural psychology (anthropology) analyzes the impact of culture and context on behavior; and abnormal/personality/forensic psychology, sociology, and psychiatry focus on deviant behavior (including for instance, industrial psychopaths). Criminological psychology studies psychological problems associated with criminal behavior, criminal investigation, and the treatment of criminals (Colman 2003).

Criminology can be defined as the study of crime, the causes of crime (etiology), crime typology, the meaning of crime in terms of law, rates, or incidence of crime, and community reaction to crime. It is a branch of sociology, and also draws heavily from law (enforcement) literature. Strictly defined, it comprises four kinds of study: *descriptive* (viz., lawbreaking frequencies, contexts, and perpetrators, as well as consequences), *explanatory* (focusing on particular breaches, or accounting for differing frequencies), *penological* (studying effects on offenders such as reform, deterrence, rehabilitation, or incapacitation), and *nomological*

---

[4] Much of this paper borrows heavily from a presentation I have made numerous times to campus and professional audiences titled "The Psychology of White Collar Crime." Sutherland (1949) coined the term "white collar crime" and described it as a crime that is "committed by a person of respectability and high social status in the course of his occupation"; despite its flawed logical status, the phrase has demonstrated surprisingly strong staying power. White collar crime variously refers to the crime perpetrator's social status, criminal behavior in an occupational role, as well as crime committed by organizations or by individuals acting in organizational capacities (see also, Geis and Meier 1977). In this paper, I have used the terms white collar crime and fraud interchangeably.

[5] To understand better the term "science" in behavioral science, I quote from the AAA Behavioral Science in the Accounting Curriculum Committee: "The differences between the deliberate research activities of the behavioral scientist and the casual observations and conclusions of the sophisticated layman are mainly matters of procedure or method. They have to do with how clearly and precisely a person formulates his concepts, how carefully and systematically he makes and records observations, and how rigorously he reasons from data to conclusions. The objective of behavioral science is to understand, explain and predict human behavior; that is to establish generalizations about human behavior that are supported by empirical evidence collected in an impersonal way by procedures that are completely open to review and replication and capable of verification by other interested scholars" (see Ashton 1982).

(law enforcement itself, including questions such as the kinds of conduct that should be prohibited by the law) (Gregory 2004).

BEHAVIORAL ROOT CAUSES OF FRAUD

Behavioral scientists have failed thus far to identify a well-defined and well-understood psychological characteristic or a set of characteristics that are diagnostic about fraud perpetrator propensity. At the same time, to say that "greed and dishonesty"—a commonly heard refrain—can account for all that went on during the "irrational exuberance" of the 1990s and the early 2000s or earlier eras would be overly simplistic.[6] After all, most people in the business world are fully law abiding market participants—they do not necessarily resort to fraud to achieve their stretch goals. From a criminology perspective, white collar crime, like other crime, can best be explained by three factors: a supply of motivated offenders, the availability of suitable targets, and the absence of capable guardians—control systems or someone "to mind the store" so to speak (Cohen and Felson 1979).[7] This is consistent with the general explanation of (white collar) crime as choice, positing that variation in crime is produced by variation in opportunities and in motivation (Shover and Bryant 1993). Criminal opportunities are presented by those vulnerable environments and opportunistically interpretable scenarios that individuals and groups see as offering attractive potential for criminal reward with little apparent risk of detection or penalty. The aggregate rate of white collar crime varies directly with the supply of criminal opportunities and with the supply of individuals and organizations predisposed or motivated to exploit them; the rate and incidence of crime varies inversely with the intensity and severity of rule enforcement (Shover 1998).[8]

In general, fluctuations in business cycles, and criminogenic cultures that conflict with accepted social, ethical, and legal norms of behavior, are correlated with increases in the rate of white collar crime. For instance, when there is a widespread belief that "everyone is getting rich" many come to believe that to pass up any opportunity is to miss the boat. Similarly, after noting the illegitimate earnings management misdeeds of companies such as Enron, Nortel, and Cisco, Fuller and Jensen (2002) have commented ruefully, "Companies do not grow in a constant fashion with each quarter's results better than last. In the long run conforming to pressures to satisfy the market's desire for impossible predictability and unwise growth leads to the destruction of corporate value, shortened careers, humiliation, and damaged companies." Along the way, it also leads otherwise honest executives to turn to the dark side. They lie, cheat, and steal in order to relieve the immense pressure to meet analyst expectations of unattainable performance, just to keep their jobs and, thus, for self-preservation. It should be noted that other countries, cultures, and languages provide a context that allows fraud to flourish in perhaps different stripes, shapes, and forms. This is why it is necessary to bring in perspectives from economic/cultural anthropology to understand how white collar crime might manifest itself in other contexts.

---

[6] Cf. The fictitious character, Gordon Gekko, played by actor Michael Douglas in the 1987 movie *Wall Street* dramatically says "Greed is good." The movie portrays corporate raiders of the 1980s era, and by illustrating the frenzied pace of mergers and acquisitions, made the theoretically justified but practically dubious idea of aligning the interests of managers and stockholders through the granting of stock options to executives, a part of popular culture.

[7] More recent research by Weisburd et al. (1995) finds that some convicted white collar criminals see such crime as a good bet as a revealed preference from their surprisingly high rate of recidivism, or repeat criminal offenses.

[8] Shover (1998) laments that "[d]espite its axiomatic status in crime-as-choice theory, the hypothesized inverse relationship between variation in use of sanctions and the rate of white-collar crime has received little attention from investigators."

Starting with Cressey (1973), the sociology and criminology literature describes fraud perpetrators as "trust violators." In other words, trust violators are people you would not normally suspect of committing fraud. Specifically, Cressey (1973) explains, "Trusted persons become trust violators when they conceive of themselves as having a financial problem which is non-shareable, are aware this problem can be secretly resolved by violation of the position of financial trust, and are able to apply to their own conduct in the situation verbalizations which enable them to adjust their conceptions of themselves as trusted persons with their conceptions of themselves as users of the entrusted funds or property" (see also, Albrecht et al. 1984). Specifically, trust violators and fraud perpetrators must be able to justify their actions to themselves and others as a psychological coping mechanism to deal with the inevitable "cognitive dissonance" (that is, a lack of congruence between their own perception of being honest and the deceptive nature of their action or behavior[9]). This explanation led to the inclusion of "rationalization" as one of the elements in the conceptual framework provided by the "Fraud Triangle" that is discussed next (see Wells 2004).

THE FRAUD TRIANGLE RE-INTERPRETED

An important conceptual framework in understanding fraud is the so-called "fraud triangle," loosely based on what policemen and detectives have referred to as "means, motives, and opportunity." Widely disseminated by the Association of Certified Fraud Examiners (ACFE), the fraud triangle has three elements, *viz.*, *Perceived Incentives/Pressures*, *Perceived Opportunities*, and *Rationalization of Fraudulent Behavior* (see Figure 1). Not surprisingly, all three elements of the fraud triangle are influenced by the fraud perpetrators' psychology. After all, personal incentives and perceived pressure drive human behavior, and the need to rationalize wrongdoing as being somehow defensible is very much psychologically rooted in the notion of cognitive dissonance. To some extent, even the assessment of opportunity—including the relatively low likelihood of being caught—depends on the perpetrator's personal, behavioral calculus. Accordingly, when trying to understand the root causes of fraud, it behooves us to seek psychological answers and explanations, not just logical ones. White collar criminals need excuses, and here's a typical list:

FIGURE 1
The Fraud Triangle: Opportunity, Pressure, and Rationalization

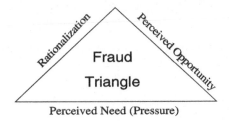

---

[9] Cf. The theory of "cognitive dissonance"—a psychologically distressing state motivating the individual to distort one or both cognitions to restore consistency—was first proposed by Stanford University social psychologist, Leon Festinger (1957). Conditions under which dissonance as discrepancy between attitudes and actions produces attitude change: actions must have consequences perceived to be negative, the actor must feel personally responsible, and arousal must be both experienced and linked to the dissonance (Joule and Beauvois 1998).

- Everyone's getting rich, so why shouldn't I?
- Taking money is just a temporary "borrowing," it will be returned when the gambling/betting winnings materialize.
- I deserve these "perks" as reasonable compensation, and the company can certainly afford it.
- This is a victimless crime, if anything, and I am not hurting anyone; in fact what I am doing is for a good cause!
- It is not really a serious matter.

Although the fraud triangle is a powerful conceptual tool, there are other factors such as the basic greed and acquisitiveness, a "revenge motive" to make the organization pay for perceived inequities, or a "catch me if you can" attitude that some white collar criminals exhibit, and these personality characteristics do not easily fit within the fraud triangle framework. Similarly, the white collar criminal's assessment of the organization's attitude toward fraud even if the perpetrator is identified (e.g., organizational inertia and reluctance to take any action, turning a blind eye, being content with a slap on the wrist, poor track record in vigorously prosecuting fraud) gets factored into the bahavioral calculus but is not obvious as a separate descriptive category. Hence, to discourage would-be fraudsters, ACFE Founder Joseph Wells advises, "Let them know you're watching!"

White collar crime is notoriously difficult to prosecute because the offenders are well connected and often are first-time offenders. Such fraud perpetrators take extreme care to conceal their activities, destroy evidence, and disrupt the audit trail. Indeed, Braithwaite (1991) has argued that white collar crime is a defining issue in criminology as it puts into sharp relief the "differentials of power and influence" as well as the dynamics of inequality in wealth, power, status, and personal reputation. Thus, even the common expression "where there's smoke, there's fire" may not quite apply, because the fraud perpetrator may introduce a smoke screen or otherwise stamp out the smoke, leaving no tell-tale evidence of fire. We should instead heed the quip used by scientists engaged in the search for extraterrestrial life: "Absence of evidence is not evidence of absence." For all these reasons, many corporate and economic crimes are not prosecuted despite their significant financial consequences, and white collar crime remains a largely unmanaged risk in organizations.

When undertaking prosecution of white collar crime cases, it is important to consider the "other fraud triangle" consisting of the vertices of "the act, the concealment, and the conversion" to ferret out and reconstruct how the fraudulent act was committed, what actions were taken by the fraudster to hide the audit trail or conceal his/her tracks, and eventually how s/he (as well as potential others) unlawfully benefited from the act.

CRIMINOLOGY, SOCIOLOGY, PSYCHOLOGY, AND THE FRAUDSTER

Sorting people into types based on distinguishing characteristics or behavioral dispositions is a common social process. The rationale in criminology behind (white collar) crime typologies is the potential to facilitate crime prevention or correctional efforts[10] for which success naturally depends on accurately identifying and addressing the specific problems

---

[10] Gibbons (2002) notes: "In order to be useful in causal inquiry or correctional intervention, typologies must meet several requirements. First, a typology must be sufficiently detailed and clear so that offenders can be reliably assigned to its categories. A second requirement is that the typology identify mutually exclusive types, so that actual offenders fall into only one slot. A third criterion is parsimony, that is, a relative limit in the number of types. Finally, typologies must be empirically congruent; that is, the typological description should closely fit the individuals in a given type, and the population under scrutiny should largely fall within the typology without a residual category of unclassified cases ... typological schemes in criminology often fail to meet these four criteria."

underlying different kinds of lawbreaking behavior (Gibbons 1965). For instance, Mr. Thomas Golden of PricewaterhouseCoopers, an experienced forensic accountant, believes that financial reporting fraud perpetrators fit one of two profiles: "greater good oriented" or "scheming, self-centered" types. Those who fit the greater good oriented profile are "otherwise honest individuals who misrepresent the numbers by rationalizing that what they are doing is best for the company." The scheming, self-centered types are "individuals who exhibit a rampant disregard for the truth, are well aware of what they are doing and who are attempting to attain goals dishonestly."[11] Given the challenges in devising accurate white collar crime typologies, it is likely that we will see an effort to distinguish types of white collar crime, i.e., crime patterns, rather than white collar criminal taxonomies. For instance, Shapiro (1980) advocates a search for behavioral patterns in characterizing different types of white collar crime such as fraud, self-dealing, and regulatory offenses. In subsequent writings, Shapiro (1990) suggests it is high time that we looked beyond "perpetrators' wardrobe and social characteristics" to "the *modus operandi* of their misdeeds and the ways in which they establish and exploit trust." As noted earlier, the concept of "abuse of trust" is a centerpiece of Cressey's (1973) characterization of white collar criminals as trust violators. A trust crime refers to the "exploitation of a fiduciary position by an agent responsible for custody, discretion, information, or property rights" (Shover 1998).[12] Two ways in which we can use behavioral science to understand the *modus operandi* of trust violators are now briefly described: the science of persuasion (Cialdini 2001, 2007; Hogan and Speakman 2006) and social engineering (Hinson 2008; Mitnick and Simon 2002).

SCIENCE OF PERSUASION

Psychologist Cialdini (2001, 2007) describes how hard-wired tendencies of human beings are cleverly exploited in influencing and persuading others. It is important to understand that when the influencer's intent is not honorable, the result is not persuasion but manipulation (Lakhani 2005). This is why the "science of persuasion" represents an important key to understanding how trust violators go about their business of manipulating others. For instance, what the convicted felon Sam Antar refers to on his website as "the art of spinning" involves swindlers' tactics such as "selling people hope," "making excuses as long as one can," or "attacking the messenger to detract scrutiny of one's own actions" that exploit human gullibility in an extreme fashion.

SOCIAL ENGINEERING

Social engineering involves systematic manipulation of others through trickery and cunning. Social engineers "toy with your trust" and are masters of the craft of gaining and using their "influence" through persuasive requests. It is only through deep familiarity with the methods and techniques adopted by social engineers that we can put up an adequate defense to pierce the "veil of deception." "Social engineering uses influence and persuasion to deceive people by convincing them that the social engineer is someone he is not, or by manipulation. As a result, the social engineer is able to take advantage of people to obtain information with or without the use of technology" (Mitnick and Simon 2002). Hinson

---

[11] Mr. Thomas Golden's characterization of financial reporting fraud perpetrator profiles are taken from Ballou et al. (2006). For descriptive convenience, the constructive labels "greater good oriented" and "scheming, self-centered" types have been furnished by this paper's author.

[12] In Genesis, Chapter 27, of *The Bible*, there is a narrative of how Jacob impersonates his elder brother, Esau, to trick his blind father into giving Jacob the inheritance that is Esau's birthright. This is a classic trust crime relating to fraudulent usurping of a sibling's property rights (mentioned in De Angelis [2000]).

(2008) notes, that instead of trying to break into computer networks and systems that are protected by technical security control measures, social engineers prefer to compromise the people who configure, use, and manage them. They cheat and lie their way past those who are naïve and/or unaware of the threat. Generally speaking, people are easier to deceive than computers, so social engineering remains a threat for all organizations, even those that have excellent technical security controls. In other words, people represent the weakest link in the systems security chain.

Yet another angle from which to appreciate the relevance of the behavioral sciences is to look at the emerging literature on industrial psychopaths. I turn to this next.

INDUSTRIAL PSYCHOPATHS

Some "con artists" might score high enough to be classified as "industrial/organizational psychopaths." Psychopathology refers to the science of diseases of the human mind. A psychopathic personality is characterized by a mental pathology with the following traits:

1. amoral and antisocial behavior,
2. inability to form meaningful personal relationships, and
3. extreme egocentricity and absence of empathy.

Several toxic elements of such personalities come to one's attention: An oversized ego frequently characterized by greed and self-aggrandizement, an obsession with material possessions, and "using" human beings to further one's own selfish goals (cf., German philosopher Kant's view to always treat another human being as an end in themselves, but never as a means to an end).

Dr. Paul Babiak observed at the 2000 Annual Meeting of the American Neuropsychiatric Association that: "Not all psychopaths end up in prison, and some of them exploit organizational chaos, and thrive in business." He went on to comment that manipulation and self-serving dishonesty are hardly unknown in the business world, for some 15 percent of top executives have been known, on average, to misrepresent their education and about one-third of all resumes contain lies. Industrial psychopaths have been described as "social predators who charm, manipulate, and ruthlessly plow their way through life, leaving a broad trail of broken hearts, shattered expectations and empty wallets ... selfishly taking what they want and doing as they please without the slightest sense of guilt or regret" (Hare 1998). Further, Cleckley (1976) notes that "goodness, evil, love, horror, and humor have no actual meaning, no power to move the psychopath. He is furthermore lacking in the ability to see that others are moved. It is as though he were colour-blind, despite his sharp intelligence, to the emotional aspect of human existence." Based on his limited research, Babiak (2000) described the following common pattern in the industrial psychopath's behavior:

- **Organizational entry:** Charming the interviewer; not a particularly difficult thing to do for expert manipulators.
- **Assessment:** Gauging utility of various members of organization during "honeymoon" period; begins to charm people in power and others of use to him/her; establishes a communication network.
- **Manipulation:** Psychopath spreads disinformation to enhance his/her image and disparage others; creates conflict among those who might pool negative information about himself/herself; uses full arsenal of social tools: rational persuasion, inspirational appeal, ingratiation, and coalition to accomplish devious goals.

- **Confrontation:** Psychopath abandons the "pawns" no longer useful to him/her and takes steps to "neutralize" the detractors whom s/he has failed to take in; raises doubts about the latter's competence or honesty.
- **Ascension:** Psychopath reaches upper echelons where he abandons his "patrons," those well up in the corporate hierarchy who have facilitated his rise to power (seen in one-third of the cases).

In summary, organizational entry, honeymoon period, manipulation, confrontation, and ascension appear to be the general routine followed by industrial psychopaths as they infiltrate and wreak havoc on corporations. Rather interestingly, Babiak and Hare (2006) have written a book in which they refer to industrial psychopaths as "snakes in suits."

SOCIOLOGY AND PSYCHOLOGY OF BOARD AND AUDITOR OVERSIGHT PROCESSES

The Sarbanes-Oxley Act has given the public company audit committee a very important role in the oversight of financial reporting matters. To discharge their newly defined monitoring and oversight function effectively, audit committees need a primer on the psychology of the fraud perpetrator(s) as well as insight about their own and the auditors' cognitive weaknesses and blindspots. One important behavioral insight is recognizing that high-level fraud is frequently a "team sport" and often involves collusion. Internal controls typically presume proper segregation of duties and, hence, are quite powerless against collusion and management override of controls. In fact, the COSO (1999) Fraud Study found that in 83 percent of the frauds examined, the CEO and the CFO had colluded. At the board level, the well-known *groupthink* bias ("many heads, one mind") should be guarded against. *Groupthink* discounts contrarian opinions or tends to sway the group into making a "feels good" decision, because maintaining group cohesiveness and solidarity is seen as more important than realistic appraisal of the facts at hand (Janis 1982). When there is an active tendency to ignore bad news due to either indifference or sheer laziness, board members may miss important signals of potential fraud. Jensen (1993) notes, "Board culture is an important component of board failure. The great emphasis on politeness and courtesy at the expense of truth and frankness in boardrooms is both a symptom and cause of failure in the control system. CEOs have the same insecurities and defense mechanisms as other human beings; few will accept, much less seek, the monitoring and criticism of an active and attentive board." Thus, it is easy to fault boards of directors for weak oversight, but we should also recognize that many of them may owe their position on the board to the CEO.

This is particularly so when the CEO also doubles up as chairman of the board. The trusted relationships that subsist between external auditors and their clients sometimes make auditors let their guard down. When encountering fraud scenarios, human tendencies can severely bias the auditors' judgments, viz., the *confirmation bias* (seeking confirmation of one's beliefs, e.g., the presumption that the audit client survived the audit firm's rigorous screening process and therefore must be trustworthy) and *selective perception* (seeing only what one wants to see, e.g., what one encounters during the audit is never attributed to fraud as there always could exist more innocuous non-error explanations for noted anomalies and exceptions). Such cognitive heuristics and biases have been documented extensively (see Kahneman et al. 1982) and limit auditors' ability to exercise an appropriate level of professional skepticism.

CONCLUDING REMARKS

While corporate governance reform legislation such as the Sarbanes-Oxley Act of 2002 can help limit the opportunity for fraud, individual ethics and integrity cannot be legislated. As such, fraud deterrence and detection should focus on how to deal with the underlying interpersonal and behavioral dynamics—the psychology of fraud perpetrators as well as the psychology of those responsible for governance, including auditors, and their interactions. The fraud triangle—consisting of opportunity, pressure, and rationalization—is a useful conceptual framework to understand the root causes of fraud and their behavioral underpinnings. However, it is also important to look at the other fraud triangle that focuses on the act, the concealment, and the conversion (that benefits the white collar criminal directly or indirectly). Most important to note, it is *human beings* who commit crimes, sometimes as agents on behalf of their organizations, so we must attempt to understand their motivations and determine both the why and the how of white collar crime. For organizations, establishing anti-fraud programs and controls is critical. To do this, understanding of behavioral factors influencing fraud perpetration is key for establishing responsive fraud deterrence and detection mechanisms and proactively managing the risk of financial fraud. Interestingly, the significance of behavioral science insights increases even more when we move into the domain of fraud investigation[13] as well as remediation.

Nisbett and Ross (1980) observe: "One of philosophy's oldest paradoxes is the apparent contradictions between the greatest triumphs and dramatic failures of the human mind. The same organism that routinely solves inferential problems too subtle and complex for the mightiest computers often makes errors in the simplest of judgments about everyday events. The errors, moreover, often seem traceable to violations of the same inferential rules that underlie people's most impressive successes." This is very similar to the colloquial observation that "what we have today are technological giants but ethical infants" (Ramamoorti and Weidenmier 2004).

Recent neuroscience research promises to shed further light on why we behave as we do, even in the highly subjective and personal domain of our morals and ethics. For several years now, anthropologists, psychologists, and evolutionary theorists have argued that our ethical and moral life evolved from nature (*cf.*, Hauser 2006). In the first book to describe how ethics may be a hardwired function of the human brain, distinguished neuroscientist, Donald Pfaff (2007) explains how specific brain circuits (and "mirror neurons") cause us to consider an action toward another as if it were happening to us, prompting us to treat others as we wish to be treated ourselves ("the Golden Rule"). He presents a convincing argument as to why humans across time and geography have such similar notions of good and bad, right and wrong, thus highlighting the cause-and-effect linkages among biology, psychology, and the humanities. So, 21st century advances in neuroscience are making human behavior a little bit more comprehensible after all (*cf.*, opening quotes to this paper). These developments bode well for the engagement of the behavioral sciences, including neuroscience, in understanding the "criminal mind" and will shed more light on the psychology of white collar crime.

---

[13] For instance, consider the highly developed ability to interview suspected fraudsters—as a human-to-human battle of wits and emotional tracking, reading faces, body language, etc., for lie detection in real time can be very psychologically demanding. It is clearly more art than science and such interviewing ability improves with experience.

APPENDIX
BEHAVIORALLY ORIENTED SOLUTIONS TO THE FRAUD PROBLEM
(adapted from Ramamoorti and Olsen 2007)

Among behavioral approaches and solutions to the fraud risk factors mentioned are:

- Sound tone at the top, with management "walking the talk"; aligning incentive structures within the organization in such a way that does not encourage fraud perpetration; an active Board and audit committee overseeing management performance and activities (as well as the work by external and internal auditors).
- Nurturing a culture of integrity and ethics, supported by an organizational code of conduct, periodic ethics audits, and enforcement of noted violations of the code; maintaining an ethics and/or whistleblower hotline; explicitly rewarding good behavior.
- Routine background checks on new and experienced hires, as well as for making senior leadership appointments (Human Resources needs to be leading this effort).
- Swift, decisive action to respond to incidents of fraud so that employees and others are aware of the organization's serious commitment to dealing with fraud issues head-on.
- Fraud awareness training, perhaps delivered by internal audit professionals or outside consultants, including description of ethics hotlines and guidance on what to do when fraud is encountered; control self-assessments that consist of process risk owners performing risk and control mapping (and including fraud risk considerations in such exercises).

REFERENCES

Albrecht, W. S., K. R. Howe, and M. B. Romney. 1984. *Deterring Fraud: The Internal Auditor's Perspective.* Altamonte Springs, FL: The Institute of Internal Auditors' Research Foundation.

Ashton, R. H. 1982. *Human Information Processing in Accounting.* Summarization of the report abstract of the Committee on Behavioral Science Content of the Accounting Curriculum. Accounting Research Monograph #17. Sarasota, FL: American Accounting Association.

Association of Certified Fraud Examiners (ACFE). 2008. *2008 Report to the Nation on Occupational Fraud and Abuse.* Austin, TX: ACFE.

Babiak, P. 2000. Psychopaths in the organization. Presentation delivered at the Eleventh Annual Meeting of the American Neuropsychiatric Association, Fort Myers, FL, February 20–22.

———, and R. D. Hare. 2006. *Snakes in Suits: When Psychopaths Go To Work.* New York, NY: HarperCollins.

Ballou, B., D. L. Heitger, and C. L. Landes. 2006. The future of corporate sustainability reporting. *Journal of Accountancy* (December).

Braithwaite, J. 1991. Poverty, power, and white collar crime: Sutherland and the paradoxes of criminological theory. *Australian-New Zealand Journal of Criminology* 24: 40–58.

Cialdini, R. B. 2001. *Influence: Science and Practice.* Needham Heights, MA: Allyn and Bacon.

———. 2007. *Influence: The Psychology of Persuasion.* New York, NY: HarperCollins.

Cleckley, H. 1976. *The Mask of Sanity.* 5th edition. St. Louis, MO: Mosby.

Cohen, I., and M. Felson. 1979. Social change and crime rate trends: A routine activity approach. *American Sociological Review* 44: 588–608.

Colman, A. M. 2003. *Oxford Dictionary of Psychology.* Oxford, UK: Oxford University Press.

Committee of Sponsoring Organizations of the Treadway Commission (COSO). 1999. *Fraudulent Financial Reporting: 1987–1997, An Analysis of U.S. Public Companies.* Fraud study. New York, NY: COSO.

Cressey, D. 1973. *Other People's Money: A Study in the Social Psychology of Embezzlement.* Montclair, NJ: Patterson Smith.

De Angelis, G. 2000. *White Collar Crime.* Philadelphia, PA: Chelsea House Publishers.

Devine, C. T. 1960. Research methodology and accounting theory formation. *The Accounting Review* (July): 387–399.

Festinger, L. 1957. *A Theory of Cognitive Dissonance.* Stanford, CA: Stanford University Press.

Fuller, J., and M. Jensen. 2002. Just SAY NO to Wall Street: Putting a stop to the earnings game. *Journal of Applied Corporate Finance* 14 (4): 41–46.

Geis, G., and R. F. Meier, eds. 1977. *White-Collar Crime: Offenses in Business, Politics, and the Professions.* New York, NY: Free Press.

Gibbons, D. C. 1965. *Changing the Lawbreaker.* Englewood Cliffs, NJ: Prentice Hall.

———. 2002. Typologies of criminal behavior. In *Encyclopedia of Crime and Justice,* 2nd edition, Volume 4, edited by J. Dressler, 1585–1591. New York, NY: MacMillan Reference USA.

Grazioli, S., K. Jamal, and P. E. Johnson. 2006. A cognitive approach to fraud detection. *Journal of Forensic Accounting* VII: 65–88.

Gregory, R. L. 2004. *The Oxford Companion to the Mind.* Oxford, UK: Oxford University Press.

Hare, R. D. 1998. *Without Conscience: The Disturbing World of Psychopaths Among Us.* New York, NY: Guilford Press.

Hauser, M. D. 2006. *Moral Minds: How Nature Designed Our Universal Sense of Right and Wrong.* New York, NY: HarperCollins.

Hinson, G. 2008. Social engineering techniques, risks and controls. *EDPACS: The EDP Audit, Control and Security Newsletter* Vol. XXXVII (4–5): 32–46.

Hogan, K., and J. Speakman. 2006. *Covert Persuasion: Psychological Tactics and Tricks to Win the Game.* Hoboken, NJ: John Wiley and Sons.

Janis, I. L. 1982. *Groupthink: A Psychological Study of Policy Decisions and Fiascoes.* Boston, MA: Houghton Mifflin Company.

Joule, R., and L. Beauvois. 1998. Cognitive dissonance theory: A radical view. *European Journal of Social Psychology* 8: 1–32.

Kahneman, D., P. Slovic, and A. Tversky, eds. 1982. *Judgment Under Uncertainty: Heuristics and Biases.* Cambridge, MA: Cambridge University Press.

Lakhani, D. 2005. *Persuasion: The Art of Getting What You Want.* Hoboken, NJ: John Wiley and Sons.

Mitnick, K., and W. L. Simon. 2002. *The Art of Deception: Controlling the Human Element of Security.* New York, NY: John Wiley and Sons.

Nisbett, R. E., and L. Ross. 1980. *Human Inference: Strategies and Shortcomings of Social Judgment.* Englewood Cliffs, NJ: Prentice Hall.

Pavlo, W., Jr., and N. Weinberg. 2007. *Stolen Without A Gun: Confessions from Inside History's Biggest Accounting Fraud—The Collapse of MCI WorldCom.* Tampa, FL: Etika Books LLC.

Pfaff, D. W. 2007. *The Neuroscience of Fair Play: Why We Usually follow The Golden Rule.* New York, NY: Dana Press.

Ramamoorti, S., and M. Weidenmier. 2004. The pervasive impact of information technology on internal auditing. Supplemental chapter for *Research Opportunities in Internal Auditing,* edited by A. Bailey, A. Gramling, and S. Ramamoorti. Altamonte Springs, FL: IIA Research Foundation.

———, and W. Olsen. 2007. Fraud: The human factor. *Financial Executive* (July/August).

Ruggiero, V. R. 1995. *Beyond Feelings: A Guide to Critical Thinking.* Fourth edition. Mountain View, CA: Mayfield Publishing Company.

Shapiro, S. P. 1980. *Thinking about White-Collar Crime: Matters of Conceptualization and Research.* Washington, D.C.: U.S. Department of Justice, National Institute of Justice.

———. 1990. Collaring the crime, not the criminal: Reconsidering "white collar crime." *American Sociological Review* (55): 346–365.

Shover, N., and K. M. Bryant. 1993. Theoretical explanations of corporate crime. In *Understanding Corporate Criminality,* edited by M. B. Blankenship. New York, NY: Garland.

———. 1998. White collar crime. In *The Handbook of Crime and Punishment,* edited by M. Tonry. Oxford, UK: Oxford University Press.

Sutherland, E. 1949. *White Collar Crime.* Foreword by D. R. Cressey. New York, NY: Holt.

Weisburd, D., E. Waring, and E. Chayet. 1995. Specific deterrence in a sample of offenders convicted of white-collar crimes. *Criminology* (33): 587–607.

Wells, J. T. 2004. *The Corporate Fraud Handbook: Prevention and Detection.* Hoboken, NJ: John Wiley and Sons.

West Virginia University. 2007. *Report of the National Institute of Justice Grant on the Model Fraud and Forensic Accounting FFA Curriculum.* Available at: http://www.ncjrs.gov/pdffiles1/nij/grants/217589.pdf

APPENDIX B

Chapter Supplements

This appendix offers descriptions, summaries, examples, and even poetry(!) related to the topics discussed throughout the book.

Supplement to the Preface: 2011 ACFE Video, *Inside the Fraudster's Mind*

In 2011, the Association of Certified Fraud Examiners (ACFE) developed a video for its members consisting of excerpts from interviews with numerous convicted white-collar felons.[1] The host for the video was Tonia Cooke, and reputed criminologist Gilbert Geis, a past president of the ACFE, provided expert commentary. Among the white-collar criminals featured in the video are Kenneth Kemp, Mark Whitacre, Barry Webne, Aaron Beam, Steve Comisar, Patrick Kuhse, Justin Paperny, Kevin Barnes, and Samuel Antar.

Arguing that fraudsters think differently than the rest of us do, the video highlights many of the white-collar criminals' "thinking errors," such as:

- **Sense of entitlement.** Fraudsters seem to believe that they have received unfair, inequitable treatment and are therefore only taking what they're owed.
- **Being overly optimistic.** Fraudsters don't believe they can ever get caught, so there's no inhibition against doing whatever it takes to make money.

- **Rationalization.** Fraudsters sincerely believe that they aren't the bad guys and that committing fraud is like an addiction: they can't stop. Short stints in jail are not a sufficient deterrent—hence the high rates of recidivism.
- **Peer or financial pressure.** Although the susceptibility is situational, CEOs are known to exert pressure on CFOs to "cook" the books and engage in aggressive accounting. Before long, it becomes outright fraud.
- **Instant gratification.** Fraudsters believe that everybody is corrupt to a certain degree and have no qualms about taking shortcuts to obtain immediate or short-term results.
- **Diffusion of harm.** White-collar crime tends to be a "faceless" crime, and fraudsters believe that fraud against the company doesn't affect the stockholders too much; they rationalize that the state has millions of taxpayers, and no individual would be affected too much. In the film, Geis remarks that "group actions involve people doing things that they would never do alone." There is comfort in knowing that everybody else is doing it.
- **Lack of remorse.** One felon says that he "didn't really feel bad. . . . When you stop caring, you'll do anything." However, fraudsters do want to keep their self-esteem, so they say it is someone else's fault to try to avoid going to prison.
- **Egoism.** Extreme competence can lead to egoism. This is different from arrogance, which is not a surefire indicator of a fraudster; not all arrogant individuals are unethical. Egoism makes fraudsters believe in their power of manipulation and their ability to talk their way out of crimes, because they are convinced that they are smarter than their victims.
- **Disregard for authority and rules.** Sam Antar, a member of the inner circle of a family business, claims that during their business management discussions, no moral concerns were ever raised. Committing fraud was just like another part of life.

Toward the end of the video, the following strategies to prevent fraud are mentioned: recognize pressure, reduce the opportunity, set an ethical tone at the top, encourage whistleblowers, develop and deploy an effective internal audit function, focus on long-term goals, and teach ethics to staff.

Supplement 1 to Chapter 3: "Greed Takes the Blame"

The following editorial is by Mr. David Freedman, the senior editor of the *Value Examiner*, a publication of the National Association of Certified Valuators and Analysts (NACVA):

I thumbed through four business bestsellers about the economic collapse of 2008–2009. All four of them blame that mother of all scapegoats, greed, among other things, for the severity of the recession. Here are mini-reviews of the four books, which were published this year:

And Then the Roof Caved In: How Wall Street's Greed and Stupidity Brought Capitalism to Its Knees, by David Faber (John Wiley & Sons)

Faber, a CNBC reporter, traces the roots of the economic collapse to failures of investment banks, mortgage lenders, ratings agencies, and the U.S. government. It all started, he says, when the Federal Reserve pushed interest rates to historic lows after September 11, 2001.

A Colossal Failure of Common Sense: The Inside Story of the Collapse of Lehman Brothers, by Lawrence G. McDonald and Patrick Robinson (Crown Business Books)

The demise of the nation's oldest investment bank was a devastating blow to the world's financial system. The authors of *A Colossal Failure,* one of whom was a former Lehman VP, blame the firm's executives as greedy, arrogant, and recklessly addicted to growth.

House of Cards: A Tale of Hubris and Wretched Excess on Wall Street, by William D. Cohan (Doubleday)

Cohan, a financial journalist, traces the beginning of Wall Street's collapse on the fall of Bear Stearns. He "vividly documents the mix of arrogance, greed, recklessness, and pettiness that took down the 86-year-old brokerage house, and then the entire economy," says *BusinessWeek.*

Fool's Gold: How the Bold Dream of a Small Tribe at J. P. Morgan was Corrupted by Wall Street Greed and Unleashed a Catastrophe, by Gillian Tett (Free Press)

A *Financial Times* journalist details how the market in securitized credit derivatives was perverted by greed, arrogance, and delusion.

What's wrong with Greed?

According to Adam Smith, capitalism succeeds because people in the marketplace are permitted to act, both individually and collectively, on the basis of enlightened self-interest. Well, who is enlightened? My view is that nobody is enlightened. So capitalism actually succeeds on the basis of the unenlightened self-interest. Which is not a lot different from greed. What do you think? [2]

Supplement 2 to Chapter 3: "Fraud Is a Bad Thing" by Michael Grayson

Fraud is a bad thing, it is true,
So why do people do, do, do?
Opportunity is one part of the reason why,
Because they think they can do it on the sly.

Incentive or pressure is the second part here.
Pressure implies that they have a fear
Of something bad happening if they do what is right,
So they do what is bad without putting up a fight.
Incentive means that if they commit fraud, they will receive
Something good for themselves if they successfully deceive
People who rely on them to do proper work
And report honestly instead of information berserk.

The ability to rationalize completes the fraud triangle.
People who know would not call this a new fangle.
The fraudsters knew it was wrong, but excuses they make—
And some people even want to let them get away with it.

Boy, that takes the cake![3]

Supplement to Chapter 4: The Mind Today: Peeking into the Brain

The material in this section, which is based on the findings of neuroscience, is evolving. The functions of the brain are important, because the more analysis of emotional material that can be done by the brain, the more accurate the individual's decision making will be—and hence, the less the chance of being defrauded.

The mind and the brain overlap; affect relates to the central nervous system and interacts with the body to express emotion. Thanks to advances in neuroscience (even neuroeconomics!), understanding of this area is rapidly accelerating and is very promising for the risk officer and the fraud investigator. Highlights of what we know now are described next.

Some interesting research into the universal nature of human emotion is being done through the Internet and *crowdsourcing*. We have seen functional magnetic resonance imaging research showing that the experience of being excluded from a game produces physical symptoms that are described as feeling like being kicked in the gut.[4]

Brain structures are beginning to show clear associations with certain emotions; for example, disgust has been correlated with the insular cortex.[5] The role of emotions in memory has been known for a long time, but recent research has shown how this relates to structures in the brain and produces actual changes at the molecular level. Psychological growth from infancy to adulthood enhances the logic of emotion, and there is now a model that correlates brain structures with the psychological functions of the mind (see Table B.1).[6]

Table B.1 Correlations between the Brain and the Mind

Depth	Part of the Brain	Psychological Function of the Mind
Deepest (oldest)	Brain stem	Visceral activation
	Diencephalon	Action tendencies
	Limbic	Discrete emotions
	Paralimbic	Blends of emotion
Highest (newest)	Prefrontal cortex	Blends of blends

In a finding that is most intriguing for crime solvers, eyewitnesses who accurately identified a criminal had a different brain pattern of activity than eyewitnesses who were adamant in their identifications but whose memories turned out to be false. This correlated to the memory center (the hippocampus), to the emotional "weigh station" (the prefrontal cortex), and to how long the eye focused on the correct face.[7]

Supplement 1 to Chapter 5: Sample Phishing E-Mail—the Case from the In-Box

For the sake of simplicity, it is worthwhile to start with a common fraudulent scheme that is familiar to all, the e-mail "phishing" attempt (just as the biologist uses the drosophila, or the common fruit fly, whose genome has been completely sequenced).

Here is a recent example. It arrived in people's e-mail inboxes shortly before New Year's Day 2012:

OFFICE OF THE UNITED NATIONS

Secretary-General Ban Ki-moon

Whitehall Court, London, SW1A 2EL

UNITED KINGDOM

Our ref: . . . UNA-UK/1347/IDR

Your ref: . . . UNA-UK/555/2011

UNITED NATION'S EMPOWERMENT PROGRAM

On behalf of UNITED NATION'S Secretary-General Ban Ki-moon and Mr. Jean-Pierre Gonnot, Acting Director, Division for Social Policy and Development. We wish to inform you of your selection as one of our Beneficiary for ongoing Financial Empowerment Program, according to the meeting held on Commission for Social Development, on 48th session (UN Headquarters, 22nd of June 2011) in collaboration with Barack Hussein Obama's Foundation in United State Of America. All participants/beneficiaries were selected randomly from Worldwide online networks Directories.

I, Ted Turner, UN Foundation Chairman, wish to inform you of your selection as one of the Beneficiary of £2.8 Million Great British Pounds Sterling, for the ongoing 2011 Financial Empowerment Program worldwide.

So, this letter is to officially inform you that your benefited funds has been accredited into Visa/ATM CARD in your favor, with ATM Card Number (4080 2010 1765 5501); Your Personal Identification Number is 343.

As this office will send to you a Visa/ATM CARD that you will use to withdraw your funds in any ATM MACHINE CENTER or Visa card outlet in the world with a maximum withdrawal of J5000 GBP daily. Furthermore, you will be required to re-confirm your Bio Data as stated below to avoid impersonation which will enable the payment committee of UN begin the delivery process of your Visa/ATM CARD.

1. Full names
2. Address
3. Country
4. Nationality
5. Phone number
6. Age
7. Occupation
8. Zip code
9. ID
10. ATM card number

You will be required to send a scanned copy of your passport or any mode of identification.

Take note that you are warned to stop further communications with any other person(s) or office(s) different from the staff of UN Foundation West Africa, Abuja Nigeria, to avoid impersonation or hitches in receiving your Empowerment Funds.

NB: This is to Initiate Poverty Eradication Worldwide/ International Financial Reform

Forward all your details reply to:

UNITED NATIONS WEST AFRICA, ABUJA NIGERIA
Secretary-General Rev. Michael Hasse
E-mail: michaelhasse900@att.net
Cell Phone Number: +234–802–280–5877

Department of Public Information, United Nations © 2010
[Online Administrator]
Ted Turner, UN Foundation Chairman
C/O: Secretary-General Ban Ki-moon and Mr. Jean-Pierre Gonnot

Supplement 2 to Chapter 5: "The Spider and the Fly " by Mary Howitt (1799–1888)

"Will you walk into my parlour?" said the Spider to the Fly,

'Tis the prettiest little parlour that ever you did spy;

The way into my parlour is up a winding stair,
And I've a many curious things to shew when you are there."

"Oh no, no," said the little Fly, "to ask me is in vain,
For who goes up your winding stair can ne'er come down again. "

"I'm sure you must be weary, dear, with soaring up so high;
Will you rest upon my little bed?" said the Spider to the Fly.
"There are pretty curtains drawn around; the sheets are fine and
    thin,
And if you like to rest awhile, I'll snugly tuck you in!"

"Oh no, no," said the little Fly, "for I've often heard it said,
They never, never wake again, who sleep upon your bed! "

Said the cunning Spider to the Fly, "Dear friend what can I do,
To prove the warm affection I've always felt for you?
I have within my pantry, good store of all that's nice;
I'm sure you're very welcome—will you please to take a slice?"

"Oh no, no," said the little Fly, "kind Sir, that cannot be,
I've heard what's in your pantry, and I do not wish to see!"

"Sweet creature!" said the Spider, "you're witty and you're wise,
How handsome are your gauzy wings, how brilliant are your eyes!
I've a little looking-glass upon my parlour shelf,
If you'll step in one moment, dear, you shall behold yourself."

"I thank you, gentle sir," she said, "for what you're pleased
    to say,
And bidding you good morning now, I'll call another day."

The Spider turned him round about, and went into his den,

For well he knew the silly Fly would soon come back again:
So he wove a subtle web, in a little corner sly,
And set his table ready, to dine upon the Fly.

Then he came out to his door again, and merrily did sing,
"Come hither, hither, pretty Fly, with the pearl and silver wing;
Your robes are green and purple—there's a crest upon your head;
Your eyes are like the diamond bright, but mine are dull as
    lead!"

Alas, alas! how very soon this silly little Fly,
Hearing his wily, flattering words, came slowly flitting by;
With buzzing wings she hung aloft, then near and nearer drew,
Thinking only of her brilliant eyes, and green and purple hue —
Thinking only of her crested head—poor foolish thing!
    At last,
Up jumped the cunning Spider, and fiercely held her fast.
He dragged her up his winding stair, into his dismal den,
Within his little parlour—but she ne'er came out again!

And now dear little children, who may this story read,
To idle, silly flattering words, I pray you ne'er give heed:
Unto an evil counsellor, close heart and ear and eye,
And take a lesson from this tale, of the Spider and the Fly.

Supplement to Chapter 7: Executive Assessment at Morrison Associates, Ltd.

The firm's executive assessment process has been utilized in several
industries at various levels of organizations. These include CEOs,
board members, chairs, and other officers in the C-suite as well as
those who report into the C-suite. Individuals and teams have participated at several points in their careers. The purpose has been
to take a team that is skilled in understanding work and individuals

and target its efforts toward the understanding of one leader in the course of a day of interviews, psychological testing, and dialogue.

That day will be unique for every individual, but for quality and consistency, we use the same agenda with every one:

Greeting with lead consultant: 15 minutes

Psychological testing: 2.5 hours

Goal setting: 20 minutes

Individual interviews:
 Personal—psychiatrist facilitation: 1 hour
 Work—MBA facilitating: 1 hour

Break

Discussion:
 What is success? Balancing work, family, and self: 30 minutes
 Dialogue on all findings: 2 hours

Adjourn: The firm's research has afforded insights into assessing success characteristics in leaders, measuring growth in self-awareness as part of transformational leadership programs, and led to the creation of high-quality educational programs.

Supplement 1 to Chapter 8: Investment Guru Ken Fisher on How to Smell a Rat

Ken Fisher, the founder, chairman, and CEO of Fisher Investments, a money management firm, is also a celebrated columnist of 25 years for *Forbes* magazine. Over the years he has come to command great respect for the analysis calls he makes. In the wake of the Wall Street financial crisis of 2008 and 2009, he wrote "How to Smell a Rat" to furnish five warning signs that investors should heed if they are not to be duped.

The five warning signs appear so obvious at first that they don't seem to need reiteration. Nevertheless, careful reflection allows one to see the merits of Fisher's sagacious advice to pay attention.

Here are the five warning signs (adapted and paraphrased):

1. **Lack of independence.** Your financial advisor also has custody of your assets. This is what is colorfully described as the "fox guarding the henhouse" problem.

2. **Spectacular returns.** Returns are so consistently great that it is almost *too good to be true.* This was true of Bernie Madoff's firm.
3. **Opaqueness and incomprehensibility.** The investing strategy isn't understandable; it's murky, flashy, or too complicated for the financial advisor to describe so you can easily understand. Complexity frequently masks fraud.
4. **Exclusivity.** Your financial advisor promotes benefits like exclusivity, which don't affect the results. Indeed, any kind of secrecy, such as being advised not to discuss your investments with others, is a way to set the wheels of shame into motion.
5. **Secondhand information.** You didn't do your own due diligence, but a trusted intermediary did. Recall that fraudsters are typically described as trust violators. Your skeptical attitude should promote a "trust but verify" orientation.[8]

Supplement 2 to Chapter 8: On the Psychology of an Unindicted Coconspirator Sought by Government as a Cooperating Witness

The following is a blog entry by Walter Pavlo, who writes about white-collar crime regularly and is reproduced with his permission. Pavlo's blog can be found at www.forbes.com.

The Life of a Cooperating Witness: Rewards and Perils

by Walter Pavlo, 1/04/2013 @ 2:05PM

This Is Accused Insider Trader Mathew Martoma's Life Now

Former SAC Capital's Mathew Martoma (38) entered his "NOT" guilty plea yesterday in Manhattan federal court (my favorite 500 Pearl Street). The government is accusing Martoma of trading on inside information associated with a tip he got on an Alzheimer's drug which had failed during test trials. The information is alleged to have allowed Martoma/SAC avoid over $260 million in losses on publicly traded stocks Elan and Wyeth.

The media has started its speculation as to when, or if, Martoma will begin his cooperation with the government in hopes of winning leniency by turning on SAC's founder and billionaire, Steve Cohen. Cooperating with the government is one way to reduce the number of years one spends in prison. Martoma's cooperation may indeed happen, but he was just arrested in November 2012, so this case has more to play out and Martoma has a lot to process. Getting arrested is not something that is easy for a person to grasp.

Martoma was approached by two FBI agents while he worked in his front yard of his Florida home in 2012. The agents told him that they had information that he had committed a crime of illegally trading in stocks. His reaction? Martoma fainted. White-collar defendants are usually not tough guys.

Tactics used by the FBI are meant to intimidate individuals and get them to cooperate in their investigation. Cooperating witnesses are powerful in persuading jurors to convict and getting other co-conspirators to plead guilty. Some agents have told me that they carry a copy of the Federal Sentencing Guideline Table as a visual aid in showing targets how much prison time they could be looking at should they consider NOT cooperating. However understandable these tactics may be at getting to the bottom of solving a crime, they are a part of the punishment of a white-collar perpetrator. Martoma's punishment is already starting whether he is found guilty or not.

There are stages of emotions that come with being the focus of a criminal indictment. Like Mr. Martoma's reaction to the FBI approaching him with information, the initial reaction was fear, absolute terror. The criminal activity presented by the agents to Martoma in his front yard had occurred in 2008, nearly 4 years prior. Martoma had forgotten about his offense those years ago until he was reminded by two concerned agents . . . then he found the floor. Shock.

The next stage is denial. Being comfortable in a successful lifestyle, it is confusing to pair the criminal actions of a person to the characteristics of a successful career, family and social status. Denial is the best coping mechanism. However, reality awaits when the job is lost, friends turn their backs and those that remain start to ask questions based on what they read in the papers. Since Martoma's arrest in November, his social calendar has probably cleared up a bit. The only meetings he's attending are with his legal team, his new friends, who come with a price tag of $750/hour. And you thought dogs were expensive when it comes to companionship. This is where Martoma is today, surrounded by paid attorneys who are giving him options and comfort . . . and believe me, one of the options they are discussing is cooperation.

As time progresses the defendant enters a stage of confusion. A wondering of "Who am I?" and "Am I that bad person I read about?" Right now, Martoma is thinking he's a good guy . . . and he probably is a good guy, but that does not mean he is not capable of doing something illegal (bad).

Confusion leads to exhaustion. Where is my life going? What is the cost of my actions? How will my family survive? How will I recover financially? The questions follow the person to bed every night, but alcohol and sleeping pills help for a while.

Then there is acceptance, a realization that the only way out of the criminal probe is to surrender and admit one's guilt. Acceptance takes a while. What is prison like? How will people view me? What will life be like after prison? You know your life must be total hell when the thought of prison seems like a relief.

Martoma's not there yet, but the case is still warm. There's a bit more processing to come for Mr. Martoma, but it will come . . . trust me.[9]

Supplement 3 to Chapter 8: Fraudster Modus Operandi— Convicted Felon Samuel Antar on the Art of Spinning

This is a blog entry from convicted felon Samuel Antar, a former CPA and the former CFO of Crazy Eddie, on how to identify possible while-collar criminals (or at least deceitful people):

> White-collar crime is a crime of persuasion and deceit. Since the white-collar criminal uses persuasion and deceit to commit their crimes, it follows that such felons are artful liars.
>
> People often ask me what characteristics I look for in other people that alert me to possible criminal activity or at least unethical and deceitful people.
>
> Not all questionable conduct is illegal. A person can be unethical or deceitful (however they are defined) without committing any illegal acts as defined under the law.
>
> However, most criminals use tools like spinning (see below) in the conduct of their crimes.
>
> **The Art of Spinning**
>
> *Sell people hope.* My cousin "Crazy Eddie" Antar taught me that "people live on hope" and their hopes and dreams must be fed

through our spin and lies. In any situation, if possible, accentuate the positive.

Make excuses as long as you can. Try to have your excuses based on at least one truthful fact even if the fact is unrelated to your actions and argument.

When you cannot dispute the underlying facts, accept them as true but rationalize your actions. You are allowed to make mistakes as long as you have no wrongful intent. Being stupid is not a crime.

Always say in words you "take responsibility," but try to indirectly shift the blame on other people and factors. You need to portray yourself as a "stand up" guy or gal.

When you cannot defend your actions or arguments, attack the messenger to detract attention from your questionable actions.

Always show your kindness by doing people favors. You will require the gratitude of such people to come to your aid and defend you.

Build up your stature, integrity, and credibility by publicizing the good deeds you have done in areas unrelated to the subject of scrutiny.

Build a strong base of support. Try to have surrogates and the beneficiaries of your largess stand up for you and defend you.

If you can, appear to take the "high road" and have your surrogates do the "dirty work" for you. After all, you cannot control the actions of your zealots.

When you can no longer spin, shut up. For example, offer no guidance to investors or resign for "personal reasons." Your surrogates and so-called friends can still speak on your behalf and defend you.

If you are under investigation always say you will "cooperate." However, use all means necessary legal or otherwise to stifle the investigators. Remember that "people live on hope," and their inclination is to believe you.

When called to testify under oath (if you do not exercise your 5th amendment privilege against self-incrimination), have selective memory about your questionable actions. It is harder to be charged with perjury if you cannot remember what you have done rather than testify and lie about it.

However, before you testify, have other friendly witnesses testify before you to defend you. You need to "lock in" their stories first (before they change their minds) so your testimony does not conflict with their testimony and your story will appear to be more truthful.

Try not to have your actions at least appear to rise to the level of criminal conduct or a litigable action. Being stupid or being unethical is not always a crime or a tortuous action.

One last rule. To be a most effective spinner, always keep your friends close and your enemies closer. The kindness you s-how your enemies will reduce their propensity to be skeptical of you.

If you see some of the above similarities in people who are in authority such as executives, politicians, and others, you are forewarned to watch out. Before a person can be a white-collar criminal, they must be deceitful and be able to follow most of the above rules of spinning.[10]

Notes

1. This summary of the 2011 ACFE *Inside the Fraudster's Mind* video was prepared by Sridhar Ramamoorti. Permission to use the video for this book and present this summary has been granted by Mr. John Warren on behalf of the Association of Certified Fraud Examiners.

2. David M. Freedman, "Greed Takes the Blame," *Value Examiner*, September–October 2009. This editorial has been reproduced in its entirety with the *Value Examiner* senior editor's permission as well as the National Association of Certified Valuators and Analysts.

3. Reproduced with permission from Michael Grayson, Chair, Accounting Department, Brooklyn College, Brooklyn, NY.

4. N. I. Eisenberger and M. D. Lieberman, "Why Rejection Hurts: The Neurocognitive Overlap between Physical and Social Pain," *Trends in Cognitive Science* 8 (2004): 294–300.

5. B. Wicker, C. Keysers, J. Plailly, J. P. Royet, V. Gallese, and G. Rizzolatti, "Both of Us Disgusted in My Insula: The Common Neural Basis of Seeing and Feeling Disgust," *Neuron* 40 (2003): 655–64.

6. Richard D. Lane and David A. S. Garfield, "Becoming Aware of Feelings: Integration of Cognitive-Developmental, Neuroscientific, and Psychoanalytic Perspectives," *Neuropsychoanalysis* 7 (1)(2005): 5–30.

7. John Medina, "Memory, the Hippocampus and the Wandering Eye," *Clinical Psychiatry News*, February 2010.

8. Adapted from Ken Fisher, *How to Smell a Rat: The Five Signs of Financial Fraud* (Hoboken, NJ: John Wiley & Sons, 2009).

9. Walter Pavlo, "This Is Accused Insider Trader Mathew Martoma's Life Now," January 4, 2013, www.forbes.com/sites/walterpavlo/2013/01/04/this-is-accused-insider-trader-mathew-martomas-life-now.

10. Samuel E. Antar, "The Art of Spinning: How to Identify Possible White-Collar Criminals or at Least Unethical and Deceitful People Who You Should Avoid," *White-Collar Fraud Blog*, December 25, 2006, www.whitecollarfraud.com. Reprinted with permission from Samuel Antar.

Bibliography

Abagnale, F. W. *Catch Me If You Can: The Amazing True Story of the Youngest and Most Daring Con Man in the History of Fun and Profit.* New York: Broadway Books, 2000.

ACFE Video, *Inside the Fraudster's Mind.* Austin, TX: Association of Certified Fraud Examiners. (Note: An accompanying self-guide was issued in March 2013.)

AICPA. *Management Override of Internal Controls: The Achilles Heel of Fraud Prevention.* New York: AICPA, 2005.

AICPA. Statement on Auditing Standards (SAS) No. 99: Consideration of Fraud in a Financial Statement Audit. New York: AICPA, 2002.

AICPA. *Professional Standards,* vols. 1 and 2. New York: AICPA, 2003.

Akerlof, G. A., and R. J. Shiller. *Animal Spirits: How Human Psychology Drives the Economy, and Why It Matters for Global Capitalism.* Princeton, NJ: Princeton University Press, 2010.

Albrecht, W. S., M. B. Romney, D. J. Cherrington, I. R. Payne, and A. V. Roe. *How to Detect and Prevent Business Fraud.* Englewood Cliffs, NJ: Prentice Hall, 1982.

Altman, M. *Behavioral Economics for Dummies.* Hoboken, NJ: John Wiley & Sons, 2012.

Anderson, D. W., S. J. Melanson, and J. Maly. "The Evolution of Corporate Governance: Power Redistribution Brings Boards to Life." *Corporate Governance* 15, no. 5 (September 2007): 780–97.

Apter, M.J. *Danger: Our Quest for Excitement.* Oxford, England: OneWorld Publications, 2007.

Ariely, D. *The (Honest) Truth about Dishonesty: How We Lie to Everyone—Especially Ourselves.* New York: HarperCollins, 2012.

Basch, M. F. *Affect: The Gateway to Action.* New York: Basic Books, 1988.

Beam, Aaron, with C. Warner. *HealthSouth: The Wagon to Disaster.* Fairhope, AL: Wagon Pub., 2009.

Benderly, B. L., M. F. Gallagher, and J. M. Young. *Discovering Culture: An Introduction to Anthropology.* New York: D. Van Nostrand Co., 1977.

Beu, D. S., and M. R. Buckley. "This Is War: How the Politically Astute Achieve Crimes of Obedience through the Use of Moral Disengagement." *Leadership Quarterly* 15 (2004): 551–68.

Biegelman, M. T., and J. T. Bartow. *Executive Roadmap to Fraud Prevention and Internal Control: Creating a Culture of Compliance.* Hoboken, NJ: John Wiley & Sons, 2006.

Bologna, G. J., and R. J. Lindquist. *Fraud Auditing and Forensic Accounting,* 2nd ed. New York: John Wiley & Sons, 1995.

Boyle, D. M., F. T. DeZoort, and D. R. Hermanson. *The Impact of Alternative Fraud Model Use on Auditors' Fraud Risk Judgments and Confidence.* Unpublished working paper, 2012.

Brooks, David. *The Social Animal.* New York: Random House, 2011.

Brosnan, Sarah F. & Frans F. de Waal, *Monkeys Reject Unequal Pay.* Atlanta: Emory University Yerkes Primate Research Center, 2003.

Burgess, E. W. "Comment" and "Concluding Comment." In G. Geis (ed.), *White-Collar Crime.* New York: Free Press, 1977.

Cameron, William Bruce. *Informal Sociology: A Casual Introduction to Sociological Thinking.* New York: Random House, 1963.

Cendrowski, Harry, James P. Martin, and Louis W. Petro. *The Handbook of Fraud Deterrence.* Hoboken, NJ: John Wiley & Sons, 2007.

Cialdini, Robert B. *Influence: The Psychology of Persuasion.* New York: HarperCollins, 2007.

———. *Influence: Science and Practice.* Needham Heights, MA: Allyn & Bacon, 2001.

Coenen, Tracy. *How to Detect Behavioral Red Flags.* Sequence Inc., December 30, 2007, www.sequenceinc.com.

Cohen, L. and M. Felson. "Social Change and Crime Rate Trends: A Routine Activity Approach." *American Sociological Review* 44 (1979): 588–608.

Cooley, C. H. *Human Nature and the Social Order.* New York: Schocken Books, 1902.

Cravens, K., E. O. Oliver, and S. Ramamoorti. "The Reputation Audit: Measuring and Managing Corporate Reputation." *European Management Journal* 21, no. 2 (April 2003): 201–212.

Cressey, Donald R. *Other People's Money: The Social Psychology of Embezzlement.* New York: Free Press, 1953.

———. *Management Fraud, Accounting Controls, and Criminological Theory.* In R. K. Elliott and J. J. Willingham (eds.), *Management Fraud: Detection and Deterrence.* New York: Petrocelli Books, 1980.

Csikszentmihalyi, Mihaly. *Flow: The Psychology of Optimal Experience.* New York: Harper & Row, 1990.

Damasio, A. *Descartes' Error: Emotion, Reason, and the Human Brain.* New York: G.P. Putnam's Sons, 1994. (Rev. ed. New York: Penguin, 2005.)

————. *The Feeling of What Happens: Body and Emotion in the Making of Consciousness.* New York: Harcourt, 1999.

Darwin, Charles, Paul Ekman, and Phillip Prodger. *The Expression of the Emotions in Man and Animals,* 3rd ed. London: HarperCollins, 1998.

Davis, J. H., F. D. Schoorman, and L. Donaldson. "Toward a Stewardship Theory of Management." *Academy of Management Review* 22, no. 1 (1997): 20–47.

Demos, Virginia. *Exploring Affect: The Selected Writings of Silvan S. Tomkins.* Cambridge, UK: Press Syndicate of the University of Cambridge, 1995.

Dooling, Richard. "Rise of the Machines." *New York Times,* October 12, 2008.

Dorrell, D. D., and G. A. Gadawski. *Financial Forensics Body of Knowledge.* Hoboken, NJ: John Wiley & Sons, 2012.

Duffield, Grace, and Peter Grabosky. *The Psychology of Fraud: Trends and Issues in Crime and Criminal Justice.* Canberra, Australia: Australian Institute of Criminology, 2001.

Eichenwald, K. *Conspiracy of Fools: A True Story.* New York: Broadway Books, 2005.

Eisenberger, N. I., and M. D. Lieberman. "Why Rejection Hurts: The Neurocognitive Overlap between Physical and Social Pain." *Trends in Cognitive Science* 8 (2004): 294–300.

Ekman, Paul, Maureen. O'Sullivan, and M. Frank, "A Few Can Catch a Liar." *Psychological Science* 10 (1999): 263–266.

Felps, Will, Terrence R. Mitchell, and Eliza Byington, "How, When, and Why Bad Apples Spoil the Barrel: Negative Group Members and Dysfunctional Groups." *Research in Organizational Behavior* 27 (2006): 175–222.

Feng, Mei, Weili Ge, Shuqing Luo, and Terry Shevlin, "Why Do CFOs Become Involved in Material Accounting Manipulations?" *Journal of Accounting and Economics* 51, nos. 1–2 (February 2011): 21–36.

Festinger, Leon. "A Theory of Social Comparison Processes." *Human Relations* 7, no. 2 (1954): 117–140.

Fisher, Ken. *How to Smell a Rat: The Five Signs of Financial Fraud.* Hoboken NJ: John Wiley & Sons, 2009.

Forbes, Peter. *Dazzled and Deceived: Mimicry and Camouflage.* New Haven, CT: Yale University Press, 2009.

Freud, Sigmund. *The Interpretation of Dreams: The Illustrated Edition.* Jeffrey Moussaieff Masson, ed. A. A. Brill, trans. New York: Sterling, 2010.

————. *New Introductory Lectures on Psychoanalysis.* James Strachey, trans. New York: W.W. Norton & Co.

Fromm, Erich. *The Crisis of Psychoanalysis: Essays on Freud, Marx, and Social Psychology.* Greenwich, CT: Fawcett, 1970.

Fuller, J., and M. C. Jensen. "Just Say No to Wall Street." Monitor Company n.d., www.latrobefinancialmanagement.com/ Research/Governance.

Furnham, A., and M. Argyle. *The Psychology of Money.* London: Routledge, 1998.

Gino, F., and M. H. Bazerman. *Slippery Slopes and Misconduct: The Effect of Gradual Degradation on the Failure to Notice Others' Unethical Behavior.* Cambridge, MA: Harvard Business School, 2007, www .people.hbs.edu/mbazerman/Papers/Gino-Baz-06-007-Slippery%20Slopes.pdf.

Goffman, Erving. *The Presentation of Self in Everyday Life.* New York: Anchor Books, 1959.

Grandin, Temple, and Sean Barron. *Unwritten Rules of Social Relationships: Decoding: Social Mysteries through the Unique Perspectives of Autism.* Arlington, TX: Future Horizons, 2005.

Greenspan, Stephen. *Annals of Gullibility: Why We Are Duped and How to Avoid It.* Westport, CT: Praeger, 2008.

Greenspan, Stephen. "Fooled by Ponzi (and Madoff): How Bernard Madoff Made Off with My Money." *eSKEPTIC,* December 23, 2008, www.skeptic.com/eskeptic/08-12-23.

Hare, Robert, and Paul Babiak. *Snakes in Suits: When Psychopaths Go to Work.* New York: HarperCollins, 2006.

Henriques, Diana B. "Madoff Will Plead Guilty; Faces Life for Swindle." *New York Times,* March 11, 2009.

————. "Two Are Charged with Helping Madoff Falsify Records." *New York Times,* November 14, 2009.

————. *The Wizard of Lies: Bernie Madoff and the Death of Trust.* New York: Times Books/Henry Holt & Company, 2012.

Hinson, G. "Social Engineering Techniques, Risks, and Controls." *EDP Audit, Control, and Security Newsletter* 37, no. 4–5 (2008): 32–46.

Hodgson, Geoff. *Capitalism, Value, and Exploitation: A Radical Theory.* Oxford, UK: Martin Robertson, 1982.

Hollinger, Paul C., and Kalia Doner. *What Babies Say Before They Can Talk.* New York: Simon & Schuster, 2003.

Howitt, Mary. "The Spider and the Fly." Poetry Archives, http://poetry.poetryx.com/poems/10524.

Hughes, Everett C. "Good People and Dirty Work." In H. S. Becker (ed.), *The Other Side*. New York: Free Press, 1964.

Iacoboni, Marco. *Mirroring People: The New Science of How We Connect with Others*. New York: Farrar, Straus & Giroux, 2008.

Jennings, Marianne M. *Seven Signs of Ethical Collapse: How to Spot Moral Meltdowns . . . Before It's Too Late*. New York: St. Martin's Press, 2006.

Jensen, Michael. "The Modern Industrial Revolution, Exit, and the failure of internal control Systems." *Journal of Finance* 48 (1993): 831–880.

Kahneman, D. *Thinking Fast and Slow*. New York: Farrar, Straus and Giroux, 2011.

Kassin, S., S. Fein, and H. R. Markus. *Social Psychology*, 8th ed. Belmont, CA: Wadsworth, Cengage Learning, 2011.

Katz, J. "Cover-Up and Collective Integrity." *Social Problem* 25 (1977): 3–17.

Khanna, V. S., E. H. Kim, and Y. Lu. *CEO Connectedness and Corporate Frauds*. Michigan Law Review: Public Law and Legal Theory Research Paper Series. Paper #283. June 2012.

Kipling, Rudyard. "The Man Who Would Be King." *Selected Stories*. New York: Penguin Classic, 2011.

Kraemer, Harry. *From Values to Action: The Four Principles of Values-Based Leadership*. San Francisco: Jossey-Bass, 2011.

Lane, Richard D., and David A. S. Garfield. "Becoming Aware of Feelings: Integration of Cognitive-Developmental, Neuroscientific, and Psychoanalytic Perspectives." *Neuropsychoanalysis* 7, no. 1 (2005): 5–30.

Lansky, Melvin R., and Andrew P. Morrison. *The Widening Scope of Shame*. Hillsdale, NJ: Analytic Press, 1997.

Ledoux, J. E. *The Emotional Brain: The Mysterious Underpinnings of Emotional Life*. New York: Simon & Schuster, 1996.

Levitt, Arthur. "Numbers Game," speech delivered at New York University, New York, September 28, 1998. www.sec.gov/news/speech/speecharchive/1998/spch220.txt.

Lewis, M. Shame: *The Exposed Self*. New York: Free Press, 1992.

Littleton, A.C., "Value and Price in Accounting," *Accounting Review* IV (September 1929): 147–154.

Lowenstein, Roger. *Origins of the Crash*. New York: Penguin Press, 2004.

———. *The End of Wall Street*. New York: Penguin Press, 2010.

Maccoby, Michael. *The Productive Narcissist: The Promise and Peril of Visionary Leadership*. New York: Broadway, 2003.

McGregor, Lynn. *The Human Face of Corporate Governance.* London: Palgrave Macmillan. 2000.

McLean, Bethany, and Peter Elkind. *The Smartest Guys in the Room: The Amazing Rise and Scandalous Fall of Enron.* New York: Penguin, 2003.

Medina, John. "Memory, the Hippocampus and the Wandering Eye." *Clinical Psychiatry News Molecules of the Mind* February 2010.

Micklethwait, John, and Adrain Wooldridge. *The Company: A Short History of a Revolutionary Idea.* New York: Modern Library Edition, 2003.

Milgram, Stanley. *Obedience to Authority: An Experimental View.* New York: Harper & Row, 1974.

Miller-Keane Encyclopedia. *Encyclopaedia and Dictionary of Medicine, Nursing, and Allied Health,* 7th ed. Philadelphia: Elsevier, 2003.

Myung, I. J., S. Ramamoorti, and A. D. Bailey, Jr. "Maximum Entropy Aggregation of Expert Predictions." *Management Science* 42, no. 10 (1996): 1420–1436.

Nathanson, Donald L. *Shame and Pride: Affect, Sex, and the Birth of the Self.* New York: W. W. Norton, 1992.

Nigrini, M. J. *Benford's Law: Applications for Forensic Accounting, Auditing, and Fraud Detection.* Hoboken, NJ: John Wiley & Sons, 2012.

———. *Forensic Analytics: Methods and Techniques for Forensic Accounting Investigations.* Hoboken, NJ: John Wiley & Sons, 2011.

Paquette, V., and J. Levesque et al. "'Change the Mind and You Change the Brain': Effects of Cognitive-Behavioral Therapy on the Neural Correlates of Spider Phobia." *Neuroimage* 18, no. 2 (2003): 401–409.

Patterson, S., and D. Fitzpatrick. "Hearings Possible on 'Whale' Loss: Senate Panel Wraps Up Report on JP Morgan's Massive Bets; Public Questioning Could Be Next." *Wall Street Journal* February 20, 2013.

Pavlo, Walt, Jr. and Neil Weinberg. *Stolen Without A Gun: Confessions from Inside History's Biggest Accounting Fraud—the Collapse of MCI WorldCom.* Tampa, FL: Etika Books, 2007.

Pope, Kelly R. *Crossing the Line: Ordinary People Committing Extraordinary Crimes.* Chicago: DePaul University, 2011. Documentary film.

Post, Jerrold. *Leaders and Their Followers in a Dangerous World: The Psychology of Political Behavior (Psychoanalysis and Social Theory).* Ithaca, NY: Cornell University Press, 2004.

———. *When Illness Strikes the Leader.* New Haven, CT: Yale University Press, 1995.

Ramamoorti, S. "The Psychology and Sociology of Fraud: Integrating the Behavioral Sciences Component into Fraud and Forensic

Accounting Curricula." *Issues in Accounting Education* 23, no. 4 (November 2008): 521–533.

Ramamoorti, S., J. W. Koletar, and D. Morrison. *Bringing Freud to Fraud: Understanding the State of Mind of the C-Level Suite/White-Collar Offender through "A-B-C" Analysis.* Institute for Fraud Prevention, 2009, www.theifp.org.

Ramamoorti, S., and S. Curtis. "Procurement Fraud and Data Analytics." *Journal of Government Financial Management* 52, no. 4 (Winter 2003): 16–24.

Ramamoorti, S., and W. Olsen. "Fraud: The Human Factor." *Financial Executive* (July-August 2007): 53–55.

Reber, A. S., R. Allen, and E. S. Reber. *Penguin Dictionary of Psychology.* London: Penguin, 2009.

Rendell, I., and H. Whitehead. "Culture in Whales and Dolphins." *Behavioral and Brain Sciences* 24 (2001): 309–382.

Roese, N. J., and J. M. Olson, eds. *What Might Have Been: The Social Psychology of Counterfactual Thinking.* Hillsdale, NJ: Lawrence Erlbaum, 1995.

Rothlein, Steve, "Noble Cause Corruption." Public Agency Training Council, 2008, www.patc.com/weeklyarticles/noble-cause-corruption.shtml.

Samenow, Stanton, E. *Inside the Criminal Mind.* New York: Times Books, 1984.

Saunders, D. R. "Psychological Perspectives on Management Fraud." In R. K. Elliott and J. J. Willingham (eds.), *Management Fraud: Detection and Deterrence.* New York: Petrocelli Books, 1980, 107–115.

Sayles, Leonard R., and Cynthia J. Smith. *The Rise of the Rogue Executive: How Good Companies Go Bad and How to Stop the Destruction.* Upper Saddle River, NJ: Prentice Hall, 2006.

Schilit, H. M., and J. Perler. *Financial Shenanigans: How to Detect Accounting Gimmicks and Fraud in Financial Reports.* New York: McGraw Hill, 2010.

Schrand, C. M., and S. L. Zechman. *Executive Overconfidence and the Slippery Slope to Fraud.* SSRN eLibrary, 2009.

Schwartz, J. M., and S. Begley. *The Mind and the Brain: Neuroplasticity and the Power of Mental Force.* New York: HarperCollins, 2003.

S.E.C. press release. "SEC Charges Illinois for Misleading Pension Disclosures." March 11, 2013, www.sec.gov/news/press/2013/2013-37.htm.

Secret, Mosi. "Ex-Legislator Guilty of Theft Gets 5-Year Prison Sentence." *New York Times*, June 15, 2013.

Simon, Herbert. "Designing Organizations for an Information-Rich World." In Martin Greenberger (ed.), *Computers, Communication, and the Public Interest.* Baltimore: Johns Hopkins Press, 1971, 40–41.

Smith, Bryan. "Rita Crundwell and the Dixon Embezzlement." *Chicago*, December 2012.

Stout, Martha. *The Sociopath Next Door.* New York: MJF Books, 2005.

Sutherland, Edwin H. *White-Collar Crime.* New York: Holt, Rinehart & Winston, 1949.

Swets, Paul. *The Art of Talking So That People Will Listen.* New York: Fireside, 1987.

Thomson, W. Lord Kelvin. *Popular Lectures and Addresses,* vol. I. London: MacMillan, 1891.

Tuleja, Tad. *Beyond the Bottom Line.* New York: Penguin Books, 1987.

Tyler, Tom R. *Why People Obey the Law.* New Haven, CT: Yale University Press, 1990.

Walker, D. M. "Integrity: Restoring Trust in American Business and the Accounting Profession." Speech given at the AICPA Leadership Conference, November 2002, www.gao.gov/cghome/2002/acpro122.pdf.

Walsh, Mary Williams. "Illinois Is Accused of Fraud by S.E.C." *New York Times*, March 11, 2013.

Wells, J. T. *Fraud Fighter: My Fables and Foibles.* Hoboken, NJ: John Wiley & Sons, 2011.

———. "Let Them Know Someone's Watching." *Journal of Accountancy* May 2002, www.journalofaccountancy.com/Issues/2002/May/LetThemKnowSomeoneSWatching.

Wicker, B., C. Keysers, J. Plailly, J. P. Royet, V. Gallese, and G. Rizzolatti. "Both of Us Disgusted in My Insula: The Common Neural Basis of Seeing and Feeling Disgust." *Neuron* 40 (2003): 655–64.

Wight, J. B. *Saving Adam Smith: A Tale of Wealth, Transformation, and Virtue.* London: Financial Times/Prentice Hall, 2002.

Wilson, James Q., and George L. Kelling. *Broken Windows: The Police and Neighborhood Safety.* New York: Manhattan Institute, 1982, www.manhattan-institute.org/pdf/_atlantic_monthly-broken_windows.pdf.

Wolfe, D. T., and D. R. Hermanson. "The Fraud Diamond: Considering the Four Elements of Fraud." *CPA Journal* 74 (December 2004).

About the Author

Dr. Sridhar Ramamoorti, ACA, CPA/CITP/CFF/CGMA, CIA, CFE, CFSA, CGAP, CRMA, CGFM, CICA, CRP, MAFF, is currently an Associate Professor of Accounting and Director, Board Culture & Behavioral Dynamics, Corporate Governance Center at Kennesaw State University (KSU). Possessing a blended academic-practitioner background, Dr. Ramamoorti is a respected thought leader and prolific speaker in the areas of governance, risk, and compliance (GRC) and has published widely.

Dr. Ramamoorti received a bachelor's degree in commerce and a diploma in mathematics and statistics from Bombay University, India, before qualifying as a chartered accountant. After working for Ernst & Whinney in the Middle East, he earned a Ph.D. in quantitative psychology at Ohio State University. He then served on the accountancy faculty at the University of Illinois at Urbana-Champaign for several years. Returning to professional accounting practice, he joined the professional standards group of Arthur Andersen & Co. at the firm's Chicago world headquarters. Subsequently, he was affiliated with the fraud investigation and dispute services practice of Ernst & Young before becoming a corporate governance partner at Grant Thornton. Prior to joining the KSU faculty, he was a principal with Infogix, Inc., and continues to be a GRC consultant to the company.

Dr. Ramamoorti has published over 30 articles in academic and professional journals such as *Management Science, International Journal of Accounting, European Management Journal, Journal of Information Systems, Financial Executive, Internal Auditor, Journal of Government Financial Management,* and *QFinance.* He has also been on authoring teams of several books and monographs, including *The Audit Committee Handbook, Internal Auditing: Assurance and Advisory Services,* the COSO and ISACA guidance on *Monitoring Internal Control Systems (and IT),* and *Research Opportunities in Internal Auditing.* He has delivered numerous keynote addresses and has presented his practice-relevant research at conferences and other events in 14 countries.

Active in the profession, Dr. Ramamoorti currently chairs the GRC Committee for Financial Executives International, as well as the Competitive Manuscript Award Committee of the American Accounting Association. He is a board member of the Institute for Truth in Accounting and Ascend. Previously, he was the inaugural chairman of the Academy for Government Accountability, a trustee of the Institute of Internal Auditors Research Foundation, and a board member of the Institute for Business and Professional Ethics at DePaul University and the Institute for Fraud Prevention at West Virginia University.

• • •

David "Daven" E. Morrison, III, MD, is an organizational psychiatrist with over 15 years of experience in working with senior corporate executives on leadership and executive functioning. The focus of his work is to deepen the capacity of senior executives to be self-aware. With a refined process of individual and senior management team consultation, he has worked successfully for companies in many industries and within multiple levels of management and management structures.

Morrison Associates, Ltd., founded in 1976, is a consulting firm that works primarily with financial service organizations such as banks, accounting firms, insurance companies, and private equity groups. The firm has assessed in depth more than 1,500 leaders at companies such as Abbott, Accenture, Amoco, Arthur Andersen, Ashta Chemical, AT&T, Bank of America, Baker-Hughes, BP, CF Industries, Chicago Tribune, Continental Bank, Conseco, Elizabeth Arden, Exxon, Food Lion, Hospira, Illinois Tool Works, Johnson & Higgins, Loyola University Medical Center, Motorola, Nabisco, Northern Trust, Schneider International, Unilever, Wachovia, the Williams Companies, and others. Concepts and experiences with these organizations have resulted in the creation of a variety of high-quality educational programs. The firm's research has afforded insights into assessing success characteristics in leaders, recognizing accounting partners who put the firm at risk, and measuring growth in self-awareness as part of transformational leadership programs.

Dr. Morrison is a graduate of Northwestern University and a diplomate of the American Board of Psychiatry and Neurology. A past president of the Academy of Organizational and Occupational Psychiatry, he is active with the Group for the Advancement of Psychiatry—Committee on Work & Organizations; Institute for Fraud Prevention; and the Tomkins Institute of Applied Studies of Motivation, Emotion and Cognition. He is a clinical assistant professor of psychiatry at Rosalind Franklin University's Chicago School of Medicine. Dr. Morrison resides in Grayslake, Illinois, with his wife, Jeanette, and their sons, Daniel and Henry.

• • •

Joseph Koletar, DPA, CFE, has over 40 years of professional experience in the public and private sectors. He had a distinguished career with the U.S. Army, the Federal Bureau of Investigation (FBI), and two of the Big Four accounting firms. Based out of North Carolina, he now works as an independent forensic consultant.

Mr. Koletar served for 25 years as a special agent and senior executive in the FBI. At the time of his retirement, he was the national program manager for the Witness Protection Program, criminal undercover operations, surveillance and aviation operations, and White House Background Investigations. Previously, he was an intelligence officer in the U.S. Army Special Security Group.

Later in his career, he was an executive in the fraud investigation and dispute advisory practices of Ernst & Young LLP and Deloitte & Touche LLP. During this time, Mr. Koletar conducted and managed investigations for clients in industries such as retail, health care, energy, and financial services. Matters addressed included executive defalcations, conflicts of interest, revenue recognition, sales commission schemes, payroll and disbursement schemes, Foreign Corrupt Practices Act, anti–money laundering controls, fraud risk vulnerability assessments, compliance testing, and crisis management preparedness. Mr. Koletar's client list includes companies such as General Motors, Johnson & Johnson, GE Capital, Credit Suisse, Columbia HCA, Dell Computer, and many premier law firms.

Mr. Koletar holds a bachelor of arts degree from Pennsylvania State University, a master of science degree in industrial administration from George Washington University, and a master of public administration and a doctor of public administration from the University of Southern California. He is an alumnus of the Program for Senior Managers in Government at Harvard University.

He has written extensively on fraud topics in professional journals, has been quoted in the *New York Times*, and interviewed on National Public Radio. In 2003, his book *Fraud Exposed: What You Don't Know Could Cost Your Company Millions* was published by John Wiley & Sons; since then, he has also written *The FBI Career Guide*, *Rethinking Risk* and authored three sections in the *Encyclopedia of Law Enforcement* (Sage Publications, 2004). Mr. Koletar serves on the editorial review board of the CPA Journal and has been a guest lecturer at the University of Pennsylvania Law School, Pennsylvania State University, Kennesaw State University, and Louisiana State University. He has spoken to groups such as the American Management Association, the American Institute of CPAs, the Institute of Internal Auditors, the New York Bar Association, and the American Corporate Counsel Association, among others.

Mr. Koletar is the former chairman of the Board of Regents of the Association of Certified Fraud Examiners (ACFE), the highest elected position in the 66,000+ member global association. He was also the chairman of the ACFE Board of Review, which deals with professional practice issues, and was named ACFE Fellow in 2003.

• • •

Kelly Richmond Pope, PhD, CPA, is an expert in the field of white-collar crime. Dr. Pope is an associate professor in the School of Accountancy and Management Information Systems at DePaul University in Chicago, as well as the founder of Helios Digital Learning Inc., a media company that offers a suite of educational, consulting, and training products and services designed to help organizations understand, identify, and prevent fraud.

Her research has been published in such journals as *Behavioral Research in Accounting*, *Auditing: A Journal of Practice and Theory*, *Journal of Business Ethics*, the *CPA Journal*, and *Journal of Accountancy*. Dr. Pope is a contributing writer for Forbes.com and *Newsweek/ The Daily Beast*. She is a former Big Four forensic accountant and the creator and executive producer of the award-winning educational white-collar crime documentary *Crossing the Line: Ordinary People Committing Extraordinary Crime*, which was a 2012 recipient of the American Accounting Association Ethics Committee's teaching award and a recipient of the 2012 teaching innovation award sponsored by the AICPA. *Crossing the Line* has been screened at the Securities and Exchange Commission in Washington, D.C.

Dr. Pope is currently serving a three-year term on the governing council of the American Institute of Certified Public Accountants. She holds a Ph.D. in accounting from Virginia Tech and is a licensed certified public accountant in North Carolina.

Index

Page numbers in *italics* refer to exhibits.